LINUX KERNEL AND DEVICE DRIVER PROGRAMMING

A SIMPLER APPROACH TO LINUX KERNEL

LINUX KERNEL AND DEVICE DRIVER PROGRAMMING

A SIMPLER APPROACH TO LINUX KERNEL

By

Mohan Lal Jangir

Development Manager

Samsung India Software Operations

Bangalore (Karnataka)

UNIVERSITY SCIENCE PRESS

(An Imprint of Laxmi Publications (P) Ltd.)

An ISO 9001:2008 Company

BENGALURU • CHENNAI • COCHIN • GUWAHATI • HYDERABAD

JALANDHAR • KOLKATA • LUCKNOW • MUMBAI • RANCHI • NEW DELHI

BOSTON (USA) • ACCRA (GHANA) • NAIROBI (KENYA)

LINUX KERNEL AND DEVICE DRIVER PROGRAMMING

Printed and bound in India
Typeset at Excellent Graphics, Delhi
First Edition: 2015
ISBN 978-93-80298-93-1

Published in India by

UNIVERSITY SCIENCE PRESS
(An Imprint of Laxmi Publications Pvt. Ltd.)

An ISO 9001:2008 Company
113, GOLDEN HOUSE, DARYAGANJ,
NEW DELHI - 110002, INDIA
Telephone : 91-11-4353 2500, 4353 2501
Fax : 91-11-2325 2572, 4353 2528
www.laxmipublications.com info@laxmipublications.com

Branches

Bengaluru	080-26 75 69 30	
Chennai	044-24 34 47 26,	24 35 95 07
Cochin	0484-237 70 04,	405 13 03
Guwahati	0361-254 36 69,	251 38 81
Hyderabad	040-27 55 53 83,	27 55 53 93
Jalandhar	0181-222 12 72	
Kolkata	033-22 27 43 84	
Lucknow	0522-220 99 16	
Mumbai	022-24 91 54 15,	24 92 78 69
Ranchi	0651-220 44 64	

C—10102/015/04
Printed at : Repro Knowledgecast Limited, Thane

Contents

Preface

Being an electrical engineering student at my undergraduate level, my exposure to Linux started rather late and was limited to C programming on Linux PC. My true interaction with Linux started during my post graduation at IIT DELHI, wherein I started learning Linux shell commands, Vi editor etc. Still my experience remained limited to user space work like programming, networking and basic system administration.

My first encounter with kernel programming happened when I was given an assignment to write a device driver for mouse. Although I could succeed in getting mouse events, I could not complete the assignment. But it left an interesting area open to me which I continued to explore till date.

The idea of sharing the experience started when I finished a self assignment to write a network device driver on 2.4 kernel. I wrote an article and published it on Linux Malta group. The article turned out to be an immensely popular which increased my faith in sharing my experience. Later, the same article was re-published in Linux Gazette magazine because Linux Malta group website went down.

Based on the responses from the readers I realized that while many good, in-fact very good, reference books are available about Linux device driver programming, still there is a void in teaching an end to end driver development. Specifically a sample and real hardware made users to do the real development from scratch.

Encouraged from this article's success, I decided to write similar articles for block, USB, char, UART drivers as well and put them together along with kernel programming articles so that a reader finds all of them in one place. That's how this book has originated. All the code samples in this book are written or re-written for 2.6.21 kernel, however wherever needed, reference to older kernel are also been given so that readers may know the difference if they have to work on older kernels.

The examples sited throughout this book are trimmed versions of the self assignments done at home on Linux running on AMD AthlonTM processor. Specifically the error handling part is either removed or is minimal for the sake of brevity. Also the driver design is kept very simple and minimal basic functions are implemented for easy understanding. This will help readers to quickly understand and then modify them to add more features, error handling and bug fixing to grasp better understanding.

Audience of This Book

This book is written for students or professionals who quickly want to learn Linux Kernel programming and device driver development. Each chapter in this book is associated with code samples and code commentary so that the readers may quickly understand.

The readers are expected to have C programming experience and minimum know how of Linux. Every chapter in this book has been written from basic so that readers have no difficulty in understanding them.

Organization of This Book

This book can be classified in three parts. The first part is from chapter 1 to chapter 6 which is about kernel programming. These chapters explain kernel functionalities, debugging mechanisms, communication mechanisms etc.

The second part is from chapter 7 to chapter 9 which is dedicated for device driver development. These chapters pick a real hardware and explain device driver development from scratch. These chapters also include references to specifications, registers, and protocols etc. which are used by the devices, so that readers find all needful data at one place.

The third part is chapter 10 which explains about some common mechanism likes memory allocation, kernel threads, inter processor communications etc.

Readers are encouraged to modify, enhance and fix the sample code specifically on non-x86 and multi-processor architectures. This will give readers more confidence in kernel and device driver programming.

—Author

Acknowledgement

At the outset, I would like to thank the publishers and editors to make this book in reality.

This book is an outcome of my learning experiments done with Linux kernel. I thank my parents and family for their blessings and support. Specially my elder brother Dr. Manoj Jangid who has been an encouraging, supporting and inspiring figure in my life.

Writing this book was a long process and I must thank my wife Devyani for providing encouragement and support throughout even though she was completely held up by our one year old son Vatsal. She patiently managed things alone when I spent hours to complete the experiments and to convert them into this book.

I feel gratitude to Linux open source community who has answered many questions on mailing lists. It was a great help from them whenever I stuck somewhere during experiments.

Lastly, I thank my article readers whose feedback and response have inspired me to write this book. It has been a pleasant experience to share my experiments with them.

—Author

1 Beginning Kernel Programming

Linux being an open source operating system gives flexibility to customize the kernel based on user needs. This means, that a user is free to include whatever needed and exclude everything else to keep the kernel size small. In this chapter, we begin with kernel compilation and then develop first kernel module.

1.1 MAKING A NEW KERNEL

Linux kernel programmers very often need to build new kernel for different hardware or for different products. This section is for beginners who are compiling kernel for the first time. If you have compiled and run new kernel previously, you can safely skip this section.

1.1.1 Know Your System

For compiling new kernel, you have to first gather information about what to include in the kernel and what can be excluded. If you are working with a new system, the hardware reference manual is your best bet. To begin with, you need to gather at least the following information:

- Processor—Manufacturer, number of cores/processors
- Bus (PCI, ISA, PCMCIA, USB etc)
- Network devices
- Display devices
- File systems to be used
- Peripheral devices

Next, you can configure the kernel to include support for required hardware.

1.1.2 Configuring and Compiling Kernel

You can download kernel source from http://www.kernel.org/. There are many ways to configure the kernel. If you are working in graphical mode, you can use "make xconfig" or "make gconfig" which provides very easy and convenient way to configure the kernel. If you don't have graphical mode but can run Tcl/Tk, you can use "make menuconfig", else you can use "make config" which works completely in text mode.

You can choose any feature to be included in kernel (built-in), or can choose to compile as module (runtime loadable module). Therefore, it is possible to keep necessary features to be built in kernel while optional features can be configured as module, and can be loaded on demand. Your configuration is saved in ".config" file in kernel tree.

Alternatively, if you have an already prepared configuration file, you can directly copy that file to .config, and can run "make oldconfig".

In older kernels, "make dep" was required after configuration to generate dependencies. However, 2.6 kernel does not need "make dep".

To compile the kernel you need the following commands:

- make—compiles compressed kernel image. If you know target name for compressed kernel image, you can use that command also. For example, for x86 architecture, you can use "make bzImage" image.
- make modules—compiles kernel modules.
- make modules_install—installs kernel modules in /lib/modules/'uname –r'/ directory. If you want to install in other directory, you can use "make modules_install INSTALL_MOD_PATH=/path/to/modules/dir" command.

The compressed kernel image is created either in main kernel tree or some architecture specific directory. For example, for x86 architecture you will find compress kernel image at arch/i386/boot/bzImage location.

1.1.3 Making initrd Image and Installing Kernel

After compiling the kernel, you need to make initrd image (initial ram disk). You can use mkinitramfs command to build initrd image. The initrd image name can be specified with –o option. Kernel version must be specified at the end. Below is an example to create initrd for 2.6.30 kernel.

```
mkinitramfs -o /boot/initrd.img-2.6.30 2.6.30
```

Next you need to copy kernel compressed image and initrd image to boot directory which can be /boot or /boot/grub based on the boot loader. Finally you need to edit boot loader configuration file (lilo.conf, grub.conf etc) to include the new kernel. Some boot loaders (like lilo) requires reinstalling boot loader after modifying boot loader configuration file.

You can reboot the system now. During next boot, you can choose to boot into the new kernel from boot loader menu.

1.2 PATCHING THE KERNEL

Sometimes it is required to patch the kernel to include source code of some work in progress or for some external feature. Two utilities 'diff' and 'patch' are useful in generating and applying patches. First let's understand how to generate a patch.

Assume that you have original kernel source in a directory named linux-old. You copy the contents of the linux-old into linux-new directory and work in linux-new directory. After finishing your changes are in linux-new directory, and you want to deliver the changes to somebody else. However, it is not a good idea to send entire linux-new directory. To deliver only the changes you made, you can create a patch and send the patch file.

The following command generates a patch for above mentioned directories.

```
diff -Nur linux-old/ linux-new/ > changes.patch
```

The N option instructs diff to treat absent files as empty. The u option instructs to generate unified format diff (which is used by patch utility). The r option instructs to look into directories recursively.

Now you can send file changes.patch to somebody else, who wants to use these changes. They can use patch utility to apply changes available in changes.patch file to linux-old directory. The patch can be applies as follows:

```
patch -p0 < changes.patch
```

The p option instructs to strip the smallest prefix containing num (digit following p option) leading slashes from each file name found in the patch file. For example, if you want to apply the patch from inside linux-old directory, you must choose –p1 option.

However, before applying a patch, it is always advisable to use —dry-run option which acts as applying patch but it really does not apply. This gives you a view of how the patch would be applied.

1.3 HELLO WORLD MODULE AND MAKEFILE

Let's write our first kernel module. Similar to main function in C application, kernel modules have init_module function which is executed when the module is inserted into the kernel using insmod command. In addition to that, modules have an exit function cleanup_module which is called when module is removed from kernel using rmmod command.

Table 1.1 illustrates a hello world kernel module.

Table 1.1

```
/* hello.c */
#include <linux/kernel.h>
#include <linux/module.h>
int init_module(void)
{
        printk("hello world\n");
        return 0;
}
void cleanup_function(void)
{
        printk("good bye\n");
        return;
}
MODULE_LICENSE("GPL");
```

The MODULE_LICENSE macro specifies kind of module; which can be GPL if you are willing to release the module under GPL license.

To compile kernel modules, you need to use kernel build. Table 1.2 illustrates a Makefile for above shown module.

Table 1.2

```
obj-m := hello.o
KDIR := /lib/modules/$(shell uname -r)/build
PWD := $(shell pwd)
default:
```

```
        $(MAKE) -C $(KDIR) M=$(PWD) modules
clean:
        $(MAKE) -C $(KDIR) M=$(PWD) clean
```

The obj-m contains kernel module image name. Note that although you mention kernel module image name with .o extension, the module will be created with .ko file extension. Therefore, this Makefile will generate a kernel module named hello.ko. The KDIR in this Makefile specifies kernel tree path.

Compile the hello.ko module using above Makefile, and insert it to the kernel using insmod command. You can remove the module from kernel using rmmod command. Alternatively, the module can be inserted using modprobe command, and can be removed using "modprobe –r" command. The modprobe command is more useful when working with real modules where some modules have symbol dependencies on other modules. In such case, modprobe loads modules in such order that modules providing symbols are loaded first and modules using those symbols are loaded later.

We'll come back to module loading in a short while. Before this let's understand kernel module Makefile.

The previous Makefile generates one kernel module from one source file. Let's see how to modify this Makefile for some more scenarios.

- Generate two separate kernel modules from two source files

Table 1.3

```
obj-m := file1.o file2.o
```

- Generate one kernel module from two source files

Table 1.4

```
obj-m := final.o
final-objs := file1.o file2.o
```

Additionally, you can use many other flags provided by kernel build for extra options. Table 1.5 illustrates one Makefile with such options.

Table 1.5

```
obj-m := hello.o
KDIR := /lib/modules/$(shell uname -r)/build
PWD := $(shell pwd)
CROSS := mips-gnu-
CFLAGS := -DMY_DEF -I path/to/header/file
default:
        $(MAKE) -C $(KDIR) M=$(PWD) V=0 modules CROSS_COMPILE=$(CROSS)
clean:
        $(MAKE) -C $(KDIR) M=$(PWD) clean
```

The CFLAGS option can be used to define extra compile options. The V option can be used to make build process verbose. If V is set to 1, the build system shows exact commands being used for compilation. Finally CROSS_COMPILE option can be used to compile the module for different target system.

If you have not worked with makefiles before, you must note that the command line starts with a TAB. If you indent it only with white spaces, you are bound to get build errors. A typical makefile has following format:

Table 1.6

```
target: dependencies
TAB command
```

1.4 LOGGING AND WATCHING PRINTS

As mentioned previously, insmod command is used for inserting a module into the kernel. However, you may not see the prints especially when you are working in graphical mode. Kernel does not send kernel prints to graphical terminals. Rather kernel chooses to write into /var/log/messages file. Therefore, all prints from your module will go to /var/log/messages file.

However it is possible to get logs on virtual terminals. To go to the first virtual terminal, you should press `Ctrl+Alt+F1`. Similarly `Ctrl+Alt+F2` for second virtual terminal and so on. `Ctrl+Alt+F7` brings you back to graphical terminal. If you choose run level 3 in /etc/inittab file, linux will always bring you to this virtual terminal mode without starting graphical mode. In "Chapter 03 – Linux Kernel Debugging", we'll see how to configure kernel to have module logs to virtual terminals.

Alternatively, dmesg or "dmesg –c" commands can be used to watch kernel logs. The –c option clears the logs after displaying.

1.5 MODULE PARAMETERS

Kernel modules can be passed command line arguments during module insertion just like applications can have command line arguments. However, the method is slightly different. Kernel provides module_param API for command line parameters. Table 1.7 illustrates a tiny kernel module which accepts one integer parameter.

Table 1.7

```
/* FILE: param.c */
#include <linux/module.h>
static int count=5;
int init_module(void)
{
        printk("count = %d\n", count);
        return 0;
}
void cleanup_module(void)
{
        printk("module removed\n");
}
module_param(count, int, 0);
MODULE_LICENSE("GPL");
```

Use Makefile similar to one shown in Table 1.5, and use following command to insert the module.

Table 1.8

```
insmod param.ko count=6
```

You will see the value of count printed during module insertion time. If you do not pass the command line parameter, the variable count uses its default initialized value.

Let's dig a little more into module_param API. This is a macro and it takes three parameters as shown below:

Table 1.9

```
module_param(name, type, permission)
```

The first parameter is command line parameter name. The second parameter is type of command line parameter which can be int, uint, short, ushort, byte etc. The third parameter specifies the permissions to change command line parameter's value via sys file system.

For every module inserted, kernel creates a directory /sys/module/<module_name> in sys file system. In this directory a sub-directory named parameters is created and a file is created for every command line parameter in this sub-directory. The permission parameter in module_param decides how the command line parameter's value can be changed using these files. Table 1.10 illustrates permission types and their effect.

Table 1.10

Permission type	Effect
0	Does not create parameters directory.
S_IRUSR	Root can read.
S_WRUSR	Root can write.
S_IRUGO	Anyone can read.
S_WRUGO	Anyone can write.

However, you must note that re-writing command line parameter via sysfs file system does not have effect until module re-reads the value. Therefore, if you want to make module command line parameter writable via sysfs file system, you must provide some way in your module to immediately re-read it.

It is possible to pass strings and array also as command line parameters. You need to use following macros to do this:

Table 1.11

```
module_param_string(name, string, string_len, permission);
module_param_array(name, type, num, permission);
```

1.6 SUMMARY

Linux kernel module support is a very versatile and distinctive feature. It provides ability to add new source code into existing kernel on the fly. This also gives a great flexibility to kernel developers who need not rebuild kernel during development phase. For example, a device driver developer can develop the device driver as kernel module and can insert & remove it in kernel multiple times.

1.7 ASSIGNMENTS

- Compile Linux kernel (any version of your choice) on desktops having different Linux distribution (like RedHat, Fedora, Ubuntu)
- Study and discuss about udev mechanism
- Compile Linux kernel for 32-bit and 64-bit machines.

1.8 REFERENCES

The Linux kernel archives-http://www.kernel.org/

2 Application and Kernel Space Communication

Linux separates the execution space between application (user) space and kernel space. It is not possible to invoke direct function call between application source code and kernel source code for security reasons. However, Linux provides some controlled methods to perform communication between the two spaces.

This chapter explores following such methods:

- system call
- proc file system
- sysfs file system
- ioctl function
- seq file interface

Before we look into these methods, first we look into buffer copying functions between user and kernel space.

2.1 BUFFER COPYING BETWEEN USER & KERNEL SPACE

As mentioned before Linux makes a clear separation between user space and kernel space. Therefore, user space pointers are not valid in kernel space. Similarly kernel space pointers are not valid in user space. However, sometimes it is required to pass buffers between user space and kernel space for data exchange or data communication. In such cases a plain memcpy does not work. Linux provides two special functions to copy data between user and kernel space as described below:

- copy_from_user – This kernel function is used for copying data from user space pointer to kernel space pointer. The function has following prototype:

Table 2.1

```
unsigned long copy_from_user (void * to, const void __user * from,
unsigned long n);
```

This function returns number of bytes which could not be copied. On success it returns 0. This function may sleep and therefore must not be called in interrupt context (more about contexts later).

- copy_to_user—This kernel function is used for copying data from kernel space pointer to user space pointer. The function has following prototype:

Table 2.2

```
unsigned long copy_to_user (void __user * to, const void * from,
unsigned long n);
```

Like copy_from_user, this function too returns number of bytes which could not be copied. On success it returns 0. This function too may sleep and therefore, must not be called in interrupt context.

2.2 SYSTEM CALL

System calls are the special functions available to user applications to request services from kernel. System calls differ from normal functions in following aspects:

- System calls pass arguments in registers (or kernel stack) while normal functions pass them on user stack.
- Each system call is identified by a unique number in kernel while normal functions are identified by their names.

System calls use interrupt 0x80 to generate an exception which is processed by kernel. The kernel then checks privilege level (a security check), and invokes appropriate system call.

Linux provides many systems calls to serve almost every need of applications. However, it is possible to add new system calls. Next section explains the method to add new system call.

Let's add the following system call to the kernel.

Table 2.3

```
unsigned int getSquare(unsigned int);
```

This is a simple system call which shall return square of the argument. Add source for this system call in file kernel/sys.c (where most of the system calls are defined).

Table 2.4

```
/* FILE: kernel/sys.c
 * New system call source code
 */
asmlinkage unsigned int sys_getSquare(unsigned int x)
{
        return x*x;
}
```

It's pretty much like ordinary function except the tag asmlinkage. The asmlinkage tag tells gcc compiler to look for arguments on kernel stack (and not in registers).

Next edit include/asm/unistd.h to add a unique number for new system call and increment total system call number.

Table 2.5

```
/* FILE: include/asm/unistd.h
 * New system call number
 */
#define __NR_getSquare 320
#define NR_syscalls    321
```

As new system call getSquare's number is 320, maximum system call number is modified to 321 (from earlier 320).

Next, create new system call's entry into system call table.

Table 2.6

```
/* FILE: arch/i386/kernel/syscall_table.S
 * New system call's entry in system call table.
 */
        .long sys_getSquare
```

That's all the changes required to add new system call. Compile the modified kernel and boot with new kernel. To check if the kernel has new system call built-in, you can use following command:

Table 2.7

```
cat /proc/kallsyms | grep getSquare
```

This command must show a symbol from kernel indicating new system call.

Before an application can use getSquare system call, a wrapper function is required which calls to sys_getSquare kernel function when applications call getSquare function. Following code shows both of them together.

Table 2.8

```
/* FILE: application.c
 * compile command: gcc application.c
 * getSquare wrapper and application calling wrapper
 */
#include <stdio.h>
#include <unistd.h>
#define __NR_getSquare 320
unsigned int getSquare(unsigned int i)
{
        return syscall(__NR_getSquare, i);
}
int main()
{
        unsigned int a=5;
        unsigned int b = getSquare(a);
        printf("b=%d\n", b);
        return 0;
}
```

The wrapper getSquare calls the system call having number 320 which is the new system call.

2.3 PROC FILE SYSTEM

Linux provides a virtual in-core file system known as proc file system which can be used to communicate between an application and kernel. The kernel must be compiled with `CONFIG_PROC_FS` option to enable the proc file system. This file system is mounted at /proc directory. This file system is called virtual because it does not exist on hard disk but in memory.

In the next example, we examine a kernel module proc.c which creates a file /proc/mydir/myfile in proc file system. Reading and writing to this file results in kernel module's functions invocation.

Table 2.9

```
/* FILE: proc.c
 * proc file system example
 */
#include <linux/kernel.h>
#include <linux/module.h>
#include <linux/proc_fs.h>
#include <asm/uaccess.h>
#include <linux/init.h>
#include <linux/version.h>
#include <stdarg.h>
#define MAX_FLAG_VALUE 5
int my_proc_flag = 1;
static int proc_read_my_flag(char *page,
        char **start, off_t off, int count, int *eof, void *data)
{
        int len;
#if (LINUX_VERSION_CODE < KERNEL_VERSION(2,6,0))
        MOD_INC_USE_COUNT;
#endif
        len = sprintf(page, "%d\n", my_proc_flag);
#if (LINUX_VERSION_CODE < KERNEL_VERSION(2,6,0))
        MOD_DEC_USE_COUNT;
#endif
        return len;
}
#define BUF_SIZE 10
static int proc_write_my_flag(struct file *file,
        const char *buffer, unsigned long count, void *data)
{
        int len=0, value = 0, i = 0;
        char buf[BUF_SIZE];
#if (LINUX_VERSION_CODE < KERNEL_VERSION(2,6,0))
        MOD_INC_USE_COUNT;
#endif
        if(count > BUF_SIZE)
                len = BUF_SIZE;
        else
                len = count;
        if(copy_from_user(buf, buffer, len)) {
#if (LINUX_VERSION_CODE < KERNEL_VERSION(2,6,0))
        MOD_DEC_USE_COUNT;
#endif
                return -EFAULT;
        }
```

```
        buf[len] = '\0';
        while(i < len-1) {
                value = value*10 + buf[i] - '0';
                i++;
        }
        if(value < 0 || value > MAX_FLAG_VALUE) {
                len = -1;
                goto out;
        }
        my_proc_flag = value;
out:
#if (LINUX_VERSION_CODE < KERNEL_VERSION(2,6,0))
        MOD_DEC_USE_COUNT;
#endif
        return len;
}
static struct proc_dir_entry *pdir = NULL;
int init_module(void)
{
        struct proc_dir_entry *pfile = NULL;
        pdir = proc_mkdir("mydir", NULL);
        if(!pdir)
                return -ENOMEM;
        pfile = create_proc_entry("myfile", 0644, pdir);
        if(!pfile)
                return -ENOMEM;
        pfile->owner = THIS_MODULE;
        pfile->read_proc = proc_read_my_flag;
        pfile->write_proc = proc_write_my_flag;
        return 0;
}
void cleanup_module(void)
{
        remove_proc_entry("myfile", pdir);
        remove_proc_entry("mydir", NULL);
        return;
}
```

Observe the use of proc_mkdir API in init_module function. This API creates /proc/mydir directory. The first argument to proc_mkdir is name of the directory. The second argument is parent directory pointer which is NULL in this case, which means mydir is created immediately below /proc.

The example then creates a file myfile in /proc/mydir directory using create_proc_entry API. The first argument of create_proc_entry is name of the file. The second argument is file permissions (read/write). The third argument is parent directory which is /proc/mydir in this case.

The read_proc and write_proc members are function pointers to the functions which will be called whenever the file is read and write respectively. If you don't want either read or write operation on the file, you can assign corresponding function pointer to NULL.

The functions proc_read_my_flag and proc_write_my_flag simply writes and reads the current value of my_proc_flag to user space buffer.

The function cleanup_module removes the myfile first, then mydir from /proc file system using API remove_proc_entry.

Following table shows Makefile for proc.c module.

Table 2.10

```
obj-m := proc.o
KDIR := /lib/modules/$(shell uname -r)/build
PWD := $(shell pwd)
default:
        $(MAKE) -C $(KDIR) M=$(PWD) modules
clean:
        $(MAKE) -C $(KDIR) M=$(PWD) clean
```

Compile the module proc.c and insert proc.ko. It must create /proc/mydir/myfile file. You can use this file in any application.

For example, following commands result in function proc_read_my_flag and function proc_write_my_flag invocation.

Table 2.11

```
root@localhost# cat /proc/mydir/myfile
1
root@localhost# echo 4 > /proc/mydir/myfile
root@localhost# cat /proc/mydir/myfile
4
```

However, you must note that the buffer pointer parameter in proc read function is actually a page. Therefore, you must not write more than page size to this buffer. If you need to write more data, you must use seq_file interface described later.

2.4 SYSFS FILE SYSTEM

While proc file system is available in both 2.4 and 2.6 kernel, the sysfs file system is available in 2.6 kernel only. This file system also is a virtual in-core file system. The kernel must be compiled with CONFIG_SYSFS=y to enable sysfs support. This file system is mounted at /sys mount point using following command (if not auto mounted).

Table 2.12

```
mount -t sysfs sysfs /sys
```

This file system is intended to export information about the devices and drivers from kernel to user space. Since it is specifically designed for devices and drivers, it follows a well defined hierarchy. However to keep the example similar to the proc file system, the next example creates a file /sys/mydir/myfile.

The sysfs file system represents directories by struct kobject while files are represented by struct attribute.

Table 2.13

```
/* FILE: sysfs.c
* sysfs file system example
 */
#include <linux/kernel.h>
#include <linux/module.h>
#include <linux/sysfs.h>
static int debug_flag = 5;
ssize_t myfile_show(struct kobject *kobj,
        struct attribute *attr, char *buffer)
{
        int ret = sprintf(buffer, "%d\n", debug_flag);
        return ret;
}
ssize_t myfile_store(struct kobject *kobj,
        struct attribute *attr, const char *buffer, size_t size)
{
        int i, flag=0;
        for(i=0; i<size; i++) {
              if(buffer[i] < '0' || buffer[i] > '9')
                    break;
              flag = flag*10 + (buffer[i] - '0');
        }
        debug_flag = flag;
        return size;
}
struct sysfs_ops myobj_ops = {0};
struct kobj_type myobj_type = {0};
struct kobject myobj = {0};
struct attribute myfile = {0};
int init_module(void)
{
        int ret;
        strcpy(myobj.name, "mydir");
        ret = kobject_register(&myobj);
        if(ret < 0)
              printk("kobject_register failed\n");
        else
              printk("kobject_register successful\n");
        myobj.ktype = &myobj_type;
        myobj_type.sysfs_ops = &myobj_ops;
        myobj_ops.show = myfile_show;
        myobj_ops.store = myfile_store;
        myfile.name = "myfile";
        myfile.mode = S_IRUGO|S_IWUSR;
        myfile.owner = THIS_MODULE;
        ret = sysfs_create_file(&myobj, &myfile);
        if(ret < 0)
```

```
                printk("sysfs_create_file failed\n");
        else
                printk("sysfs_create_file successful\n");
        return 0;
}
void cleanup_module(void)
{
        sysfs_remove_file(&myobj, &myfile);
        kobject_unregister(&myobj);
        return;
}
MODULE_LICENSE("GPL");
```

Module sysfs.c uses API kobject_register to create directory /sys/mydir. The read and write function pointers to the kobject are defined in struct sysfs_ops using members show and store. The struct sysfs_ops itself is inside struct kobj_type which is inside kobject.

The example then uses API sysfs_create_file to create /sys/mydir/myfile. The first argument to the API is kobject (directory) while second argument is the attribute (file).

The function cleanup_module removes first myfile, then mydir using sysfs_remove_file and kobject_unregister APIs.

Following table shows a Makefile for sysfs.c module.

Table 2.14

```
obj-m := sysfs.o
KDIR := /lib/modules/$(shell uname -r)/build
PWD := $(shell pwd)
default:
        $(MAKE) -C $(KDIR) M=$(PWD) modules
clean:
        $(MAKE) -C $(KDIR) M=$(PWD) clean
```

Insert the module sysfs.ko which shall create /sys/mydir/myfile. Similar to proc file system, this file too can be used in any application. Following table shows an example:

Table 2.15

```
root@localhost# cat /sys/mydir/myfile
5
root@localhost# echo 4 > /sys/mydir/myfile
root@localhost# cat /sys/mydir/myfile
4
```

2.5 IOCTL FUNCTION

The character device driver provides a function ioctl which can be used to communicate with kernel space. Originally this function was used to control the device driver behavior; however it is very common to use this function in dummy character device drivers only for application to kernel communication.

Following example registers a character device driver and its ioctl function. The character device drivers shall be discussed in detail in another chapter.

Table 2.16

```
/* FILE: ioctl.c
 * ioctl example
 */
#include <linux/kernel.h>
#include <linux/module.h>
#include <linux/fs.h>
#define DUMMY_MAJOR 56
#define DUMMY_DEVICE "dummy"
long dummy_unlocked_ioctl(struct file* file,
                          unsigned int cmd, unsigned long arg)
{
        switch(cmd)
        {
              case 0x01:
                    printk("command 1: arg = %lu\n", arg);
                    break;
              default:
                    printk("command = 0x%x\n, arg = %lu", cmd, arg);
        }
        return 0;
}
struct file_operations dummy_ops = {
        owner: THIS_MODULE,
        unlocked_ioctl: dummy_unlocked_ioctl,
};
int init_module(void)
{
        if(register_chrdev(DUMMY_MAJOR, DUMMY_DEVICE, &dummy_ops) < 0)
              printk("major number %d not available\n", DUMMY_MAJOR);
        return 0;
}
void cleanup_module(void)
{
        unregister_chrdev(DUMMY_MAJOR, DUMMY_DEVICE);
}
MODULE_LICENSE("GPL");
```

The module registers a character device using register_chrdev API. The device has only ioctl operation defined using unlocked_ioctl member. Note that, the file_operations structure has a member ioctl as well which can also be used for the same purpose. However it is recommended to use unlocked_ioctl so that kernel need not hold kernel big lock while doing the ioctl operation which does not really require the lock.

The ioctl receives two parameters from use space, cmd and arg; which will be passed as arguments in ioctl call in application as we see shortly.

Following table shows Makefile for ioctl module.

Table 2.17

```
obj-m := ioctl.o
KDIR := /lib/modules/$(shell uname -r)/build
PWD := $(shell pwd)
default:
	$(MAKE) -C $(KDIR) M=$(PWD) modules
clean:
	$(MAKE) -C $(KDIR) M=$(PWD) clean
```

Insert ioctl.ko module and create a device node to access the device as shown below:

Table 2.18

```
root@localhost# insmod ioctl.ko
root@localhost# mknod /dev/dummy c 56 0
```

The command mknod creates a character device (option c) /dev/dummy with major number 56 (equal to DUMMY_MAJOR) and minor number 0.

Now the ioctl function of the module can be invoked from application using ioctl system call as shown below:

Table 2.19

```
/* FILE: ioctl_app.c
 * compile command: gcc ioctl_app.c
 */
#include <stdio.h>
#include <sys/ioctl.h>
#include <errno.h>
#include <fcntl.h>
int main()
{
        int fd = open("/dev/dummy", O_RDWR);
        if(fd < 0) {
              printf("open: %s\n", strerror(errno));
                    return -1;
        }
        if(ioctl(fd, 1, NULL) < 0) {
              printf("ioctl: %s\n", strerror(errno));
              return -1;
        }
        printf("ioctl success\n");
        return 0;
}
```

The arguments of ioctl system call are descriptor to the character device, the command and command argument. The second and third argument to ioctl system call shall be received in second and third argument of dummy_unlocked_ioctl function in kernel space.

2.6 SEQ_FILE INTERFACE

Although introduced in 2.4 kernel, the seq_file interface has become more popular in 2.6 kernel. This interface provides method to create files similar to proc file system, but provides more generic functions to perform read/write.

Creating seq_file interface involves at least following steps:

- create an entry in proc file system
- assign file_operations to the entry
- the open function of the file_operations must assign seq_operations
- seq_operations must provide start, stop, next and show functions

The start and next functions return a void pointer. Based on return value, a decision is made as show in Figure 2.1. It illustrates execution sequence of above mentioned functions when a seq_file is opened.

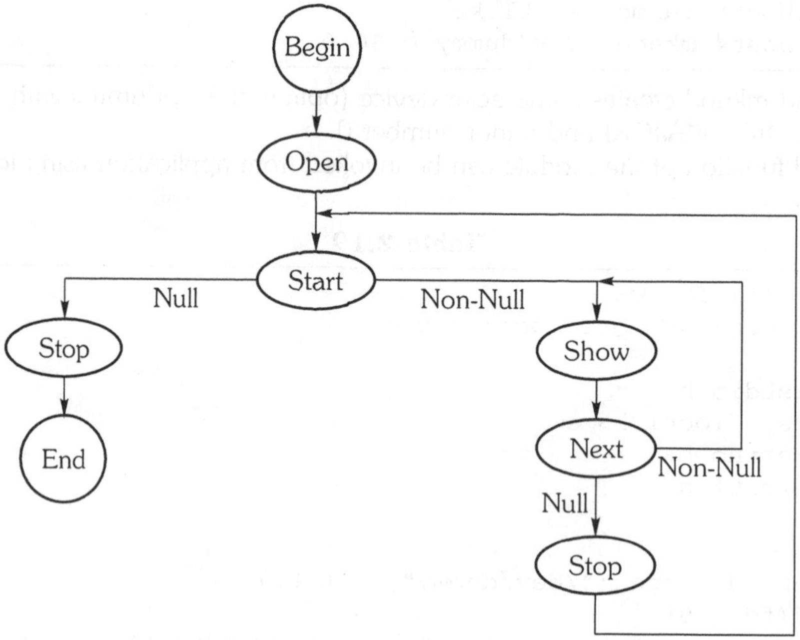

Figure 2.1

As shown, the show function is called after start function if start function returns non-null pointer. Similarly, show function is called after every next function if next function returns non-null. This state machine is executed until the seq_file EOF occurs, in which case the state machine moves to END state.

Table 2.20 illustrates a kernel module which creates a seq_file in /proc directory.

Table 2.20

```
/* FILE: seq.c */
#include <linux/module.h>
#include <linux/proc_fs.h>
#include <linux/seq_file.h>
#define SIZE 8
```

```
static int *array = NULL;
void* myseq_start(struct seq_file *m, loff_t *pos)
{
        int i;
        printk("%s\n", __FUNCTION__);
        if(*pos >= SIZE)
              return NULL;
        array = kmalloc(SIZE*sizeof(int), GFP_KERNEL);
        for(i=0; i<SIZE; i++)
              array[i] = i+1;
        printk("first *pos = %llu\n", *pos);
        return array;
}
void myseq_stop(struct seq_file *m, void *v)
{
        printk("%s: %p\n", __FUNCTION__, array);
        if(array) {
              kfree(array);
              array = NULL;
        }
        return;
}
void* myseq_next(struct seq_file *m, void *v, loff_t *pos)
{
        int *q = v;
        printk("%s: v=%p, *v=%d\n", __FUNCTION__, v, *q);
        (*pos)++;
        if(*pos < SIZE)
              return &array[*pos];
        return NULL;
}
int myseq_show(struct seq_file *m, void *v)
{
        int *q = v;
        printk("%s: v=%p, *v=%d\n", __FUNCTION__, v, *q);
        seq_printf(m, "%d ", *q);
        return 0;
}
static struct seq_operations myseq_op = {
        .start =     myseq_start,
        .next =      myseq_next,
        .stop =      myseq_stop,
        .show =      myseq_show
};
static int myseq_open(struct inode *inode, struct file *file)
{
        printk("%s\n", __FUNCTION__);
```

```
        return seq_open(file, &myseq_op);
}
static struct file_operations myseq_file_operations = {
        .open        = myseq_open,
        .read        = seq_read,
        .llseek      = seq_lseek,
        .release     = seq_release,
};
static struct proc_dir_entry *entry;
int init_module(void)
{
        printk("seq_file module inserted\n");
        entry = create_proc_entry("myseq_file", 0444, NULL);
        if (entry)
              entry->proc_fops = &myseq_file_operations;
        return 0;
}
void cleanup_module(void)
{
        printk("seq_file module removed\n");
        remove_proc_entry("myseq_file", NULL);
}
MODULE_LICENSE("GPL");
```

As shown above, the init_module function creates a proc entry using create_proc_entry function which is very similar to proc file module. Next it assigns file_operations to the entry. In file_operations, we only define new function for open member, while rest is standard seq interface functions.

In myseq_open function, we assign seq_operations to the file. Here we define four functions myseq_start, myseq_stop, myseq_next and myseq_show. These functions are called whenever the file created by create_proc_entry is read.

The myseq_start function allocates and initializes a memory (which is to be read from user space). The myseq_next function increments offset to point to next memory location until it reaches the end. The myseq_show function simply appends memory contents to the seq_file buffer. Finally myseq_stop is called after myseq_next returns NULL.

You must note that for contents to be displayed in user space, the module uses seq_printf function. This function is very similar to sprintf function except that first argument is seq_file.

Table 2.21 illustrates makefile for the seq.c

Table 2.21

```
obj-m := seq.o
KDIR := /lib/modules/$(shell uname -r)/build
PWD := $(shell pwd)
default:
        $(MAKE) -C $(KDIR) M=$(PWD) modules
clean:
        $(MAKE) -C $(KDIR) M=$(PWD) clean
```

Compile this module and insert it. You will see a file /proc/myseq_file. You can use "cat /proc/myseq_file" to read the file. You'll see following output:

Table 2.22

```
root@localhost# cat /proc/myseq_file
1 2 3 4 5 6 7 8 root@localhost#
```

As mentioned before, in contrary of proc file, seq_file interface can be used to read data even more than one page size.

2.7 SUMMARY

Application to kernel communication methods are very essential part of application development. The kernel works as service provider and applications make use of services provided by kernel. The kernel does all verification to make sure that any rouge application does not try to access any invalid range. If any application tries to access invalid range, the kernel kills that application by delivering SIGSEV signal.

2.8 ASSIGNMENTS

- Study and discuss netlink sockets
  Hint: netlink sockets are special sockets to convey networking information between user space and kernel space.
- Study and discuss mmap.
  Hint: mmap is a way to establish memory mapping between two different address spaces.

2.9 REFERENCES

- Netlink sockets-http://qos.ittc.ku.edu/netlink/html/
- Linux Memory Mapping-http://www.scs.ch/~frey/linux/memorymap.html

3 Linux Kernel Debugging

Kernel debugging is an interesting and challenging task for every kernel programmer. It requires additional knowledge, information and sometimes additional resources for kernel debugging.

In this chapter we discuss different methods for kernel debugging. Depending upon the problem, situation and resources, all or some of them can be used. This chapter discusses following methods of kernel debugging:

- printk
- proc file system
- oops tracing
- kdb
- serial console
- kgdb
- kernel support

3.1 PRINTK

Like printf which is extensively used in applications to print a message, printk provides a way to print a message or variables in kernel space. However, the difference is not only of user space and kernel space, but there are many more as discussed below.

A typical printk statement looks like

```
printk("<4>" "Hello world!\n");
```

As you see, printk has additional information in arguments. The printk has ability to selectively print a message based on the priority. This priority is passed as first argument in string form which concatenates with the format string. The priorities are as follows:

Table 3.1

Priority	Meaning
"<0>"	KERN_EMERG
"<1>"	KERN_ALERT
"<2>"	KERN_CRIT
"<3>"	KERN_ERR
"<4>"	KERN_WARNING
"<5>"	KERN_NOTICE
"<6>"	KERN_INFO
"<7>"	KERN_DEBUG

As you see, lower is the number higher is the priority. The priorities behavior can be controlled by `/proc/sys/kernel/printk` file. Typically this file looks like below:

```
root@localhost# cat /proc/sys/kernel/printk
7       4       1       7
```

The file has four digits. Each digit provides a way to change printk behavior. Their meanings are as follows:

- First digit indicates current console log level. Only messages with priority higher than this will be printed on console. In above example, every printk except KERN_DEBUG will be printed on console.
- Second digit is default level for messages without priority. It means that it is possible to have printk statement like
  ```
  printk ("Hello world!\n");
  ```
  Since above statement does not indicate priority explicitly, it is given default priority.
- Third digit is minimum console level. This indicates minimum (highest priority) value to which digit one can be set *i.e.,* digit one will always be greater than or equal to digit three.
- Fourth digit is default console log level. This indicates default value of digit one.

Third and fourth digits are required by syslogd. The syslogd can change current console log level, and can reset it to the default value from fourth digit. But syslogd can not set current log level less than minimum console level specified in third digit.

In kernel debugging, you frequently need to print kernel parameters. The following table lists format string for different kernel storage types.

Table 3.2

Type	Format string
(unsigned) int	%u %d
(unsigned) long	%lu %ld
(unsigned) long long	%llu %lld
size_t	%zu
ssize_t	%zd
u64	%llu
s64	%lld
loff_t	%llu

You must understand that excessive printk statements may cause kernel to slow down, and therefore unnecessary printk statements must be removed after debugging.

3.2 PROC FILE SYSTEM

As explained in Chapter 2: APPLICATION & KERNEL SPACE COMMUNICATION, you can create file(s) in /proc file system which have effect of calling kernel functions whenever read or written.

This mechanism provides a way for run time control debugging. For example:

Table 3.3

```
int debug_flag = 0;
if(debug_flag) {
        printk("Hello world!\n");
}
```

Above code prints line "Hello world" only if debug_flag has a non-zero value. The debug_flag can be controlled by a file in /proc file system and therefore debugger has a choice to enable or disable it at run time.

Similarly statistics can be retrieved by read function of /proc file which can be helpful in debugging.

3.3 OOPS TRACING

If you are a kernel programmer you must have seen mysterious kernel oops message whenever something goes wrong in kernel. Although 2.6 kernel gives a human readable stack trace, it was not so friendly in 2.4 series.

It is possible to get some help from oops message and debug the kernel. To understand oops tracing, let's take an example module which references NULL pointer and causes oops. Following table shows such module:

Table 3.4

```
/* File: crashmod.c */
int fun2(void)
{
        int a=5, *p;
        printk("%s\n", __FUNCTION__);
        p = &a;
        printk("a = %d\n", *p);
        *p = *p +5;
        printk("a = %d\n", *p);
        p = NULL;
        printk("a = %d\n", *p);
        return 0;
}
int fun1(void)
{
        printk("%s\n", __FUNCTION__);
        fun2();
        return 0;
}
int init_module(void)
{
        printk("inserting crash module\n");
        fun1();
        return 0;
}
```

This module reference a NULL pointer in function fun2 which causes kernel oops. Below tables shows Makefile for crashmod.c module.

Table 3.5

```
KTREE = /usr/src/linux-2.6.21.5
obj-m := crash.o
crash-objs := crashmod.o
CFLAGS += -O0
```

```
default:
        make -C $(KTREE) SUBDIRS='pwd' modules
clean:
        make -C $(KTREE) SUBDIRS='pwd' clean
```

Note the –O0 flag in addition to default CFLAGS. This is required so that objdump can generate well understandable code as we see shortly.

This module generates following oops when inserted to kernel using insmod.

Table 3.6

```
[  127.828276] BUG: unable to handle kernel NULL pointer dereference
at virtual
address 00000000
[  127.855763]  printing eip:
[  127.867641] *pde = 00000000
[  127.879158] Oops: 0000 [#1]
[  127.890463] SMP
[  127.900969] Modules linked in: crash
[  127.912990] CPU:  0
[  127.912991] EIP:     0060:[<f887c068>]    Not tainted VLI
[  127.912993] EFLAGS: 00010286    (2.6.21.5-minix #18)
[  127.948751] EIP is at fun2+0x68/0x81 [crash]
[  127.960331] eax: 00000000   ebx: f887c480   ecx: ffffffff   edx:
00000046
[  127.974283] esi: f887c480   edi: f887c480   ebp: f4dc3e80   esp:
f4dc3e70
[  127.988041] ds: 007b   es: 007b   fs: 00d8  gs: 0033   ss: 0068
[  128.000625] Process insmod (pid: 5178, ti=f4dc2000 task=c1d72a90
task.ti=f4dc
2000)
```

Observe the EIP line shown in bold letters. This line yields following information:

- Oops occurred in module named crash.
- Oops occurred in function fun2.
- The function fun2 size is 0x81 bytes. Oops occurred at offset 0x68.

This is pretty good information to start with. However, if the code is compiled with –O0 option, it is possible to get exact location using objdump utility as shown below:

Table 3.7

```
root@localhost# objdump -S crash.ko > crash.s
root@localhost# cat crash.s
int fun2(void)
{
        0:      55                          push   %ebp
        1:      89 e5                       mov    %esp,%ebp
        3:      83 ec 10                    sub    $0x10,%esp
                int a=5, *p;
        6:      c7 45 f8 05 00 00 00        movl   $0x5,-0x8(%ebp)
```

```
            printk("%s\n", __FUNCTION__);
    d:      c7 44 24 04 00 00 00     movl    $0x0,0x4(%esp)
    14:     00
    15:     c7 04 24 05 00 00 00     movl    $0x5,(%esp)
    1c:     e8 fc ff ff ff           call    1d <fun2+0x1d>
            p = &a;
    21:     8d 45 f8                 lea     -0x8(%ebp),%eax
    24:     89 45 fc                 mov     %eax,-0x4(%ebp)
            printk("a = %d\n", *p);
    27:     8b 45 fc                 mov     -0x4(%ebp),%eax
    2a:     8b 00                    mov     (%eax),%eax
    2c:     89 44 24 04              mov     %eax,0x4(%esp)
    30:     c7 04 24 09 00 00 00     movl    $0x9,(%esp)
    37:     e8 fc ff ff ff           call    38 <fun2+0x38>
            *p = *p +5;
    3c:     8b 45 fc                 mov     -0x4(%ebp),%eax
    3f:     8b 00                    mov     (%eax),%eax
    41:     8d 50 05                 lea     0x5(%eax),%edx
    44:     8b 45 fc                 mov     -0x4(%ebp),%eax
    47:     89 10                    mov     %edx,(%eax)
            printk("a = %d\n", *p);
    49:     8b 45 fc                 mov     -0x4(%ebp),%eax
    4c:     8b 00                    mov     (%eax),%eax
    4e:     89 44 24 04              mov     %eax,0x4(%esp)
    52:     c7 04 24 09 00 00 00     movl    $0x9,(%esp)
    59:     e8 fc ff ff ff           call    5a <fun2+0x5a>
            p = NULL;
    5e:     c7 45 fc 00 00 00 00     movl    $0x0,-0x4(%ebp)
            printk("a = %d\n", *p);
    65:     8b 45 fc                 mov     -0x4(%ebp),%eax
    68:     8b 00                    mov     (%eax),%eax
    6a:     89 44 24 04              mov     %eax,0x4(%esp)
    6e:     c7 04 24 09 00 00 00     movl    $0x9,(%esp)
    75:     e8 fc ff ff ff           call    76 <fun2+0x76>
            return 0;
    7a:     b8 00 00 00 00           mov     $0x0,%eax
}
    7f:     c9                       leave
    80:     c3                       ret
```

The objdump utility can generate interleaved C and assembly source code with –S option (As mentioned earlier, this requires kernel modules to be compiled with –O0).

In above objdump output, look at source line above offset 0x68 where oops occurred. This clearly tells the culprit line is:

`printk("a = %d\n", *p);`

this de-referenced an illegal pointer.

3.4 KDB

KDB is an inbuilt kernel debugger which can be helpful at times to examine memory and data structure contents.

KDB patches are available at ftp://oss.sgi.com/www/projects/kdb/download. You must apply appropriate patches to your kernel to include KDB functionality.

Download KDB patches and apply them as follows:

Table 3.8

```
root@localhost:/usr/src/linux# bunzip2 kdb-v4.4-2.6.21-common-1.bz2
root@localhost:/usr/src/linux# bunzip2 kdb-v4.4-2.6.21-i386-1.bz2root
@localhost:/usr/src/linux# patch -p1 < kdb-v4.4-2.6.21-common-1
root@localhost:/usr/src/linux# patch -p1 < kdb-v4.4-2.6.21-i386-1
```

Compile the kernel with following KDB options:

Table 3.9

```
CONFIG_KDB=y
# CONFIG_KDB_MODULES is not set
CONFIG_KDB_OFF=y
CONFIG_KDB_CONTINUE_CATASTROPHIC=0
# CONFIG_KDB_USB is not set
```

The option CONFIG_KDB_OFF=y keep KDB turned off by default. You can say n if you want to enable it by default. After system has booted, KDB can be turned on or off by writing 1 or 0 respectively in file /proc/sys/kernel/kdb. Alternatively, this can be done by passing "kdb=on" or "kdb=off" flag with kernel boot options. There is another option "kdb=early" to enable early kdb control during boot process.

The option CONFIG_KDB_CONTINUE_CATASTROPHIC controls kdb behavior whether to continue or not if a kernel panic occurs. CONFIG_KDB_USB can be used if you have a USB keyboard.

If kdb is enabled, it will automatically activate if a kernel panic or oops occurs. Alternatively it can be activated in a running kernel by pressing pause key.

Let's use kdb to debug the ioctl kernel module explained in Chapter 2: APPLICATION & KERNEL SPACE COMMUNICATION. Insert the ioctl kernel module and press pause key to activate kdb. Following table shows a kdb debug session.

Table 3.10

```
Entering kdb(current = 0xc0520480, pid 0) on processor 0 due to
keyboard Entry
[0] kdb> bp dummy_unlocked_ioctl
Instruction [i] BP#0 at 0xf887e060 ([ioctl] dummy_unlocked_ioctl) is
enabled globally adjust 1
[0] kdb> bl
Instruction [i] BP#0 at 0xf887e060 ([ioctl] dummy_unlocked_ioctl) is
enabled globally adjust 1
[0] kdb> go
root@localhost:/root# ./a.out
Instruction [i] breakpoint #0 at 0xf887e060 (adjusted)
```

```
0xf887e060     dummy_unlocked_ioctl     int3
Entering kdb(current = 0xf46d0560, pid 6154) on processor 0 due to
Breakpoint @ 0xf887e060
[0]kdb> bt
Stack traceback for pid 6154
0xf46d0560     6154     6143     1 0  R   0xf46d0710     *a.out

esp            eip            Function(args)
0xf3d95f48     0xf887e060     [ioctl] dummy_unlocked_ioctl
0xf3d95f54     0xc0181f28     do_ioctl + 0x28
0xf3d95f70     0xc018219f     vfs_ioctl + 0x21f
0xf3d95f98     0xc0182269     sys_ioctl + 0x39
0xf3d95fb4     0xc0104154     sysenter_past_esp + 0x5d
[0]kdb> ss
SS trap at 0xf887e061 dummy_unlocked_ioctl + 0x1: mov %esp, %ebp
[0]kdb> ss
SS trap at 0xf887e063 dummy_unlocked_ioctl + 0x3: sub $0xc, %esp
[0]kdb> go
ioctl success
root@localhost:/root#
```

In above example, kdb is activated when pause key is pressed. We set a breakpoint using bp command on function dummy_unlocked_ioctl. The bl command lists the breakpoints and go command continues kernel execution normally.

Later when ./a.out is executed which invokes ioctl function of the character device driver as explained in Chapter 2: APPLICATION & KERNEL SPACE COMMUNICATION, the dummy_unlocked_ioctl function is called. As soon as this function is called, kdb stops kernel execution and drops to kdb shell.

As you see in above debug session, kdb can not be used for source level debugging (it shows assembly code), however it can be useful at times. Following table shows some important kdb commands.

Table 3.11

Command	Usages	Description
md	<vaddr>	Display memory contents
mdp	<paddr> <bytes>	Display physical memory
mm	<vaddr> <contents>	Modify memory contents
go	[<vaddr>]	Continue execution
rd		Display registers
rm	<reg> <contents>	Modify registers
bt	[<vaddr>]	Show traceback
btp	<pid>	Display stack for process <pid>
dmesg		Display syslog buffer
bp	[<vaddr>]	Set/Display breakpoints
bl	[<vaddr>]	Display breakpoints
bc	<bpnum>	Clear breakpoint
ss		Single step

Of course kdb has much more commands than shown here. It's very powerful and handy tool and provides lot of options to examine memory and data structures.

In addition to pause key, kdb can be activated through serial console as follows:

- Setup the serial console as explained in next section.
- A user level application must open serial port, so that kernel starts receiving commands on serial port.
- Use Ctrl-A key from serial consol to activate kdb (Note that in minicom, Ctrl-A is reserved for other purpose. You can change the kdb activation key by modifying kdb_serial_str[]).

Some patches have been submitted by Dan Aloni to activate kdb over network as well. Refer to "KDB over the network using netconsole" at http://lwn.net/Articles/211485/ for more details.

3.5 USING SERIAL CONSOLE

It is possible to redirect kernel messages to a remote host using serial port. This method is very common for debugging embedded systems or target boards which do not have own console.

You need to connect the target board to remote host using a null modem cable (having female connector at both ends). If remote host does not have a serial port, you can use USB to serial convector to connect with target board.

To let kernel know so that it redirects all kernel messages on serial port, you need to pass some boot options to kernel as shown below:

Table 3.12

```
title    Ubuntu 8.04, kernel 2.6.21-5-devel
root     (hd0,6)
kernel   /boot/vmlinuz-2.6.21.5-devel root=/dev/hda1 ro console=tty0
console=ttyS0,115200n8
initrd   /boot/initrd.img-2.6.21.5-devel
```

The boot option console=ttyS0,115200n8 instructs kernel to mirror all print messages to ttyS0 also. 115200n8 specifies serial port configuration. Same configuration must be made at remote host serial terminal.

3.6 KGDB

This is most convenient method of debugging Linux kernel however some setup work is required in order to use it. Using kgdb, it is possible to debug Linux kernel step by step, the way you use gdb to debug applications.

To setup kgdb, you need two machines; a development machine and a target machine. Development machine is the one where you have kernel source, kgdb patches and compile the kernel or modules whereas target machine is the one where you run the kernel to be debugged. The two machines must be connected by network as well as by serial port using null modem cable.

Before compiling the kernel on development machine, you have to download appropriate kgdb patches for your kernel and apply. Following table shows typical kgdb configuration during kernel compilation.

Table 3.13

```
CONFIG_KGDB=y
CONFIG_KGDB_CONSOLE=y
```

```
# CONFIG_KGDB_ONLY_MODULES is not set
CONFIG_KGDB_8250_NOMODULE=y
CONFIG_KGDB_8250=y
CONFIG_KGDB_SIMPLE_SERIAL=y
CONFIG_KGDB_BAUDRATE=115200
CONFIG_KGDB_PORT_NUM=0
CONFIG_EARLY_PRINTK=y
```

In particular, CONFIG_KGDB_PORT_NUM and CONFIG_KGDB_BAUDRATE must be set correctly.

Load the new compiled kernel to target machine and give following boot options:

Table 3.14

```
kgdbwait kgdb8250=0,115200
```

These boot options instructs kernel to wait to connect from remote gdb. The two options to kgdb8250 are serial port number and baud rate.

If you boot the target machine with new kernel, you observe that target machine boot process halts and it waits for gdb connection from a remote host.

Go back to development machine. Use gdb to load kernel image and connect to target machine as follows:

Table 3.15

```
root@localhost# gdb vmlinux
(gdb) set remotebaud 115200
(gdb) target remote /dev/ttyS0
(gdb) continue
```

Hereafter you can put breakpoints anywhere in kernel functions and can debug step by step as you debug Linux applications.

3.7 SERIAL CONSOLE LOGIN

Getting a login prompt at serial console is very useful to debug kernel hangs. It is because the serial console login works over UART driver which generally works even if some kernel process has hanged. This not only provides a shell to work on and examine system state but also provides way to use debug utilities like sysrq (explained shortly).

The getty program is used to get login prompt at a serial console. However on different Linux flavors, you may find different ways to enable the getty. The most common way to enabling getty is to create following (or similar) entry in /etc/inittab.

Table 3.16

```
s0:2345:respawn:/sbin/agetty -L -f /etc/issueserial 115200 ttyS0
vt100
```

You may refer to inittab manual page for more details on the script format.

3.8 SYSRQ

Sysrq (also known as Magic sysrq key) is very handy tool to debug kernel hangs. To use sysrq, you must compile the kernel with CONFIG_MAGIC_SYSRQ. If you have the kernel compiled with CONFIG_MAGIC_SYSRQ, you will see following proc files:

- /proc/sys/kernel/sysrq – It is used to enable or disable sysrq functionality. You can disable sysrq functionality by writing 0 to this file while writing 1 to this file enables all sysrq features. A value of greater than 1 indicates a bit-mask which enables/disables sysrq functionalities selectively. For more details on this, refer to Linux documentation on sysrq.
- /proc/sysrq-trigger – It is used to trigger sysrq functionality. If you are using a serial console, you can use serial console to write sysrq command in this file. Some of sysrq commands are listed in Table 3.17. For complete list of sysrq commands, refer to Linux documentation on sysrq.

Table 3.17

Command	Action
b	immediately reboots the system
l	shows stack back-trace of all active CPU
m	displays system memory information
p	displays current registers and flags
t	displays list of all processes and their information
0-9	sets kernel console level

In addition to /proc/sysrq-trigger, the sysrq commands can also be trigger using some key combination like:

- Alt + SysRq + command (from local keyboard if working)
- Ctrl + A + F + command (from minicom serial console)

Any serial console provides some or other way of sending "BREAK" command on serial interface. This "BREAK" command can be used along with sysrq-command key to send sysrq command.

3.9 USING KERNEL SUPPORT

Linux kernel provides some support for debugging. You can enable some or all of following options to make kernel more verbose. Following table shows some of configuration options which can be selectively enabled to make kernel more verbose.

Table 3.18

```
CONFIG_DEBUG_SPINLOCK=y
CONFIG_DEBUG_MUTEXES=y
# CONFIG_DEBUG_STACKOVERFLOW is not set
# CONFIG_DEBUG_STACK_USAGE is not set
```

3.10 SUMMARY

Linux kernel debugging is a very challenging task especially on embedded systems. Methods described in this chapter can be used based on situation and applicability for debugging.

3.11 ASSIGNMENTS

- Make kgdb setup for 32-bit and 64-bit machines, and put breakpoint at some kernel function of your choice.
- Use this kgdb setup to debug a kernel module loaded by you.
- Although objdump analysis works very well with code compiled with–O0. However, code with–O2 can also be debugged using "*objdump–Dslx test.o>test.i*" or "*objdump–prefix-address–S–l test.o>test.i*" command. Compile a module with–O2, and try to debug using objdump.
- Understand console driver concept.

3.12 REFERENCES

- netconsole-http://www.kernel.org/doc/Documentation/networking/netconsole.txt
- kdb over netconsole-http://lwn.net/Articles/211485/
- console driver-http://ar.linux.it/docs/sercons/sercons.html
- Linux kernel documentation-Documentation/sysrq.txt

4 Delayed Execution

Linux kernel programming or device driver programming very often requires delaying the code execution. For example, deferring IO based work for later time as it is very slow process or retransmitting a message after certain timeout. Linux kernel provides several mechanisms to delay the execution. This chapter discusses following such mechanisms and illustrates them with examples.

- Kernel ticks – jiffies
- Kernel timers
- Softirq and tasklet
- Work queue

4.1 KERNEL TICKS – JIFFIES

Linux kernel keeps track of number of ticks since the kernel has booted in a global variable called jiffies. The number of ticks per second depends upon HZ which is defined to 100 in most of the systems, therefore jiffies is incremented every 10 ms.

Following sample code illustrates a busy wait mechanism using jiffies:

Table 4.1

```
#include <linux/module.h>
#include <linux/jiffies.h>
int init_module(void)
{
        unsigned long now;
        printk("HZ = %ld\n", HZ);
        now = jiffies;
        while (jiffies < now + 5*HZ);
        return 0;

}
```

The insmod command shall return after 5 seconds for above module. Since this is a busy wait, the CPU does nothing useful. Above code can be changed as shown below to yield the CPU while waiting for timeout.

Table 4.2

```
#include <linux/module.h>
#include <linux/jiffies.h>
int init_module(void)
{
        unsigned long now;
        printk("HZ = %ld\n", HZ);
        now = jiffies;
        while (jiffies < now + 5*HZ)
            schedule();
        return 0;
}
```

The global variable jiffies is defined as volatile and therefore in the while loop, every time latest jiffies value is read.

Alternatively, for small delays, Linux kernel provides usleep function which takes number of microseconds to sleep as argument.

4.2 KERNEL TIMERS

The Linux kernel provides timers which can invoke a function call after given time has elapsed. Following example illustrates a simple timer mechanism:

Table 4.3

```
#include <linux/module.h>
#include <linux/timer.h>
static struct timer_list timer;
static unsigned int a = 6;
static void timeout_fn(unsigned long arg)
{
        unsigned int *q = (unsigned int*)arg;
        printk("timer expired\n");
        printk("Arg = %u\n", *q);
        return;
}
int init_module(void)
{
        printk("timer module inserted\n");
        init_timer(&timer);
        timer.function = timeout_fn;
        timer.data = (unsigned long)&a;
        timer.expires = jiffies + 5*HZ; /* 5 seconds */
        add_timer(&timer);
        return 0;
}
```

```
void cleanup_module(void)
{
        printk("timer module removed\n");
        return;
}
MODULE_LICENSE("GPL");
```

The structure timer_list represents a timer. The timer must be initialized using init_timer function before using. The function member of timer_list is assigned to the function (time out handler) which is to be invoked after timer expiry. The data member is assigned to any value which is passed back to time out handler function as argument. The field expires is assigned the timeout value in term of jiffies.

The timer is now initialized completely and is ready to start. The timer is started using add_timer function.

Insert this module and wait for 5 seconds. You will see the "timer expired" message exactly 5 seconds later than "timer module inserted".

Note that this timer mechanism is one shot timer *i.e.*, once the timer expires it does not restart automatically. If you want a periodic timer, you must reassign expires value and restart is using add_timer.

To deactivate a timer, you can use del_timer function. However, in SMP system it is possible that some CPU is running the time out handler function while another CPU is doing del_timer. Therefore in such situations you must use del_timer_sync function. The del_timer_sync function makes sure that time out handler has finished executing on other CPUs. The functions have following prototype:

Table 4.4

```
int del_timer (struct timer_list *timer);
int del_timer_sync(struct timer_list *timer);
```

Since del_timer_sync waits for time out handler to complete, you must ensure that you donít hold any lock which prevents time out handler to complete. Also del_timer_sync must not be called from interrupt context (more on it later).

The cleanup_module function in Table 4.3 example should be completed as follows:

Table 4.5

```
void cleanup_module(void)
{
        printk("timer module removed\n");
        del_timer_sync(&timer);
        return;
}
```

Now it is safe to remove module even before 5 seconds (after insmod).

It must be noted that the time out handler function is called in interrupt context therefore this function must not sleep at any point of time. Also, the timer memory must either be statically allocated or must be allocated using kmalloc. You must never call add_timer for a timer defined on stack.

Finally, the function mod_timer can be used to modify expiry time of a timer; and function timer_pending can be used to check if a timer is running or not. These functions have following prototype:

Table 4.6

```
int mod_timer(struct timer_list *timer, unsigned long expires);
int timer_pending(const struct timer_list * timer);
```

The second argument in mod_timer function specifies new absolute timeout value in jiffies. The function works well even if the timer is not running currently. The mod_timer function can be called only for those timers which have been initialized using init_timer function.

4.3 INTRODUCTION TO SOFTIRQ

The kernel timers, as discussed, provide mechanism to defer work for predefined and fixed amount of time. However, the kernel also provides mechanism to defer work which shall be executed later and as soon as possible. This mechanism, which was originally introduced as bottom-halves in ancient kernel, proposes to divide a work between important and not so important; and the idea is to do important work immediately and defer not so important work for later point of time.

For example, kernel receives a packet from network. Now kernel has two jobs, the first one is to deliver the packet to application via networking stack, while other is to prepare itself to receive further packets. Of course both jobs are mandatory to execute but kernel makes a choice here. Kernel only receives the packet and enqueues it (to deliver it to application at later point of time) and prepare itself to receive further packets. When kernel is not processing interrupts, kernel will deliver the previously queued packet to application.

This mechanism was originally known as bottom halves, where a work is divided in two parts, the top half and the bottom half. The top half is performed while interrupts are disabled while bottom half is performed later when interrupts are enabled. Thus, interrupts are disabled only for short time (rather than during entire work execution).

2.6 kernel has a better mechanism called softirq. Whenever an external device generates an interrupt, an interrupt handler is invoked. While this interrupt handler is running, the interrupts are disabled. This is called hardirq context. The interrupt handler does minimal work and restores interrupts. Later kernel invokes softirq functions which do remaining work in softirq context.

As of now Linux kernel defines following softirqs in include/linux/interrupt.h file.

- HI_SOFTIRQ
- TIMER_SOFTIRQ
- NET_TX_SOFTIRQ
- NET_RX_SOFTIRQ
- BLOCK_SOFTIRQ
- TASKLET_SOFTIRQ
- SCHED_SOFTIRQ

Each softirq has its unique number. The softirq is defined by open_softirq function which has following prototype:

Table 4.7

```
void open_softirq(int nr, void (*action)(struct softirq_action*),
void
*data);
```

The first argument nr is softirq's unique number. The second argument action is the softirq handler and third argument data is passed as it is to softirq handler when invoked. All softirqs are stored in softirq_vec array.

Whenever kernel wants to defer some work to the softirq, kernel raises that softirq using raise_softirq function. For example, if kernel receives a packet from network and wants to defer packet processing, kernel invokes raise_softirq(NET_RX_SOFTIRQ) after doing minimal important work in interrupt handler.

After an interrupt handler terminates, kernel checks if any softirq is pending. If softirq is pending then kernel invokes do_softirq function. This function check which softirqs are pending and invokes corresponding softirq handler (registered in action argument in open_softirq function). A skeleton of __do_softirq function is illustrated below:

Table 4.8

```
        pending = local_softirq_pending();
        /* ... snip ... */
        h = softirq_vec;
         do {
                if (pending & 1) {
                        h->action(h);
                }
                h++;
                pending >>= 1;
        } while (pending)
```

As shown in above table, the __do_softirq function checks each softirq if it is raised. If the softirq is set then corresponding handler is called. If there are too many softirq being raised then this function further defers softirq to ksoftirq daemon (not shown in this table).

While you are free to use any of these softirqs, you are not encouraged to add new softirq until you have genuine reason for it; because for most of device driver deferring requirement, the TASKLET_SOFTIRQ is suffice.

4.4 UNDERSTANDING TASKLETS

Similar to kernel timers, tasklets provide mechanism to defer work for later execution. But tasklets are used to defer work and then execute it at a time chosen by kernel. The tasklets are run by TASKLET_SOFTIRQ softirq. Therefore all tasklet functions run in softirq context.

Table 4.9 illustrates simple example of tasklet.

Table 4.9

```
#include <linux/module.h>
#include <linux/interrupt.h>
static struct tasklet_struct tasklet;
static unsigned int a = 6;
```

```
static void deffered_fn(unsigned long arg)
{
        unsigned int *q = (unsigned int*)arg;
        printk("deffered function executed\n");
        printk("Arg = %u\n", *q);
        return;
}
int init_module(void)
{
        printk("tasklet module inserted\n");
        tasklet_init(&tasklet, deffered_fn, (unsigned long)&a);
        tasklet_schedule(&tasklet);
        return 0;
}
void cleanup_module(void)
{
        printk("tasklet module removed\n");
        tasklet_kill(&tasklet);
        return;
}
MODULE_LICENSE("GPL");
```

Similar to timer_list structure for kernel timers, we have tasklet_struct for tasklets, which is used for defining a tasklet. The tasklet is initialized by tasklet_init function which takes three arguments. The first argument is the tasklet to be initialized (tasklet_struct). The second argument is tasklet handler or tasklet function; and the third argument is data which is passed to tasklet function as it is.

After initializing the tasklet, it can be scheduled for execution using tasklet_schedule function. On a normal system (nominally loaded), you will observe that deffered_fn is called as soon as you insert the module because softirqs are run after every interrupt handler (therefore tasklet also run after every interrupt handler because as mentioned earlier tasklets are run by TASKLET_SOFTIRQ). Similar to timers, tasklet memory (struct tasklet_struct) must be allocated either statically or by kmalloc.

The tasklet can be stopped by tasklet_kill function as shown in cleanup_module function. Additionally, tasklets can be enabled or disabled using tasklet_enable and tasklet_disable functions. If a tasklet is disabled using tasklet_disable function, it will not be executed until it is enabled again using tasklet_enable function.

Generally you run tasklet using TASKLET_SOFTIRQ softirq. However, if you want to run your tasklet at higher priority than other softirqs, you must run it using HI_SOFTIRQ using tasklet_hi_schedule function. The HI_SOFTIRQ softirq is first one to run among all softirqs. The above described functions have following prototype:

Table 4.10

```
void tasklet_enable(struct tasklet_struct *tasklet);
void tasklet_disable(struct tasklet_struct *tasklet);
void tasklet_hi_schedule(struct tasklet_struct *tasklet);
```

As mentioned earlier, kernel timers and tasklet have many things in common as described below.

- Tasklets are also one shot and must be re-scheduled by tasklet function or any other function to run again.
- Tasklets run in softirq context and therefore tasklet functions can not sleep.

All softirqs have CPU specific data. Therefore, a tasklet runs on the same CPU that schedules it. As illustrated in Table 4.8 (__do_softirq skeleton table), all softirqs are executed in order, therefore on a CPU at a time only one softirq can run, which implies on a CPU at a time only one tasklet can run. However, it is possible that other CPU is running some other softirq or tasklet. The tasklet_action function, which is softirq handler for TASKLET_SOFTIRQ, makes sure that same tasklet is not running at more than one CPU by calling function tasklet_trylock. The tasklet is executed only if tasklet_action is able to get the lock.

4.5 UNDERSTANDING WORKQUEUES

The deferring mechanism discussed so far does not allow the deferred function to sleep. However, often some functions have to sleep or wait for memory allocation, event completion, lock holding, IO completion etc. Linux kernel provides workqueue mechanism which allows deferred function to sleep.

There are two ways to use workqueue interface. First one is to use kernel's workqueue and other one is to use your own workqueue. Since work queue handler function are allowed to sleep, a single lazy such function will cause other functions also to be delayed. Therefore if you are using kernel's workqueue, make sure that your deferred function does not sleep too much. If it does, then better use your own workqueue.

Following examples illustrates a small module which uses kernel's workqueue.

Table 4.11

```
#include <linux/module.h>
#include <linux/workqueue.h>
struct my_work {
        struct work_struct work;
        void* data;
}my_work;
static unsigned int a = 6;
static void deffered_fn(struct work_struct *work)
{
        struct my_work *mwp = container_of(work, struct my_work, work);
        unsigned int *q = mwp->data;
        printk("deffered function executed\n");
        printk("Arg = %u\n", *q);
        return;
}
int init_module(void)
{
        printk("workqueue module inserted\n");
        my_work.data = &a;
        INIT_WORK(&my_work.work, deffered_fn);
        schedule_work(&my_work.work);
```

```
        return 0;
}
void cleanup_module(void)
{
        printk("workqueue module removed\n");
         flush_scheduled_work();
        return;
}
MODULE_LICENSE("GPL");
```

The one difference in deferred function prototype from softirq and timers is that the deferred function takes only one argument of type work_struct. Therefore, to pass any data to workqueue deferred function, you should define your own structure (similar to my_work) which contains work_struct and data (Although in kernel earlier than 2.6.20, the workqueue function prototype was similar to tasklet where argument was passed during workqueue initialization. However to reduce the workqueue structure size, this modification was made).

As shown in init_module function, the data member of my_work is assigned to the data which is required in deferred function. Then INIT_WORK macro is used to initialize the work_struct which takes the deferred function as second argument. The schedule_work function queues the work_struct into kernel's workqueue.

Later kernel runs the workqueue and deferred function is invoked. The container_of macro can be used to derive my_work structure and thus data member.

Before unloading the module, you must make sure to call flush_scheduled_work function which guarantees that no deferred function is pending after module unloading.

To use your own workqueue, you must first create the workqueue. Following kernel module illustrates an example.

Table 4.12

```
#include <linux/module.h>
#include <linux/workqueue.h>
struct my_work {
        struct work_struct work;
        void* data;
}my_work;
static unsigned int a = 6;
static void deffered_fn(struct work_struct *work)
{
        struct my_work *mwp = container_of(work, struct my_work, work);
        unsigned int *q = mwp->data;
        printk("deffered function executed\n");
        printk("Arg = %u\n", *q);
        return;
}
static struct workqueue_struct *myqueue = NULL;
int init_module(void)
{
        printk("workqueue module inserted\n");
```

```
        myqueue = create_workqueue("myqueue");
        my_work.data = &a;
        INIT_WORK(&my_work.work, deffered_fn);
        queue_work(myqueue, &my_work.work);
        return 0;
}
void cleanup_module(void)
{
        printk("workqueue module removed\n");
        flush_workqueue(myqueue);
        destroy_workqueue(myqueue);
        return;
}
MODULE_LICENSE("GPL");
```

The macro create_workqueue is used to create a workqueue. The only argument is takes it name of the workqueue, which can be used to identify the worker thread in processes running on system using command "ps –aux". Initialization of work_struct is done same way using INIT_WORK macro. However queuing is done using queue_work function which takes the workqueue pointer and work_struct pointer as arguments.

The work queue can be destroyed using destroy_workqueue function as shown in cleanup_module function. However, before destroying the workqueue, you must flush the workqueue using flush_workqueue function so that no deferred functions are pending.

It must be noted that on SMP system, the create_workqueue creates per CPU worker thread (although it is transparent to workqueue creating code and you need not really worry about it). However, if you want to create single worker thread across CPUs, you must use create_singlethread_workqueue function.

The schedule_work and queue_work function defers the work to be executed later but as soon as possible. However, workqueues also provide mechanism to delay the work for some certain time. Following kernel module illustrates an example.

Table 4.13

```
#include <linux/module.h>
#include <linux/workqueue.h>
struct my_work {
        struct delayed_work dwork;
        void* data;
}my_work;
static unsigned int a = 6;
static void deffered_fn(struct work_struct *work)
{
        struct delayed_work *dwp = container_of(work, struct
delayed_work, work);
        struct my_work *mwp = container_of(dwp, struct my_work, dwork);
        unsigned int *q = mwp->data;
        printk("deffered function executed\n");
        printk("Arg = %u\n", *q);
        return;
```

```
}
static struct workqueue_struct *myqueue = NULL;
int init_module(void)
{
        printk("workqueue module inserted\n");
        myqueue = create_workqueue("myqueue");
        my_work.data = &a;
        INIT_DELAYED_WORK(&my_work.dwork, deffered_fn);
        queue_delayed_work(myqueue, &my_work.dwork, 5*HZ);
        return 0;
}
void cleanup_module(void)
{
        printk("workqueue module removed\n");
        cancel_delayed_work(&my_work.dwork);
        destroy_workqueue(myqueue);
        return;
}
MODULE_LICENSE("GPL");
```

For this purpose, you have to use delayed_work structure which has work_struct member in it. To initialize the delayed_work structure INIT_DELAYED_WORK macro must be used, and queue_delayed_work function is used to queue the work. Note that the third argument of queue_delayed_work is delay in terms of relative jiffies.

The cancel_delayed_work function is used to cancel the queued work. Before destroying the workqueue, you must either flush it or you must cancel queued work. If you destroy the queue without doing any of them, and any delayed function is pending; kernel panic is likely to occur.

On a final note, work queue memory (struct work_struct) must be allocated either statically or by using kmalloc.

4.6 SUMMARY

Following table lists prototype of all workqueue functions together.

Table 4.14

```
void destroy_workqueue(struct workqueue_struct *wq);
int queue_work(struct workqueue_struct *wq, struct work_struct *work);
int queue_delayed_work(struct workqueue_struct *wq, struct delayed_work
*work, unsigned long delay);
void flush_workqueue(struct workqueue_struct *wq);
void flush_scheduled_work(void);
void flush_delayed_work(struct delayed_work *work);
int schedule_work(struct work_struct *work);
int schedule_delayed_work(struct delayed_work *work, unsigned long
delay);
int flush_work(struct work_struct *work);
int cancel_delayed_work(struct delayed_work *work);
INIT_WORK(_work, _func)
INIT_DELAYED_WORK(_work, _func)
create_workqueue(name)
```

4.7 ASSIGNMENTS

- Write a portable module using LINUX_VERSION_CODE and KERNEL_VERSION macros which can use any prototype of workqueue. Compile it for Linux kernel 2.6.10 and 2.6.30

4.8 REFERENCES

- Bottom haves in kernel 2.4 version-http://tldp.org/LDP/tlk/kernel/kernel.html

5 Kernel—Locking and Synchronization

One of the basic objectives of any operation system is to provide uniform and distributed access of system resources to the applications. Since the resources are limited and users are more, contention is likely to occur. Similarly data structures can be accessed by many users and therefore data structure may be corrupted if not accessed in well defined manner.

To solve such problems, Linux kernel defines many primitives which can be used by different processes to wok in co-operative manner. In this chapter we discuss such primitives and learn how to use them.

In particular, this chapter covers following topics:

- Execution contexts
- Locking primitives
- Event primitives

5.1 EXECUTION CONTEXTS

At any point of time, the kernel code executes in some context. As a rule of thumb, kernel code never executes by itself. An application or an interrupt or an event causes some kernel code to run. Therefore, the kernel context can be identified from the source that caused kernel code to execute.

For example, an application calls a system call whenever it needs some service from kernel. The kernel runs some code to serve the application. Therefore the kernel context can be called as user context or process context. Similarly if an external device generates an interrupt, an interrupt handler is invoked to service the interrupt. Therefore, the kernel context can be called as interrupt context. After every interrupt servicing, kernel checks if any softirq is pending. If yes, then kernel runs softirq. This context can be called as softirq context.

While writing kernel code, you must know which context the code is going to execute. This helps in selecting correct locking mechanism and understanding correct execution sequence.

Out of these contexts, interrupt context has highest priority. Softirq context has next higher priority, and process context has lowest priority. This means, that if kernel is servicing some system call to an application, and an interrupt occurs; kernel will stop process context and will serve the interrupt. Therefore, kernel changes execution context from process context to interrupt context on every interrupt. After interrupt context kernel enters to softirq context and then again resumes process context.

In other words, an interrupt context can interrupt both softirq context and process context, while softirq context can interrupt process context. For non-preemptible kernels, one process context cannot interrupt another process context, while for preemptible kernels; a process context can be interrupted by another process context. On a SMP system, it is possible that different CPUs run different contexts.

Interrupt context and softirq context have certain restrictions because the code executing in these contexts is not allowed to sleep. It implies that

- memory allocation in interrupt context must be done only with GFP_ATOMIC flag while process context can use GFP_KERNEL.
- It must not call schedule function or any other function which leads to schedule function.
- It must not wait for any lock.

A kernel thread execution can be treated as process context, although it really does not have a user process associated with.

5.2 LOCKING PRIMITIVES

Linux kernel provides a rich set of locking primitives. However a judicious choice must be made before using them. A locking primitive that is suitable for one case may not be at all suitable in another case. This section describes Linux locking primitives and explains their use cases.

5.2.1 Semaphores

Semaphores are the oldest Unix style locking primitives to protect concurrent access to critical section by multiple processes. Semaphores are of two types, binary semaphore and counting semaphore. A binary semaphore allows access to resource to only one process at a time, while counting semaphore can allow resource access to as many processes as many resources available.

Table 5.1 illustrates an example of semaphores

Table 5.1

```
#include <linux/module.h>
#include <linux/sched.h>
#include <linux/kthread.h>
static struct semaphore sem;
static struct task_struct *k1, *k2;
static int kthread1(void *arg)
{
        printk("kthread1 started\n");
        down(&sem);
        /* critical section code */
        up(&sem);
        do_exit(0);
        return 0;
}
static int kthread2(void* arg)
{
        printk("kthread2 started\n");
```

```
        down(&sem);
        /* critical section code */
        up(&sem);
        do_exit(0);
        return 0;
}
int init_module(void)
{
        printk("lock module inserted\n");
        sema_init(&sem, 1);
        k1 = kthread_run(kthread1, NULL, "kthread1");
        k2 = kthread_run(kthread2, NULL, "kthread2");
        return 0;
}
void cleanup_module(void)
{
        printk("lock module removed\n");
        return;
}
MODULE_LICENSE("GPL");
```

The sema_init function initializes the semaphore to a value 1 which means only one process can access it at a time (*i.e.*, a binary semaphore). The init_module function creates two threads which access a common critical section. Any thread can run first, and calls function down which reduces semaphore value to 0. Now a thread or process has to wait at function down function until some thread or process calls function up on the same semaphore.

You must note that although semaphore works on integer count, you must never try to modify the value directly. You must always use down and up function for locking and unlocking the semaphore. Also, you must not lock an already locked semaphore in same thread.

If you want to use a counting semaphore, you can pass number of maximum processes allowed in second argument of sema_init. For example, if you have 5 buffers and therefore 5 processes can use one buffer each. However if 6th process arrives, that has to wait until a previous process releases it. In such cases you can use counting semaphores.

It must also be noted that if a semaphore is not available, the process is put to sleep. This implies that you must not use semaphores in interrupt context and softirq context because those context are not allowed to sleep. Therefore, a semaphore is suitable to prevent concurrent access only between threads and processes *i.e.*, between process contexts.

If you don't want a thread to sleep while waiting for semaphore, you can use down_trylock function. This function either acquires the semaphores or returns 0 (failure to acquire the semaphore). You must not access the critical section if down_trylock has failed.

Table 5.2 lists prototype of functions related to semaphore.

Table 5.2

```
void sema_init(struct semaphore* sem, int value);
void down(struct semaphore* sem);
void up(struct semaphore* sem);
int down_trylock(struct semaphore* sem);
int down_interruptible(struct semaphore* sem);
```

5.2.2 Mutex

Mutexes derive their name from "mutual exclusion". Mutexes are nothing but better semaphores, however mutexes can only be locked an unlocked (like binary semaphore, and unlike counting semaphores). Since semaphores and mutexes share similar properties, same rules apply to mutexes which described for semaphores. Therefore, mutexes also used for mutual exclusion in process context only.

Table 5.3 lists prototype of functions related to mutexes.

Table 5.3

```
void mutex_lock(struct mutex *lock);
void mutex_unlock(struct mutex *lock);
int mutex_trylock(struct mutex *lock);
int mutex_lock_interruptible(struct mutex *lock);

mutex_init(mutex)
```

So what is difference between a semaphore and mutex! Well, the answer comes from the definition that mutexes are better semaphore in the sense that mutexes are associated with an owner. Therefore, a mutex must be unlocked by the same process/thread which locked it, while semaphores can be taken by one thread and can be released by another thread.

Table 5.4 illustrates a code which is legal to use with semaphores but illegal to use with mutexes.

Table 5.4

```
#include <linux/module.h>
#include <linux/sched.h>
#include <linux/kthread.h>
#define USE_SEMAPHORE
static int lock_flag = 0;
#ifdef USE_SEMAPHORE
static struct semaphore my_lock;
#define INIT_LOCK(x) sema_init(x, 1)
#define LOCK(x) down(x)
#define UNLOCK(x) up(x)
#else
DEFINE_MUTEX(my_lock);
#define INIT_LOCK(x)  mutex_init(x)
#define LOCK(x) mutex_lock(x)
#define UNLOCK(x) mutex_unlock(x)
#endif
static int kthread1(void *arg)
{
        printk("kthread1 started: %p\n", current_thread_info());
        LOCK(&my_lock);
        printk("kthread1 aquired my_lock\n");
        lock_flag = 1;
        do_exit(0);
        return 0;
}
static int kthread2(void* arg)
```

```
{
        printk("kthread2 started: %p\n", current_thread_info());
        while(lock_flag != 1);
              schedule();
        UNLOCK(&my_lock);
        printk("kthread2 released my_lock\n");
        do_exit(0);
        return 0;
}
int init_module(void)
{
        struct task_struct *k1, *k2;
        printk("lock module inserted\n");
        INIT_LOCK(&my_lock);
        k1 = kthread_run(kthread1, NULL, "kthread1");
        k2 = kthread_run(kthread2, NULL, "kthread2");
        return 0;
}
void cleanup_module(void)
{
        printk("lock module removed\n");
        return;
}
MODULE_LICENSE("GPL");
```

In this example, kthread1 acquires the lock while kthread2 releases the lock. While this goes all right with semaphores, mutexes don't like it. If you are running an SMP system, you will get an unpleasant warning from kernel in mutex mode.

Following code snippets from different parts of kernel show how mutexes are associated with an owner.

Table 5.5

```
struct mutex
{
        /* snip */
#if defined(CONFIG_DEBUG_MUTEXES) || defined(CONFIG_SMP)
        struct thread_info      *owner;
#endif
        /* snip */
};
void __sched mutex_lock(struct mutex *lock)
{
        /* snip */
        mutex_set_owner(lock);
}
static inline void mutex_set_owner(struct mutex *lock)
{
        lock->owner = current_thread_info();
}
```

```
static    inline    void    __mutex_unlock_common_slowpath(atomic_t
*lock_count, int nested)
{
        /* snip */
        debug_mutex_unlock(lock);
        /* snip */
}
void debug_mutex_unlock(struct mutex *lock)
{
        /* snip */
        DEBUG_LOCKS_WARN_ON(lock->owner != current_thread_info());
        /* snip */
}
#define DEBUG_LOCKS_WARN_ON(c)                                    \
({                                                                \
        /* snip */                                                \
        if (!oops_in_progress && unlikely(c)) {                   \
              if (debug_locks_off() && !debug_locks_silent)       \
                    WARN_ON(1);                                   \
        }                                                         \
        /*snip */                                                 \
})
```

Another difference (although not functional difference) between semaphore and mutex comes from function down_trylock and mutex_trylock. If function down_trylock fails to acquire the semaphore it returns 0, while if mutex_trylock fails to acquire mutex it returns 1! Therefore, if you are porting code from semaphores to mutexes or vice-versa you must be very careful with respect to these functions.

5.2.3 Interrupt Control

While semaphores and mutexes are good for preventing concurrent access to critical section by multiple processes or threads, these cannot be used if a critical section is shared between process context and interrupt context, or between a process context and softirq context.

As mentioned earlier, an interrupt context can interrupt a process context even when the process context is inside a critical section. Therefore, a lock can not prevent mutual exclusion between an interrupt context and process context. The only way to achieve this is; the process context before entering critical section has to make sure that interrupt does not occur at all by disabling interrupts. Since interrupts are disabled the process context is safe against preemption. Unlike semaphores and mutexes where every process context has to lock and unlock; in this particular case only process context disables and enables interrupts. Interrupt handler code need not care as a process context cannot execute as long as interrupt context is executing.

Table 5.6 illustrates an example on how to achieve mutual exclusion between interrupt context and process context. The example is based on interrupt number 18 which is assigned to eth0 interface on the system where this example is worked out. This example shares the interrupt with eth0 interface. Therefore, the interrupt handler in Table 5.6 is called whenever a packet is received on interface eth0.

Table 5.6

```
#include <linux/module.h>
#include <linux/interrupt.h>
#include <linux/kthread.h>
static int kthread1(void *arg)
{
        printk("kthread1 started\n");
        local_irq_disable();
        /* critical section */
        local_irq_enable();
        do_exit(0);
        return 0;
}
static irqreturn_t int_handler(int irq, void* p_dummy)
{
        printk("interrupt context executed\n");
        /* critical section */
        return IRQ_NONE;
}
static int dummy;
int init_module(void)
{
        static struct task_struct *k1;
        printk("interrupt module inserted\n");
        if(request_irq(18, int_handler, IRQF_SHARED, "sample", &dummy)
        < 0)
              printk("interrupt installation failed\n");
        else
              k1 = kthread_run(kthread1, NULL, "kthread1");
        return 0;
}
void cleanup_module(void)
{
        printk("interrupt module removed\n");
        free_irq(18, &dummy);
        return;
}
MODULE_LICENSE("GPL");
```

As shown in above example, the int_handler is called whenever a packet is received on eth0. Therefore this function is called in interrupt context while function kthread1 is called in process context. Since both function access same critical section, function kthread1 disables interrupt before entering to critical section, and enables them after coming out of critical section.

The function local_irq_disable disables interrupts on local CPU. It means, in an SMP systems interrupt context may still executed on other CPUs. Therefore, example shown in Table 5.6 is safe only for uni-processor systems.

The local_irq_disable function makes sure that interrupts are disabled, and therefore interrupt context does not execute. This in turn implies that softirq context also does not occur. Therefore, local_irq_disable protects a process context from both interrupt context and softirq context.

However, if a process context is sharing critical section only with softirq context (and not with interrupt context), these functions (local_irq_disable & local_irq_enable) are overkill as they prevent interrupt context also. To prevent concurrent access between a process context and a softirq context local_bh_disable and local_bh_enable functions can be used. Function local_bh_disable makes sure that softirqs are not executed until local_bh_enable is called.

Table 5.7 shows an example of synchronized access between process context and softirq context.

Table 5.7

```
#include <linux/module.h>
#include <linux/kthread.h>
#include <linux/timer.h>
static int kthread1(void *arg)
{
        printk("kthread1 started\n");
        local_bh_disable();
        /* critical section */
        local_bh_enable();
        do_exit(0);
        return 0;
}
static void timeout_fn(unsigned long arg)
{
        printk("interrupt context executed\n");
        /* critical section */
        return;
}
struct timer_list timer;
int init_module(void)
{
        static struct task_struct *k1;
        printk("interrupt module inserted\n");
        init_timer(&timer);
        timer.function = timeout_fn;
        timer.data = 0;
        timer.expires = jiffies + 1*HZ; /* 1 second */
        k1 = kthread_run(kthread1, NULL, "kthread1");
        add_timer(&timer);
        return 0;
}
void cleanup_module(void)
{
        printk("interrupt module removed\n");
        return;
}
MODULE_LICENSE("GPL");
```

Since the timer handler is called in softirq context (called by TIMER_SOFTIRQ), the kthread1 function must protect the critical section from softirq by calling local_bh_disable. However, if a critical section is shared among process context, softirq context and interrupt context all, then local_irq_disable must be used. It must be noted that local_bh_disable disables softirq on local CPU only. Therefore the example in Table 5.7 is safe only on uni-processor systems.

5.2.4 Spinlocks

In previous section, we discussed how to disable or enable interrupts. However, as mentioned, the interrupts are disabled only on local CPUs. Device driver developers have to make sure that the drivers work on uni-processor as well as for SMP systems.

Letís consider a scenario where a process context is executing on CPU0, another process context is executing on CPU1, an interrupt context is executing on CPU2 and another interrupt context is executing on CPU3; and all of them access a common critical section.

To prevent concurrent access to critical section in this scenario, local_irq_disable alone is not enough because interrupts on other CPUs are still enabled. While this can be done by disabling interrupts on all CPUs, it is rarely done in kernel as it is very costly. To help in such situation, a combination of local_irq_disable and spinlock is used.

Spinlock is a lock where an execution thread loops until it acquires the lock *i.e.*, it keeps spinning without doing any useful work until the lock is available. This is required because interrupt context can not sleep, and therefore an interrupt context will spin in a busy wait loop until the lock is acquired and then proceed.

Now letís go back to the problem defined and understand how combination of spinlock and local_irq_disable solves it. If a process context has acquired the spinlock, other process context or interrupt context executing on other CPUs can not acquire the lock, and have to wait. Therefore the process context is safe from process context and interrupt context running on other CPUs. However, this process context can be interrupted by local interrupt context. To prevent this, the process context does local_irq_disable. Since local interrupts are disabled, interrupt context will not occur on local CPU.

Linux kernel provides spin_lock_irq function to do above function (*i.e.*, spinlock + local_irq_disable). Table 5.8 illustrates how three functions operating in different contexts on different CPU are prevented from concurrent access to same critical section.

Table 5.8

```
static spinlock_t lock = SPIN_LOCK_UNLOCKED;
static int kthread1(void *arg)
{
        printk("kthread1 started in process context\n");
        spin_lock_irq(&lock);
        /* critical section */
        spin_unlock_irq(&lock);
        do_exit(0);
        return 0;
}
static irqreturn_t int_handler(int irq, void* p_dummy)
{
        printk("interrupt context executed\n");
        spin_lock_irq(&lock);
        /* critical section */
        spin_unlock_irq(&lock);
```

```
        return IRQ_NONE;
}
static void timeout_fn2(unsigned long arg)
{
        printk("softirq context 2 executed\n");
        spin_lock_irq(&lock);
        /* critical section */
        spin_unlock_irq(&lock);
        return;
}
```

It must be noted that both process context and interrupt context have to call spin_lock_irq and spin_unlock_irq (unlike local_irq_disable/local_irq_enable in previous section).

A spinlock before using must be initialized either by spin_lock_init function or by SPIN_LOCK_UNLOCKED.

Functions spin_lock_irq and spin_unlock_irq must be used when you know that interrupts are enabled. However, sometimes, a developer may not know it exactly because of many other unknown functions in source code. In such situations, spin_lock_irqsave and spin_unlock_irqrestore functions can be used. The function spin_lock_irqsave additionally saves current interrupt status which is restored by spin_unlock_irqrestore function.

Table 5.9 lists important functions/macros related to spin locks. Note that although many of them are defined as macros, those have been mentioned as function prototype only to understand argument type.

Table 5.9

```
#include <linux/spinlock.h>
/* macros. illustrated as function prototype */
local_irq_disable()
local_irq_enable()
spin_lock_init(spinlock_t* lock)
spin_lock_irq(spinlock_t* lock)
spin_unlock_irq(spinlock_t* lock)
spin_trylock_irq(spinlock_t* lock)
spin_lock_irqsave(spinlock_t* lock, unsigned long flags)
spin_unlock_irqrestore(spinlock_t* lock, unsigned long flags)
spin_trylock_irqsave(spinlock_t* lock, unsigned long flags)
spin_lock(spinlock_t* lock)
spin_unlock(spinlock_t* lock)
spin_trylock(spinlock_t* lock)
spin_lock_bh(spinlock_t* lock)
spin_unlock_bh(spinlock_t* lock)
spin_trylock_bh(spinlock_t* lock)
/* functions */
void local_bh_disable(void);
void local_bh_enable(void);
```

5.2.5 Locking Summary

This section presents a summary of locking mechanism in Table 5.10 for Uni-processor (UP) and Symmetrical Multi Processing (SMP) sytems.

Table 5.10

	process context	**softirq context**	**interrupt context**
process context	UP down, up, mutex_lock, mutex_unlock SMP down, up, mutex_lock, mutex_unlock	UP local_bh_disable, local_bh_enable SMP spin_lock_bh spin_unlock_bh	UP local_irq_disable local_irq_enable SMP spin_lock_irqsave spin_lock_irqrestore
softirq context		SMP spin_lock_bh spin_unlock_bh	UP local_irq_disable local_irq_enable SMP spin_lock_irqsave spin_lock_irqrestore
interrupt context			SMP spin_lock_irqsave spin_lock_irqrestore

5.3 EVENT MECHANISMS

In addition to locking, many times kernel developers need event mechanisms where a certain execution thread has to wait until some event occurs or until some conditions is met. Linux kernel provides a rich set of functions to accomplish this kind of activity. This section describes such functions with examples.

5.3.1 Completion

Completion primitives can be used without fear of race conditions, where a process or thread has to sleep until some event occurs. Table 5.11 illustrates an example of completion primitives.

Table 5.11

```
#include <linux/module.h>
#include <linux/sched.h>
#include <linux/kthread.h>
static struct task_struct *k1, *k2;
static struct completion done;
static int kthread1(void *arg)
{
        printk("kthread1 started.. will wait for event completion\n");
        wait_for_completion(&done);
        printk("kthread1: event completed\n");
        do_exit(0);
        return 0;
}
```

```
static int kthread2(void* arg)
{
        unsigned long now = jiffies;
        printk("kthread2 started\n");
        while(jiffies < now + 5*HZ)
              schedule();
        printk("kthread2: indicating completion event\n");
        complete(&done);
        do_exit(0);
        return 0;
}
int init_module(void)
{
        printk("completion module inserted\n");
        init_completion(&done);
        k1 = kthread_run(kthread1, NULL, "kthread1");
        k2 = kthread_run(kthread2, NULL, "kthread2");
        return 0;
}
void cleanup_module(void)
{
        printk("completion module removed\n");
        return;
}
MODULE_LICENSE("GPL");
```

A completion primitive is defined using struct completion. The completion primitive must be initialized using init_completion before using it. The kthread1 is put to sleep by wait_for_completion function. Later kthread2 calls complete function on the completion primitive on which kthread1 is waiting. Therefore, kthread1 execution is resumed.

It is possible for more than one thread or process to wait for same event using same completion primitive. In that case, complete function wakes up only one of sleeping threads. If you want to wake-up all of the sleeping threads, you can use complete_all function, or you can call complete function as many times as many threads to be woken up.

Completion primitives are safe from race condition even if the complete function is called before wait_for_completion function. In such case wait_for_completion will return immediately.

There are more functions available for meeting different requirements as described below:

- wait_for_completion_timeout—This function returns if either complete function is called or given time elapses. A zero return value indicates timeout, while a positive return value indicates complete function called.
- wait_for_completion_interruptible—This function returns if either complete function is called or the call is interrupted. A negative return value indicates interrupt occurred.
- wait_for_completion_interruptible_timeout—This function returns if either complete function is called or call is interrupted or given time elapses. A positive return value indicates complete function is called, zero return value indicates timeout occurred while negative return value indicates the call is interrupted.

Timeout value is provided in relative jiffies. In following section we will see that other primitives too provide similar set of functions. We'll shortly see an example as well.

A process which calls non-interruptible functions is put in TASK_UNINTERRUPTILBE state. If a system call invokes non-interruptible functions, then the user process which calls this system call will not return even if Ctrl+C is pressed because signals are not delivered to a task which is in TASK_UNINTERRUPTIBLE state. You will see such processes in D state in ps listing. However, if the system call invokes interruptible functions, then the user process will be terminated when Ctrl+C is pressed.

Table 5.12 lists prototype of all completion and family functions.

Table 5.12

```
void init_completion(struct completion *x);
void wait_for_completion(struct completion *x);
int wait_for_completion_interruptible(struct completion *x);
unsigned long wait_for_completion_timeout(struct completion *x,
unsigned long timeout);
long wait_for_completion_interruptible_timeout(struct completion *x,
unsigned long timeout);
void complete(struct completion *x);
void complete_all(struct completion *x);
```

5.3.2 Sleeping

In this section we use wait_event and family functions to achieve same results to completion primitive. In addition to completion primitives, wait_event primitives are associated with a condition argument, and therefore the calling process or thread is put to sleep until the condition is met. Table 5.13 illustrates an example.

Table 5.13

```
#include <linux/module.h>
#include <linux/sched.h>
#include <linux/kthread.h>
static struct task_struct *k1, *k2;
static wait_queue_head_t waitq;
static int flag = 0;
static int kthread1(void *arg)
{
        printk("kthread1 started.. will wait for event completion\n");
        wait_event(waitq, flag == 1);
        printk("kthread1: event completed\n");
        do_exit(0);
        return 0;
}
static int kthread2(void* arg)
{
        unsigned long now = jiffies;
        printk("kthread2 started\n");
        while(jiffies < now + 5*HZ)
              schedule();
        printk("kthread2: indicating completion event\n");
```

```
        flag = 1;
        wake_up(&waitq);
        do_exit(0);
        return 0;
}
int init_module(void)
{
        printk("sleep module inserted\n");
        init_waitqueue_head(&waitq);
        k1 = kthread_run(kthread1, NULL, "kthread1");
        k2 = kthread_run(kthread2, NULL, "kthread2");
        return 0;
}
void cleanup_module(void)
{
        printk("sleep module removed\n");
        return;
}
MODULE_LICENSE("GPL");
```

A wait queue is defined by wait_queue_head_t. The wait queue must either be statically allocated or be allocated using kmalloc function. The wait queue must be initialized by init_waitqueue_head function before using it. The wait_event function puts the calling thread to sleep on the wait queue until the condition mentioned in second argument is true. However, you must note that later only condition being true does not wake it up, but another thread or process must call wake_up function on the wait queue.

Just like completion primitives, it is possible for more than one process to sleep on the same wait queue. The function wake_up will wake up all of the sleeping processes on the wait queue. You must note that while wait_evnet function takes wait_queue_head_t as argument, the wake_up function takes pointer to wait_queue_head_t as argument.

Again, similar to completion primitives, wait_event family too provides several functions for meeting different requirements. Table 5.14 lists prototype of all functions (most of them are actually defined as macros).

Table 5.14

```
wait_event(wq, condition)
wait_event_timeout(wq, condition, timeout)
wait_event_interruptible(wq, condition)
wait_event_interruptible_timeout(wq, condition, timeout)
wake_up(x)
wake_up_interruptible(x)
```

Table 5.15 illustrates one example of wait_event_interruptible_timeout function and how to use its return values.

Table 5.15

```
#include <linux/module.h>
#include <linux/sched.h>
```

```
#include <linux/kthread.h>
static struct task_struct *k1;
static wait_queue_head_t waitq;
static int flag = 0;
static int kthread1(void *arg)
{
        long ret;
        printk("kthread1 started.. will wait for
event/interrupt/timeout \n");
        ret = wait_event_interruptible_timeout(waitq, flag == 1,
        5*HZ);
        if(ret < 0)
              printk("interrupted\n");
        else if(ret == 0)
              printk("timed out\n");
        else
              printk("event completed\n");
        do_exit(0);
        return 0;
}
int init_module(void)
{
        printk("sleep module inserted\n");
        init_waitqueue_head(&waitq);
        k1 = kthread_run(kthread1, NULL, "kthread1");
        return 0;
}
void cleanup_module(void)
{
        printk("sleep module removed\n");
        return;
}
MODULE_LICENSE("GPL");
```

As shown in above example, the wait_event_interruptilbe_timeout can return on three conditions (i) some threads call wake_up_interruptible for the wait queue, (ii) time out occurs and (iii) the call is interrupted. As shown in example, the return value can be used to know reason of call return.

5.3.3 Exclusive Sleeping

In previous section, we discussed that it is possible for more than one process to sleep or wait on same wait queue. When all of processes are woken up together, system performance is degraded. Also for most practical purpose, most of them will go to sleep again possibly because of resource limitation.

Linux kernel provides an extension of functions discussed in previous sections such that out of all sleeping processes only one of them will be woken up. This is referred as exclusive sleeping and corresponding functions can be identified by exclusive suffix in function names. Table 5.16 illustrates an example of exclusive sleeping.

Table 5.16

```
#include <linux/module.h>
#include <linux/sched.h>
#include <linux/kthread.h>
static struct task_struct *k0, *k1, *k2;
static wait_queue_head_t waitq;
static int flag = 0;
static int kthread0(void *arg)
{
        printk("kthread0 started.. will wait for event completion\n");
        wait_event_interruptible_exclusive(waitq, flag == 1);
        printk("kthread0: event completed\n");
        do_exit(0);
        return 0;
}
static int kthread1(void *arg)
{
        printk("kthread1 started.. will wait for event completion\n");
        wait_event_interruptible_exclusive(waitq, flag == 1);
        printk("kthread1: event completed\n");
        do_exit(0);
        return 0;
}
static int kthread2(void* arg)
{
        unsigned long now = jiffies;
        printk("kthread2 started\n");
        while(jiffies < now + 5*HZ)
              schedule();
        printk("kthread2: indicating completion event\n");
        flag = 1;
        wake_up_interruptible(&waitq);
        do_exit(0);
        return 0;
}
int init_module(void)
{
        printk("exclusive sleep module inserted\n");
        init_waitqueue_head(&waitq);
        k0 = kthread_run(kthread0, NULL, "kthread0");
        k1 = kthread_run(kthread1, NULL, "kthread1");
        k2 = kthread_run(kthread2, NULL, "kthread2");
        return 0;
}
void cleanup_module(void)
{
        unsigned long now;
        wake_up_interruptible(&waitq);
```

```
        now = jiffies;
        printk("waiting for 2 seconds\n");
        while(jiffies < now + 2*HZ)
              schedule();
        printk("exclusive sleep module removed\n");
        return;
}
MODULE_LICENSE("GPL");
```

As shown in the above example, there are two threads (kthread0 & kthread1) which call the function wait_event_interruptible_exclusive on same wait queue and same condition. When kthread2 calls wake_up_interruptible, out of the two waiting threads only one is woken-up while second thread continues to sleep. Later during module removal, again one thread is woken-up, and this time the second thread too wakes up.

It is possible for exclusive and non-exclusive processes to wait on same wait queue. In such a case wake_up function will wake up all non-exclusive processes and one exclusive process. If you want to awake all non-exclusive as well as all exclusive processes, you can use wake_up_all function.

Table 5.17 lists all exclusive sleep functions' prototype.

Table 5.17

```
wait_event_interruptible_exclusive(wq, condition)
void prepare_to_wait_exclusive(wait_queue_head_t *q, wait_queue_t
*wait, int state);
void add_wait_queue_exclusive(wait_queue_head_t *q, wait_queue_t
*wait);
```

Some of above function are helpful in process's manual sleeping control described in next section.

5.3.4 Manual Sleeping

Although for kernel developers the functions discussed in previous section should suffice, yet sometimes a finer control is required. In such cases processes can sleep manually which is nothing but a wait queue sleep function inflated.

Table 5.18 illustrates an example of a process sleeping manually.

Table 5.18

```
#include <linux/module.h>
#include <linux/sched.h>
#include <linux/kthread.h>
static struct task_struct *k1, *k2;
static wait_queue_head_t waitq;
static int flag = 0;
static int kthread1(void *arg)
{
        DEFINE_WAIT(wait);
        printk("kthread1 started.. will wait for event completion\n");
        while(flag != 1)
{
```

```
        prepare_to_wait(&waitq, &wait, TASK_INTERRUPTIBLE);
        if(flag == 1)
              break;
        schedule();
        }
        finish_wait(&waitq, &wait);
        if(signal_pending(current))
              printk("signal delivered to the thread while
              sleeping\n");
        printk("kthread1: event completed\n");
        do_exit(0);
        return 0;
}
static int kthread2(void* arg)
{
        unsigned long now = jiffies;
        printk("kthread2 started\n");
        while(jiffies < now + 5*HZ)
              schedule();
        printk("kthread2: indicating completion event\n");
        flag = 1;
        wake_up(&waitq);
        do_exit(0);
        return 0;
}
int init_module(void)
{
        printk("manual sleep module inserted\n");
        init_waitqueue_head(&waitq);
        k1 = kthread_run(kthread1, NULL, "kthread1");
        k2 = kthread_run(kthread2, NULL, "kthread2");
        return 0;
}
void cleanup_module(void)
{
        printk("manual sleep module removed\n");
        return;
}
MODULE_LICENSE("GPL");
```

As shown in example, function kthread1 repeatedly calls prepare_to_wait and schedule function until the condition becomes true. You must call finish_wait after the function is out of repetitive waiting. Since a signal might be delivered while the process was waiting, you must check if any signal is pending using signal_pending function.

In older kernels, you will find finer version of manual sleep as shown below:

Table 5.19

```
static int kthread1(void *arg)
{
        DEFINE_WAIT(wait);
        printk("kthread1 started.. will wait for event completion\n");
        for(;;)
        {
              add_wait_queue(&waitq, &wait);
              set_current_state(TASK_INTERRUPTIBLE);
              if(flag == 1)
                    break;
              schedule();
        }
        remove_wait_queue(&waitq, &wait);
        set_current_state(TASK_RUNNING);
        if(signal_pending(current))
              printk("signal delivered to the thread while
              sleeping\n");
              printk("kthread1: event completed\n");
        do_exit(0);
        return 0;
}
```

5.4 SUMMARY

Although locks and synchronization mechanism described in this chapter are enough for kernel developers to avoid race conditions and safeguard critical section, yet there are many other kinds of locks which are needed in special circumstances. For example, where there are more readers and less writer, read-write locks can be used. Similarly, RCU (read-copy-update) locks can be helpful in systems where memory access is much slower than CPU. Therefore, a judicious selection of locks is very important in system performance.

5.5 ASSIGNMENTS

- Write a kernel module which sleeps forever. Check its behavior on uni-processor and multi-processor system. Discuss results and behavior.
- Study and discuss RCU concept.

5.6 REFERENCES

- RCU-http://lwn.net/Articles/262464/
- Interrupt handling-http://www.stillhq.com/pdfdb/000447/data.pdf

6 Linux Networking Subsystem

Linux provides a layered, flexible and versatile networking subsystem. It's up to date including all network technologies like IP, IPv6, ATM, IPX etc. The networking subsystems are often referred as stack owing to their layered design.

There are some core data structures operating under all such subsystems. This chapter addresses a few such important data structures and then explains mechanism to install new protocol handlers.

This chapter is divided among following sections:

- Packet buffer sk_buff
- Network device netdev
- Registering protocol handlers
- IP packet processing & route lookup

6.1 PACKET BUFFER

In Linux kernel packets are represented by struct sk_buff which is defined in header file include/linux/skbuff.h. This section describes packet buffer management APIs which mainly operate on following fields in sk_buff structure.

Figure 6.1 shows a typical sk_buff and some of important fields:

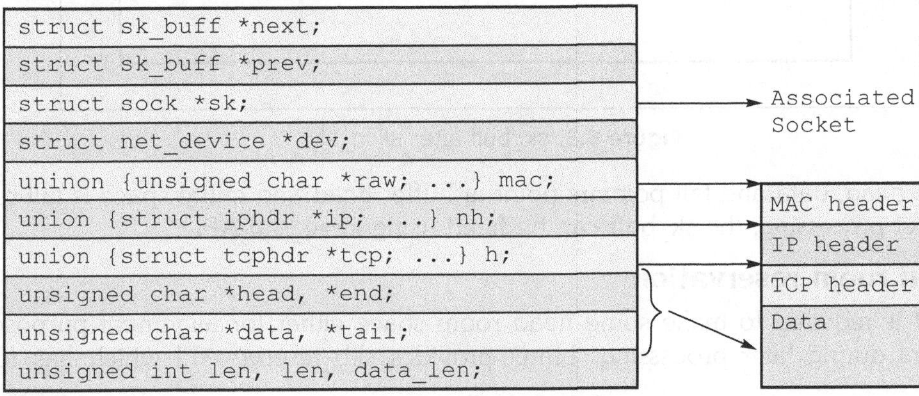

Figure 6.1. sk_buff

As shown in Figure 6.1, the sk_buff has meta-data and actual data in separate buffers. The meta-data contains pointers for L2, L3 and L4 layers. The actual data is pointed by following pointers:

- head – pointer to packet buffer head
- data – pointer to actual start of data
- tail – pointer to end of data
- end – pointer to packet buffer end
- len – actual data length

Therefore a typical packet buffer looks as follows:

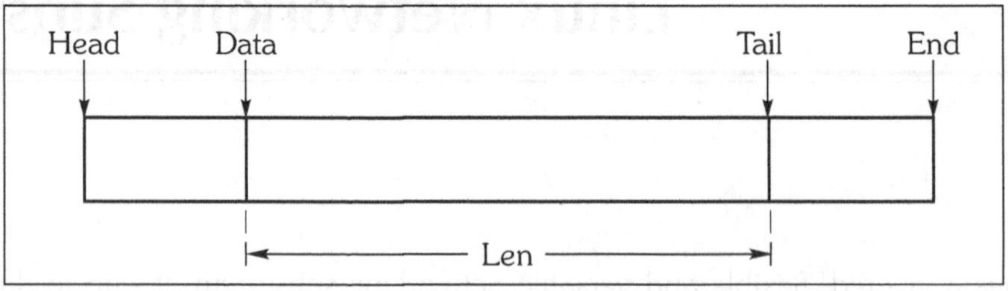

Figure 6.2. A typical packet buffer

The space between head pointer and data pointer is called head room, while space between tail pointer and end pointer is called tail room. Obviously data and tail pointers are always bounded by head and end pointer.

6.1.1 Packet buffer allocation

A packet buffer is allocated using alloc_skb API. The API has following prototype

```
struct sk_buff *alloc_skb (unsigned int size, gfp_t priority);
```

The first argument is packet buffer size while second argument is priority which can be GFP_KERNEL, GFP_ATOMIC etc (see memory allocation for more details) depending upon the context in which packet buffer allocation is done.

Pictorial view of sk_buff after allocation is illustrated in Figure 6.3.

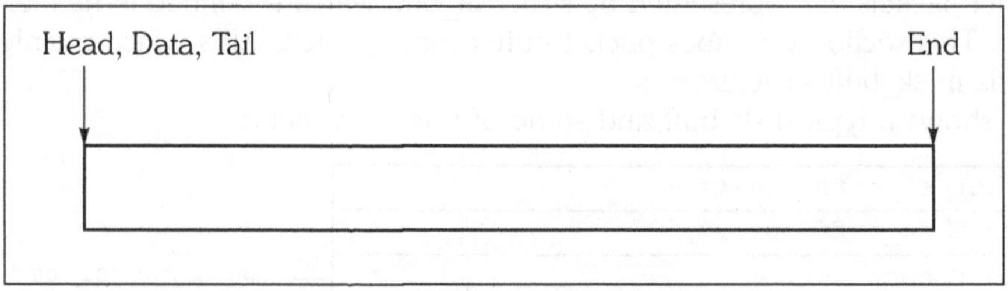

Figure 6.3. sk_buff after alloc_skb

As shown, head, data and tail pointers point at buffer head and entire space is tail room. After packet processing, the sk_buff can be freed using kfree_skb API.

6.1.2 Head room reservation

Sometimes it is required to make some head room space either for alignment purpose or for some headers during later processing. Linux provides skb_reserve API which has following prototype:

```
void skb_reserve (struct sk_buff *skb, int len2);
```

Pictorial view of sk_buff after head room reservation is illustrated in Figure 6.4.

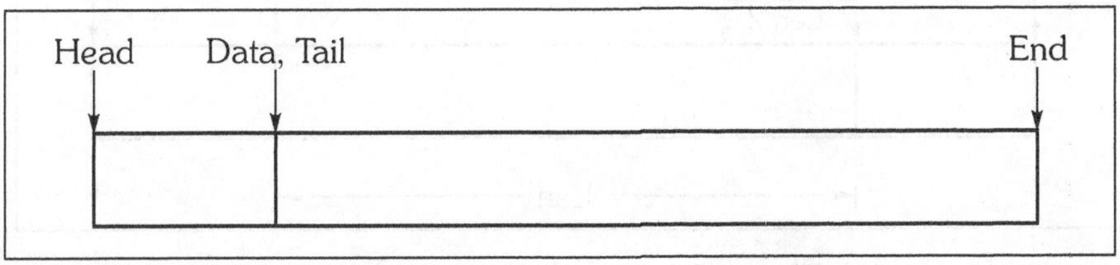

Figure 6.4. sk_buff after skb_reserve

As shown in Figure 6.4, skb_reserve moves both data and tail pointers towards end pointer by len2, thus increasing head room and decreasing tail room. This operation has no effect on packet length. It should be noted that skb_reserve should be called only on empty (just allocated) buffers.

6.1.3 Appending contents at packet end

To append new or more contents in existing packet, Linux provides skb_put API which has following prototype:

```
unsigned char *skb_put (struct sk_buff *skb, unsigned int len2);
```

Pictorial view of sk_buff after data insertion at head is illustrated in Figure 6.5.

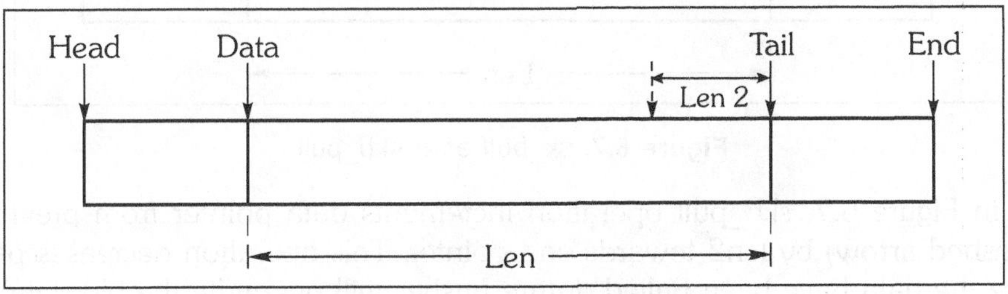

Figure 6.5. sk_buff after skb_put

As shown in Figure 6.5, skb_put moves tail pointer from existing position to new position by length len2 towards end pointer (previous tail pointer location is shown by dashed arrow). The data pointer is not touched during this operation. This API increases packet length by len2.

It must be noted that, skb_put only moves tail pointer to create space between previous tail pointer and new tail pointer. The contents must be copied externally starting from previous tail pointer (dashed arrow) which is returned by skb_put API.

6.1.4 Adding contents at packet start

API skb_push is used to add more contents at packet start which has following prototype:

```
unsigned char *skb_push (struct sk_buff *skb, unsigned int len2);
```

Figure 6.6 shows pictorial view of packet buffer after skb_push operation.

As shown in Figure 6.6, the skb_push API moves data pointer from previous position (shown by dashed arrow) to new position by len2 towards head pointer. This operation does not affect tail pointer but increases packet length by len2.

Again, it must be noted that packet contents must be copied externally from new data pointer location which is returned by skb_push API.

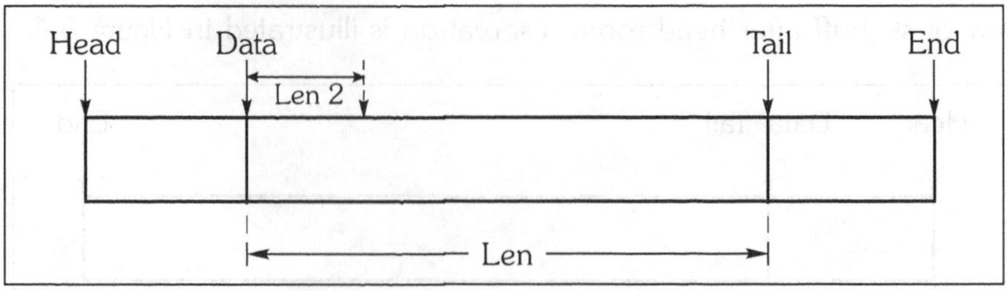

Figure 6.6. sk_buff after skb_push

6.1.5 Removing contents from packet start

To remove packet contents at packet start, Linux provides skb_pull API which has following prototype:

```
unsigned char *skb_pull (struct sk_buff *skb, unsigned int len2);
```

The pictorial view of sk_buff after skb_pull operation is shown in Figure 6.7.

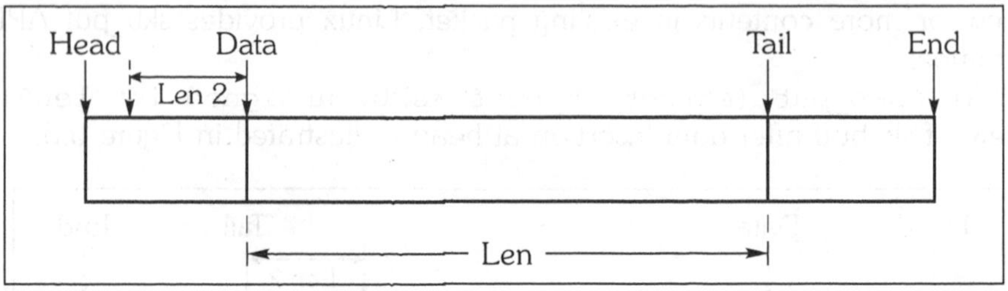

Figure 6.7. sk_buff after skb_pull

As shown in Figure 6.7, skb_pull operation increments data pointer from previous location (shown by dashed arrow) by len2 towards end pointer. This operation decreases packet length by len2. Once the data have been pulled, future pushes will overwrite the old data.

6.1.6 Removing contents from packet end

To remove packet contents from packet end, Linux provides skb_trim API which has following prototype:

```
void skb_trim (struct sk_buff *skb, unsigned int len2);
```

The pictorial view of sk_buff after skb_trim operation is shown in Figure 6.8.

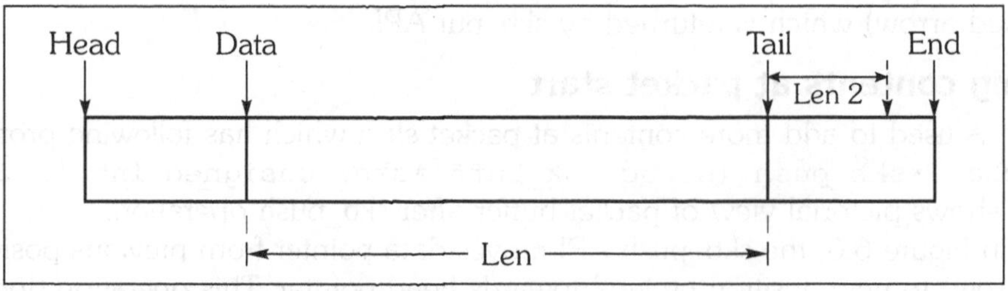

Figure 6.8. sk_buff after skb_trim

As shown in Figure 6.8, the tail pointer is moved from previous position (shown by dashed arrow) to new position by len2 offset towards head pointer. This operation decreases packet length by len2. Once the buffer is trimmed, future skb_put will overwrite the old data.

There are certainly much more APIs available for packet buffer management, however above described APIs are enough for basic packet processing. For more details on packet processing APIs, look in net/core/skbuff.c file.

6.1.7 Non Linear Buffers

The SKB buffers discussed so far are linear buffers. Although very uncommon yet the SKB can be non-linear. In this case the SKB will have paged data. Non-linear buffers are useful during sendmsg() system call or during file system file being sent directly over socket.

Figure 6.9 shows a schematic diagram of non-linear buffer:

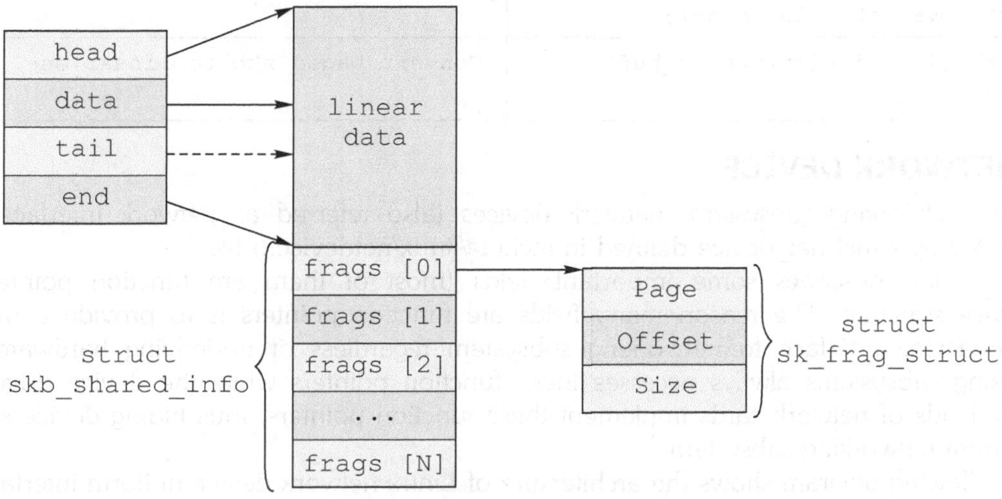

Figure 6.9. Non-linear SKB

There are some special properties of non-linear buffers:

- skb->data_len is non-zero for non-linear buffers (for linear buffers skb->data_len is always zero)
- Amount of non-paged data (linear data) at skb->data can be calculated as (skb->len – skb->data_len). Alternatively skb_headlen() function can be used for same purpose.
- It is invalid to do skb_put() or skb_trim() operations on non-linear buffers as data does not end at tail pointer because data extends beyond tail pointer in skb_shared_info structure. That's the reason tail pointer is shown by a broken arrow in Figure 6.9.

You can use following APIs to operate upon non-linear buffers.

Table 6.1: Non-linear buffer APIs

API	Description
void *skb_header_pointer(const struct sk_buff *skb, int offset, int len, void *buffer);	The return pointer could be one of two things. First, if what you asked for is directly in the skb->data linear data area, you are given a direct pointer into there. Else, you are given the buffer pointer you passed in.

`int skb_copy_bits(const struct sk_buff *skb, int offset, void *to, int len);`	Copy some data bits from skb to kernel buffer.
`void skb_fill_page_desc(struct sk_buff *skb, int i, struct page *page, int off, int size) ;`	Fills the ith page vector to point to page at offset off of size size. It also updates the nr_frags member to be one past i.
`int skb_copy_datagram_iovec(const struct sk_buff *from, int offset, struct iovec *to, int size);`	Copy a datagram to an iovec.
`int skb_linearize(struct sk_buff *skb);`	Convert paged skb to linear one.

6.2 NETWORK DEVICE

In Linux networking subsystem, network devices (also referred as network interfaces) are represented by struct net_device defined in include/linux/netdevice.h file.

This section describes some important fields (most of them are function pointers) of net_device structure. The reason many fields are function pointers is to provide a uniform network device interface to networking subsystem regardless of underlying hardware. The networking subsystems always accesses these function pointers while the device drivers for different kinds of network cards implement these function pointers, thus hiding device specific details from networking subsystem.

The following diagram shows the architecture of Linux network device uniform interface:

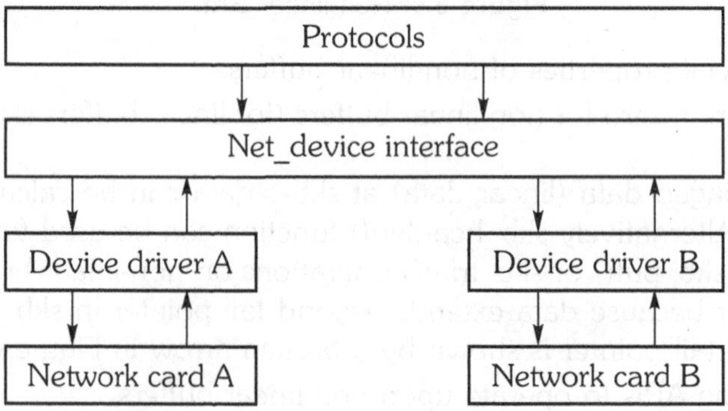

Figure 6.10. Linux network device interface

Following table lists important fields of net_device structure:

Table 6.2: net_device structure fields

Field	`char name[IFNAMSIZE]`
Description	Name of the device. If name does not contain any name, Linux kernel self assigns a name eth*N* where *N* is a suitable numeric. For example, if the system already has eth0 and eth1, then new net_device will be assigned eth2.

Field	unsigned long base_addr
Description	The memory mapped base IO address.
Field	unsigned char dev_addr[MAX_ADDR_LEN]
Description	Interface specific hardware address (MAC address).
Field	unsigned char addr_len
Description	Hardware address length. For Ethernet, hardware address length is 6.
Field	unsigned char broadcast[MAX_ADDR_LEN]
Description	Link layer broadcast address.
Field	hard_header_len
Description	Size of link layer header. For Ethernet, link layer header length is 14.
Field	unsigned int irq
Description	Device's interrupt number.
Field	int (*open) (struct net_device*)
Description	This device specific function is called whenever the device is activated (for example "ifconfig eth0 up" will activate eth0). This function must register system resources the device needs (IO ports, IRQ, DMA etc) and turn on the hardware.
Field	int (*stop) (struct net_device*)
Description	This device specific function is called whenever the device is deactivated (for example "ifconfig eth0 down" will deactivate eth0). This function must release all system resources previously acquired by the device.
Field	int (*hard_start_xmit) (struct sk_buff*,struct net_device)
Description	This device specific function transfers the packet contents on wire.
Field	struct net_device_stats* (*get_stats) (struct net_device*)
Description	This function returns device statistics.
Field	struct list_head poll_list
Description	This is list node used to en-queue the device to CPU specific poll_list whenever the device has received packets and are ready to be processed.
Field	int (*poll) (struct net_device*, int *quota)

Description	Device specific polling function if device supports, else it is assigned to process_backlog function.
Field	void* priv
Description	Private data to the driver. Device driver are free to use it any way they want.

Although the net_device structure has many more fields (refer to netdevice.h), Table 6.2 describes basic and important ones which are required or implemented by a network device driver.

You must have observed that there is no function pointer to receive packets in net_device structure. It's because the packet receiving mechanism is asynchronous and is handled by a queuing mechanism (poll_list field). Every driver receives a packet from wire and en-queues at tail while a softirq (dedicated for network packet receiving) de-queues them and deliver to protocol stacks as shown below:

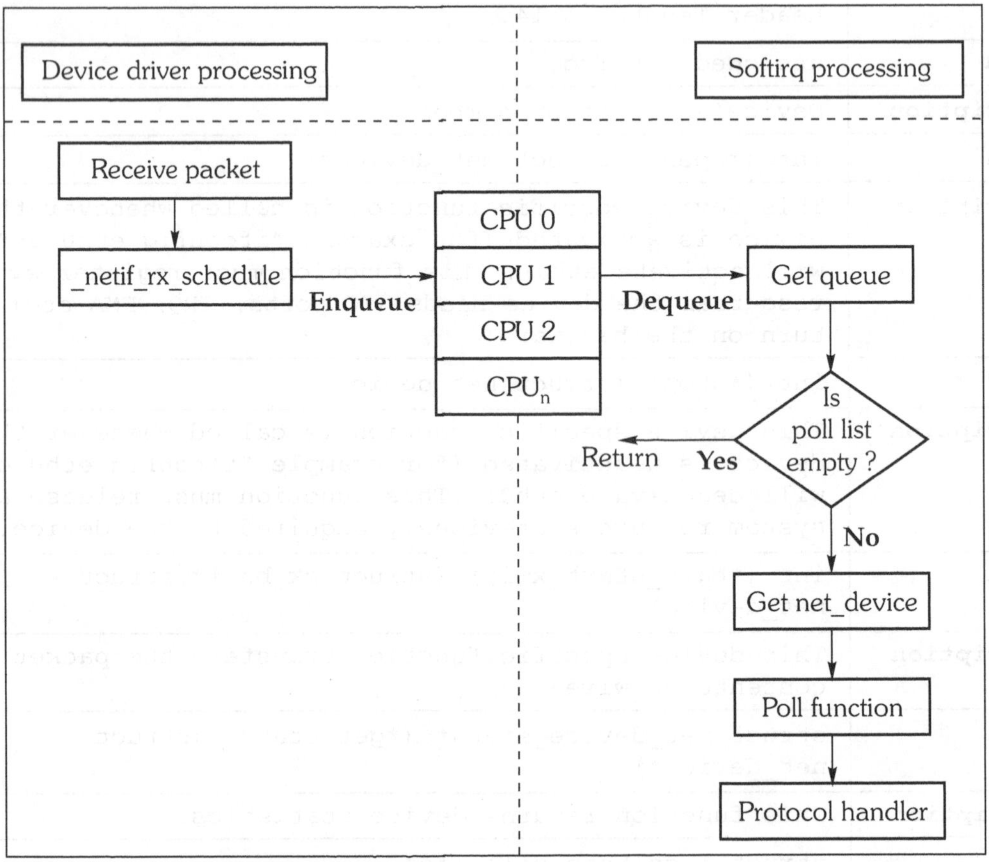

Figure 6.11. net_device packet receiving mechanism

Above diagram will be revisited shortly in forthcoming section which discusses IP packet journey in Linux kernel.

The Linux netdev architecture has recently proposed a new architecture called NAPI. In contrast to earlier netdev architecture where device driver received and copied the packet in sk_buff and queued the packet; the NAPI approach queues the device which has received the packet and let the device poll function to copy the packet in sk_buff. Deferring packet copy functionality from device driver to softirq improves device driver performance. Since NAPI drivers use polling mechanism, the interrupts are disabled as soon as first packet arrives. Then the driver calls the poll function until all packets are processed. If there is no further packet left to process, the driver re-enables interrupt and enters interrupt mode again. Therefore it reduces number of interrupts delivered to the device driver.

6.3 REGISTERING PROTOCOL HANDLERS

Linux networking supports almost all standard protocols. Yet it is sometimes required to introduce new protocols. Linux provides very elegant API to add hooks without affecting existing protocols.

6.3.1 Network Layer Protocol

This section illustrates an example to add a hook to capture ARP packets (Although ARP is not strictly network layer protocol; this section assumes any protocol above Ethernet as network layer protocol).

Linux provides following APIs to add or remove network layer protocols:

Table 6.3

```
void dev_add_pack (struct packet_type *pt);
void dev_remove_pack (struct packet_type *pt);
```

Following table shows a simple example to capture ARP packets.

Table 6.4

```
/* FILE: proto.c */
#include <linux/kernel.h>
#include <linux/module.h>
#include <linux/proc_fs.h>
#include <linux/netdevice.h>
unsigned int arp_count = 0;
static int proc_read_my_flag(char *page,
          char **start, off_t off, int count, int *eof, void *data)
{
        int len=0;
        len += sprintf(page+len, "arp_count = %d\n", arp_count);
        arp_count = 0;
        return len;
}
int my_arp_rcv(struct sk_buff* skb, struct net_device *dev, struct
packet_type *pt, struct net_device *orig_dev)
{
        arp_count++;
        kfree_skb(skb);
        return 0;
}
static struct packet_type my_arp_pkt_type = {
```

```
        .type = __constant_htons(ETH_P_ARP),
        .func = my_arp_rcv,
};
int init_module(void)
{
        struct proc_dir_entry *pfile = NULL;
        pfile = create_proc_entry("myfile", 0444, NULL);
        if(!pfile)
                return -ENOMEM;
        pfile->owner = THIS_MODULE;
        pfile->read_proc = proc_read_my_flag;
        pfile->write_proc = NULL;
        dev_add_pack(&my_arp_pkt_type);
        return 0;
}
void cleanup_module(void)
{
        dev_remove_pack(&my_arp_pkt_type);
        remove_proc_entry("myfile", NULL);
        return;
}
```

The packet_type structure has two important fields, type and func. The type field holds the protocol value and func field holds the protocol handler. The example usage this packet_type structure instance to register the protocol using dev_add_pack API. The example module removes the protocol using dev_remove_pack API. You must always pass a global structure to these APIs because kernel stores the argument pointer in a list.

The protocol handler simply increments a counters and frees the packet. The counter can be read via proc file system. The proc file system code shown in this example is very similar to the one discussed earlier in Chapter 2: APPLICATION & KERNEL SPACE COMMUNICATION.

To test this module, you can use arping utility to send ARP requests to default gateway. The ARP replies from gateway will be captured by new protocol handler which can be verified by the counter read.

6.3.2 Transport Layer Protocol

To add a transport layer protocol (above network layer), Linux provides following API

Table 6.5

```
int inet_add_protocol (
struct net_protocol *prot, unsigned char protocol);
int inet_del_protocol (
struct net_protocol *prot, unsigned char protocol);
```

The struct net_protocol has a member handler which holds the protocol handler. The member has following type:

```
int (*handler) (struct sk_buff *skb);
```

Unlike dev_add_pack, inet_add_protocol does not allow overwriting existing protocol. Therefore you can only add new protocols but cannot coexist with already installed protocols.

6.4 IP PACKET JOURNEY IN KERNEL

After understanding Linux networking subsystem, let's have a look at the IP packet processing path. Packet path from device driver to netdev are different for NAPI drivers and non-NAPI drivers. Following section lists those paths:

6.4.1 Non-NAPI device drivers

- Driver allocates a skb and copies the packet contents from hardware to the skb.
- Driver queues the packet using netif_rx call which in turn calls napi_schedule to raise network softirq (NET_RX_SOFTIRQ).
- Kernel later invokes network softirq function net_rx_action.
- The function net_rx_action invokes device poll function. Non-NAPI devices have process_backlog as their poll function.
- The process_backlog function invokes netif_receive_skb which distributes the packet to appropriate protocol handlers.

6.4.2 NAPI device drivers

- Driver processes interrupt to recognize packet arrival and en-queues the device. The driver disables further interrupts.
- Drivers calls napi_schedule function to raise network softirq.
- Kernel later invokes network softirq function net_rx_action.
- The function net_rx_action invokes device specific poll function. NAPI devices have their specific poll function which allocates a skb and copies data from hardware to skb.
- The poll function then invokes netif_receive_skb which distributes the packet to appropriate protocol handlers.
- The poll function keeps removing packets from hardware buffer until all packets are removed. If no further packets are left in hardware buffer, the driver exits poll mode and enters interrupt mode by enabling interrupts.

For IP packets, Linux kernel had established ip_rcv function (using dev_add_pack) as protocol handler and therefore netif_receive_skb delivers the packet to ip_rcv function.

Figure 6.12 shows the control flow during IP packet processing:

The ip_rcv function performs basic sanity checks (checksum, length etc) on the received packet and then calls ip_rcv_finish function. The ip_rcv_finish function makes routing decision (skb->dst->input) based on which packet is either forwarded to another host or delivered to local host.

For making routing decision, ip_rcv_finish calls ip_route_input function. The ip_route_input function looks into routing cache, and if an entry is found in routing cache the function returns appropriate skb->dst value. However if ip_route_input fails to find a routing entry in routing cache, it invokes ip_route_input_slow function which creates a destination entry from FIB lookup.

Therefore, at the end of ip_rcv_finish, a decision can be made based upon skb->dst entry.

If the packet is to be delivered to local host, function ip_local_deliver is called which may perform reassembly if required and calls ip_local_deliver_finish. This function ends IP layer processing and invokes appropriate protocol hander for the transport protocol based on protocol value in IP header.

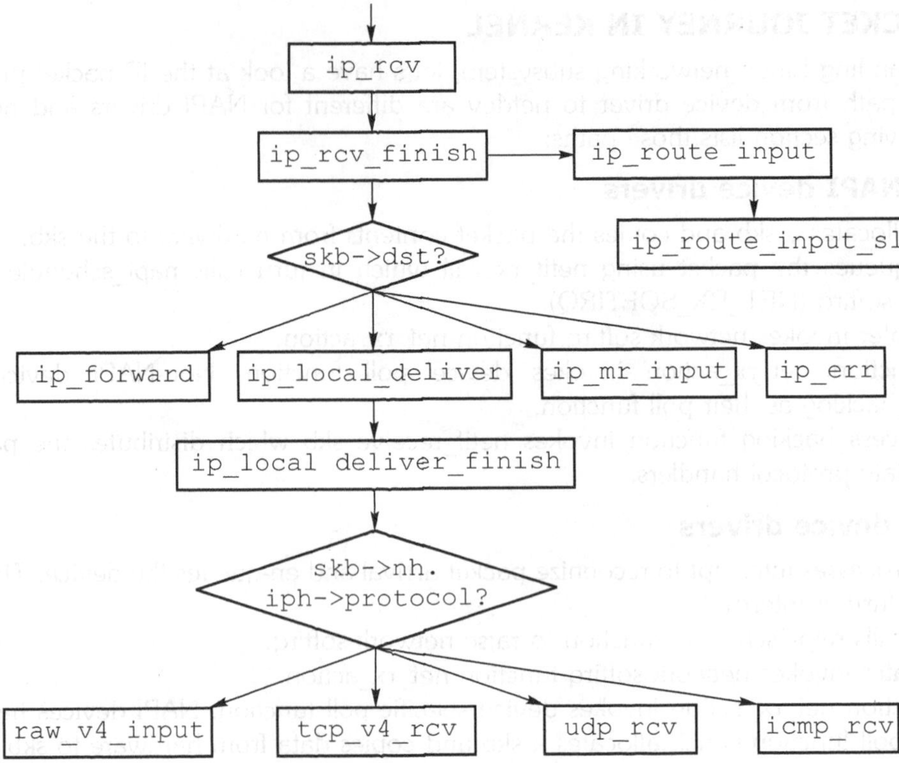

Figure 6.12. Inbound IP packet processing

For UDP packets, Linux kernel establishes udp_rcv function (using inet_add_protocol) as protocol handler. Similarly for TCP packets, the protocol handler is tcp_v4_rcv function. If the packet is UDP, it is given to udp_rcv function. The transport layer handlers find appropriate socket to which the packet is to be delivered and the processes waiting for packets on those sockets are woken-up.

6.5 ROUTE LOOKUP

As mentioned in previous section, the function ip_rcv_finish performs route lookup using ip_route_input and ip_route_input_slow functions. The ip_route_input performs lookup in "routing cache" (can be accessed by "route –C" command) while ip_route_input_slow performs lookup in FIB (Forwarding Information Base). These route lookup functions take input parameters in form of struct flowi, and perform a route lookup based on these parameters.

Figure 6.13 shows routing cache data structures and their relation.

The routing cache is stored in a global pointer rt_hash_table which points to a hash table. This hash table stores one entry for each destination for which route lookup has been done previously. The routing entries are stored in struct rtable which stores dst_entry (protocol independent part) and flowi (route key). The input() and output() functions of dst_entry decide packet processing path (*i.e.*, local delivery or forwarding).

As mentioned previously, if ip_rcv_finish fails to find a destination entry (or route entry) in routing cache, it calls ip_route_input_slow function which does FIB lookup. The FIB lookup consists of two parts. It firsts does a policy lookup to find an appropriate routing table, and then it finds a route in the routing table.

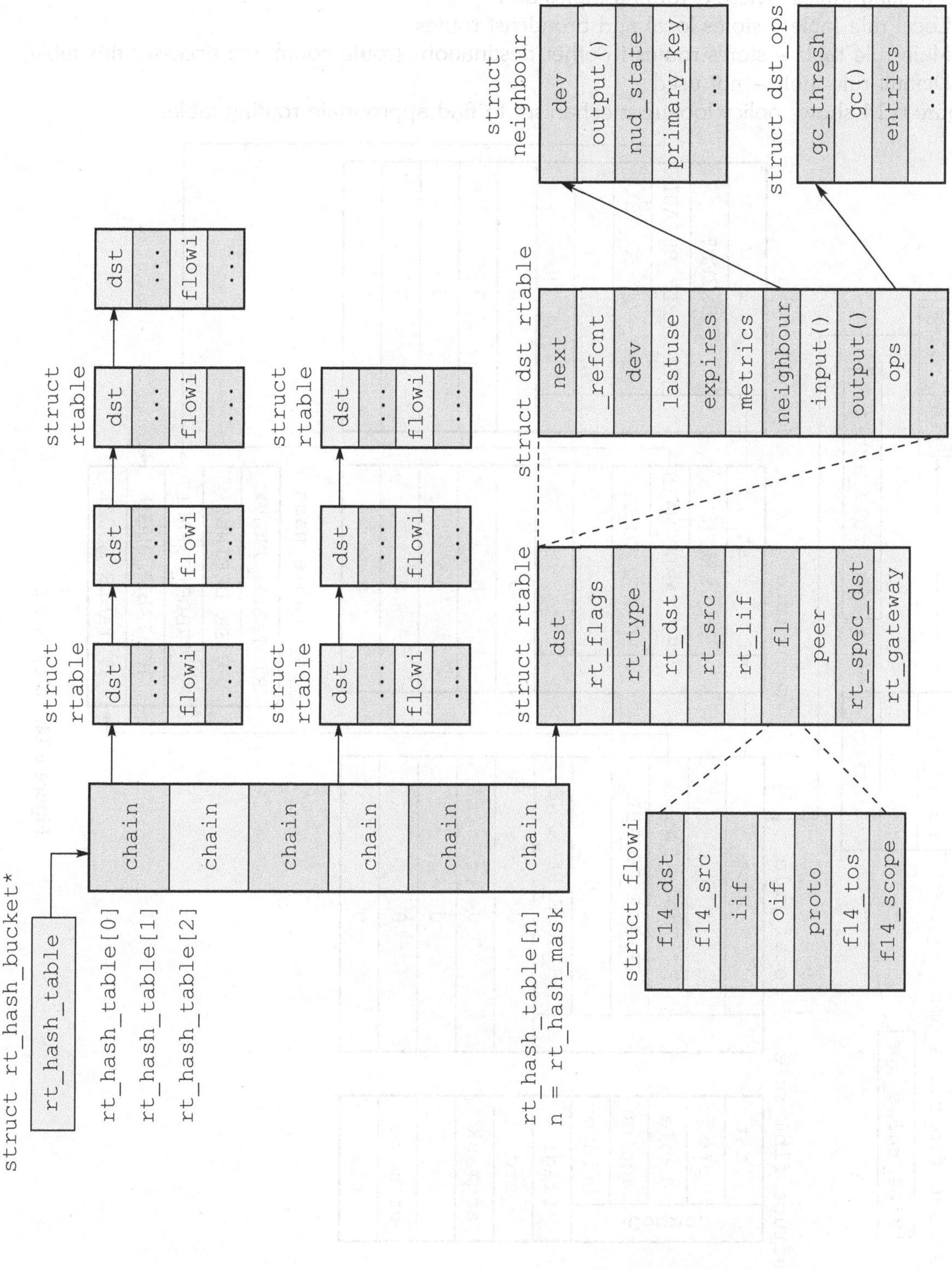

Figure 6.13. Routing Cache

The Linux kernel can support multiple routing tables if it is compiled with CONFIG_IP_MULTIPLE_TABLES option. However without this option, Linux kernel supports only 3 routing tables. These 3 routing tables are:

- Local rule table – stores local and broadcast routes.
- Main rule table – stores routes to other destinations (route command accesses this table)
- Default rule table – not used

Figure 6.14 shows policy lookup mechanism to find appropriate routing table.

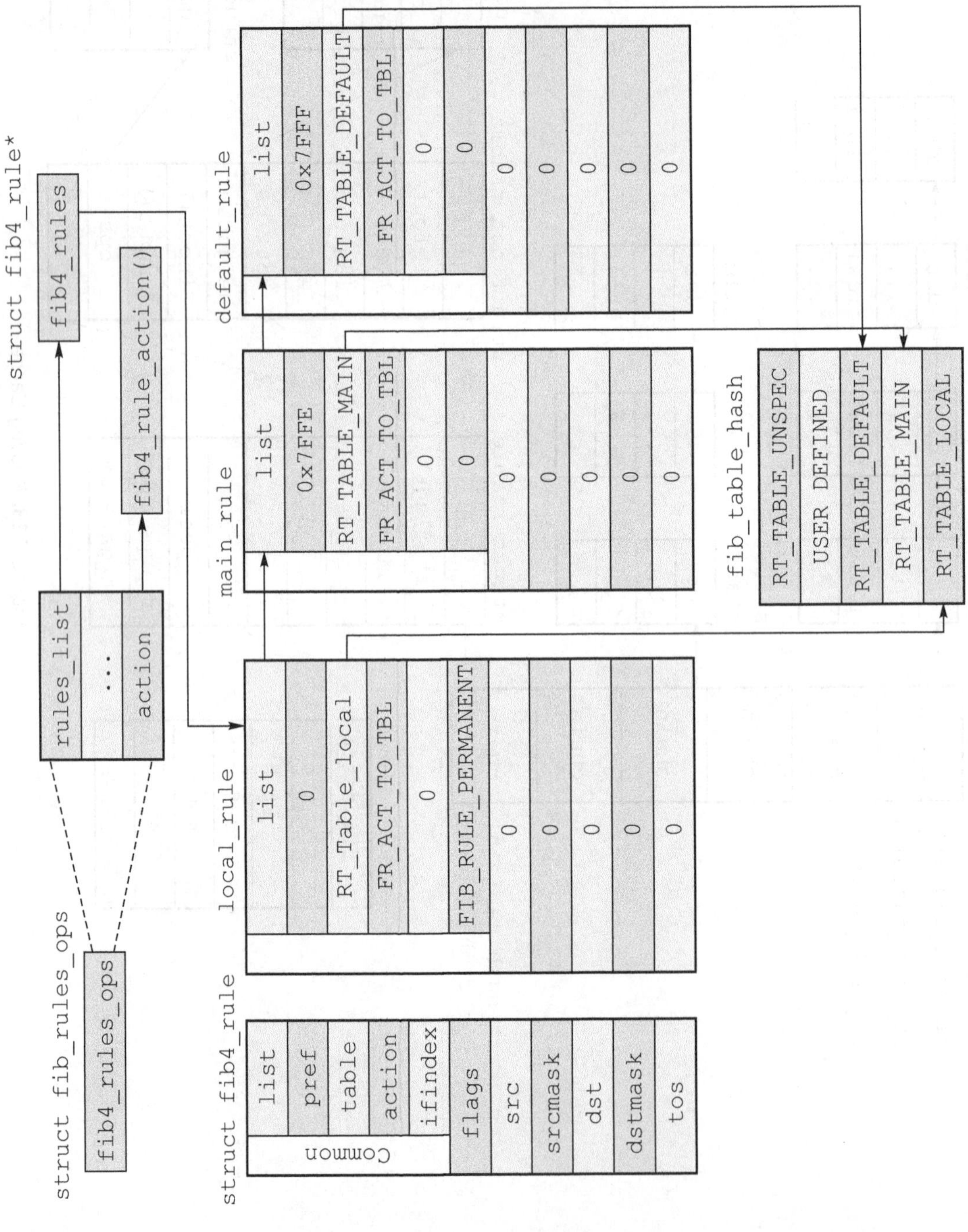

Figure 6.14. Policy lookup

The ip_route_input_slow function that is responsible for FIB lookup calls the fib_lookup function. The fib_lookup function calls fib_rules_lookup function which iterates through all rules in fib4_rules_ops global list. If kernel is not compiled with option CONFIG_IP_MULTIPLE_TABLES then there are only 3 rules (local_rule, main_rule and default_rule). The fib_rules_lookup matches input flowi parameters to those in rule list and if a rule is matched then action function is called which is fib4_rule_action. The fib4_rule_action function first checks rule action type. If the rule action type is FR_ACT_TO_TBL, it gets the routing table corresponding to this rule, and then calls the function pointed by tb_lookup field as explained in Figure 6.15. The tb_lookup function points to fn_hash_lookup function.

Figure 6.15 shows the data structures associated with routing table.

A routing table is stored in fib_table structure. This structure contains a field tb_data which actually contains fn_hash structure. The fn_hash structure has an array of fn_zone structure; one element for each netmask length. Therefore, the arrary size is 33 (from netmask length 0 to netmask length 32). All the routes of same netmask length are stored in same fn_zone structure. The fn_zone structure contains a pointer fz_hash which points to a hash table (therefore all routes of same netmask length are stored in one hash table). The number of buckets in the hash_table is represented by fz_divisor field. Each element in this hash table is fib_node structure. Therefore, a fib_node structure represents a unique network mask. The fib_node structure contains fib_alias structure. The fib_alias structure is used to differentiate between different routes to same destination based on some parameters like TOS etc. Finally fib_alias structure contains fib_info structure which stores next hop information in fib_nh field.

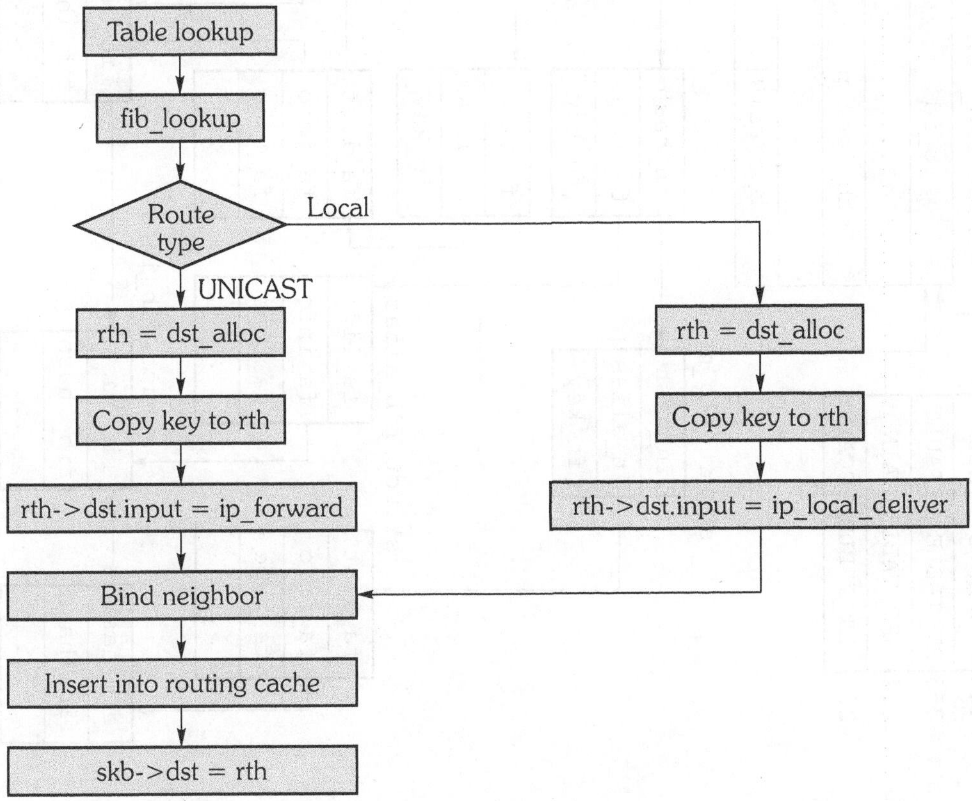

Figure 6.15. FIB lookup operations

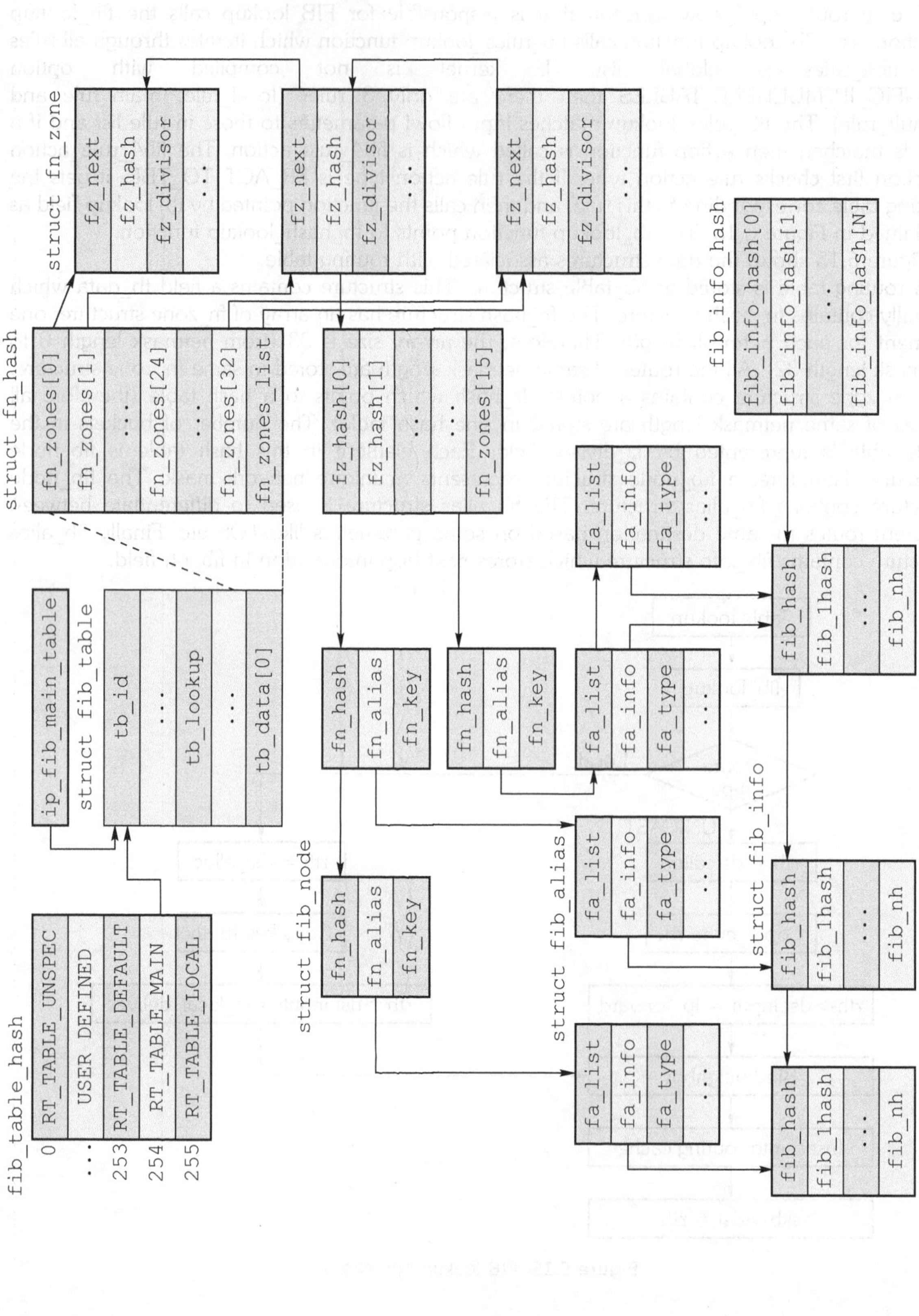

Figure 6.16. Routing table

To do a route lookup, the kernel first finds an appropriate routing table (say main table which is also pointed by ip_fib_main_table). The tb_lookup field is a function pointer which performs route lookup on given table. As mentioned previously, the tb_lookup points to fn_hash_lookup. The fn_hash_lookup function uses fn_zone_list field of fn_hash function to do route lookup. The fn_zone_list points to last element of fn_zones arrary (*i.e.*, of netmask length 32). It is because routing is done on LPM (longest prefix match) basis. If a match is not found in the hash table of fn_zones[32], then kernel moves to fn_zones[31] using the fz_next pointer. Kernel repeats this until a match is found and then a new destination entry is created with matched information.

After a route lookup is done successfully in FIB, the result is stored in routing cache for faster lookup next time. Figure 6.16 shows the operations after FIB lookup.

6.6 SUMMARY

Data networking is an important feature of any operating system and Linux is no exception. With growth of telecommunication networks, connected embedded systems; Linux networking stack is now widely used.

6.7 ASSIGNMENTS

- Write a new kernel function (build it with kernel tree) to display routing table. Invoke this function through a proc file created by you.
- Study about Linux network hooks (NF_IP_PRE_ROUTING, NF_IP_LOCAL_IN, NF_IP_FORWARD, NF_IP_LOCAL_OUT, AND NF_IP_POST_ROUTING). Write a module using Linux network hooks (NF_HOOK). Modify the captured skbs.
- Understand Linux netfilters. Configure a firewall on your Linux system using iptables.

6.8 REFERENCES

- Understanding Linux Network Internals by Christian Benvenuti
- Netfilters-http://en.wikipedia.org/wiki/Netfilter

7 Developing UART (Serial Port) Device Driver

This chapter shall describe a step by step and incremental method to develop device driver for UART chip which controls serial port on Linux box or Linux boards. The chapter shall cover following sections:

- Setup
- Compiling kernel for UART driver development
- Understanding UART and its functions
- Understanding UART registers
- Developing 'polling write' UART driver
- Upgrading to 'interrupt based write' UART driver
- Upgrading to 'interrupt based read' UART driver
- Assignments

7.1 SETUP

For UART driver development in this chapter, we need following:

- A PC with at least one serial port running Linux. If you have more than one serial port use COM1 (ttyS0).
- Another PC with at least one serial or USB port running Linux or Windows.
- In case of USB port on another PC, a USB to serial converter required.
- A null modem cable (both ends having female serial connector)

Before starting driver development, lets setup serial communication in a running kernel. Connect null modem cable between serial port on development host and remote host. Run minicom or hyperterminal (we shall refer the remote host application as serial console) on remote host with following configuration (more details about the configuration parameters later):

- Baud Rate – 57600
- Data Bits – 8
- Flow Control – None
- Parity – None
- Stop Bits – 1

Compile following application on development host and execute to communicate with remote host serial console.

Table 7.1

```
/* FILE: serial_app.c */
/* compile command: gcc -o serial_app serial_app.c */
#include <stdio.h>
#include <string.h>
#include <fcntl.h>
#include <errno.h>
#include <termios.h>
int main()
{
        int fd, i, ret;
        struct termios options = {0};
        unsigned char data[64] = {0};
        time_t rawtime;
        time(&rawtime);
        sprintf(data, "Local time is: %s\r", ctime (&rawtime));
        fd = open("/dev/ttyS0", O_RDWR);
        if(fd < 0) {
                printf("Open /dev/ttyS0: %s\n", strerror(errno));
                return -1;
        }
        cfsetispeed(&options, B57600);
        options.c_cflag &= ~PARENB; /* Clear parity enable */
        options.c_iflag &= ~INPCK; /* Enable parity checking */
        options.c_cflag &= ~CSTOPB;
        options.c_cflag &= ~CSIZE;
        options.c_cflag |= CS8;
        /* set options */
        if (tcsetattr(fd, TCSANOW, &options) != 0) {
                printf("tcsetattr: %s\n", strerror(errno));
                return 0;
        }
        ret = write(fd, data, strlen(data) ) ;
        printf("write returns %d\n", ret);
        close(fd);
        return 0 ;
}
```

On execution of the application on development host, you should see system date string generated by the application appearing in serial console at remote host.

We shall continue to use this application for testing UART device driver.

7.2 COMPILING KERNEL FOR UART DRIVER DEVELOPMENT

The Linux kernel has a very flexible and versatile driver for common UART (complying with 8250, 16450 series and family). We must disable existing driver in Linux kernel so that it does not conflict with the new UART driver we are going to insert.

Go to kernel source directory and invoke “make xconfig” or “make gconfig”. Go to ‘drivers’, then to ‘Character devices’, then to ‘serial drivers’ and disable ‘8250’ support as shown below:

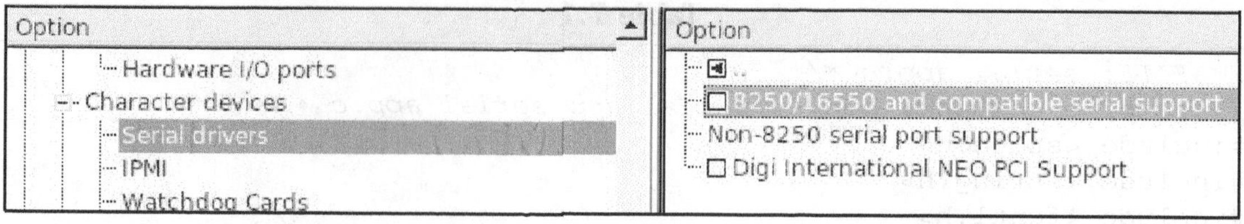

Figure 7.1

Recompile the kernel and boot the system with new kernel. To verify if everything is as expected, files /proc/ioports and /proc/interrupts must not have any entry for ‘serial’ driver. More specifically ports 0x2f8-0x2ff and 0x3f8-0x3ff must not be occupied. Similarly IRQ 4 must not be occupied (more about these parameters later).

7.3 UNDERSTANDING UART FUNCTIONS

This section describes UART receiving and transmission functions, configuration parameters and accessing method.

7.3.1 Transmission and Reception

UART stands for Universal Asynchronous Receiver/Transmitter. The UART performs a parallel to serial conversion during transmission and from serial to parallel conversion during receiving. The UART transmits or receives data using RS-232 specifications.

For transmitting data out, UART has a “Transmit Holding Register” also known as THR. CPU can write outgoing byte in THR. From THR the byte is transferred to an internal shift register which is not accessible to CPU. From shift register, the byte is transmitted bit by bit (Bit 0 first, bit 7 last) on the serial line. Similarly for receiving, the UART receives the byte (bit by bit) in a shift register. Once entire byte is received, the byte is transferred in “Receiver Buffer Register” also known as RBR where CPU can read it. In some UART RBR is also referred as RHR (Receiver Holding Register).

Early UARTs had only one byte THR and RBR where CPU can read and write only one byte at a time. This caused serial drivers to under perform because CPU has to process interrupts after every byte transmission or reception. To increase the performance, later UART were designed with 16 bytes size (or more) FIFO where CPU can read and write data in bigger chunk of 16 (or 14) bytes, thereby increasing system performance. Here a point must be noted that UART can not have very large FIFO because the driver has no control over the data already sent to FIFO. Therefore even after receiving a stop signal from peer UART, the data in FIFO shall be transmitted.

7.3.2 UART Configuration

There are some parameters which control UART transmission, reception and flow control behavior. A brief explanation of the parameters is in order.

- Baud Rate – Baud rate represents the number of bits transmitted per second including parity and stop bits (which are removed by peer UART). Therefore, the actual data rate is less than the baud rate. It is measured in bps (bits per second).

- Parity Bit – UART can add an extra bit to the outgoing byte for error detection and correction purpose. The receiver UART performs the same calculation on the byte and compares with parity bit to verify if the byte has been received correctly.

The parity can be 'Even Parity' or 'Odd Parity'. In even parity, the number of high bits (logical 1) will always be even. Therefore, if the information has odd number of high bits, another high bit will be added. However, if the information has even number of high bits, a low bit will be added.

The odd parity is similar to even parity with only difference that number of high bits will always be odd.

- Stop Bit—The UART adds extra one or two bits at the end of byte to mark end of frame. This is required because if receiver UART has not understood start of byte correctly, it may read the byte wrong. The stop bits help in re-synchronizing and discarding current frame if frame error has occurred.
- Data Word Length—RS232 specifications devises a method where the information can be transmitted bit by bit. The information must be split in data words. The data word length can be configured between 5 to 8 bits.
- Flow Control—Flow control is a mechanism between two UARTs where each UART can inform to other about its current receiving capacity. If a UART is not in position to receive any more data, it sends a signal to the peer UART. On receiving this signal, the peer UART stops transmission and waits for another signal to restart the transmission.

7.3.3 Accessing UART

As we discussed in section 7.3.1, the UART has certain registers which can be accessed by CPU. The UART device driver has the responsibility of reading and writing to those registers; thereby making data transfer over serial port possible.

The UART registers are available as IO ports starting a specific port number. The port numbers are set by BIOS and Linux or any other OS uses same port numbers. The UART also has capability of generating an interrupt when some data is received on serial port. The interrupt is required to get CPU attention so that the data can be read from the RBR. Typical values of IO ports and interrupt number are shown in below table:

Table 7.2

Device	Port Range	IRQ
ttyS0, COM1	0x3F8-0x3FF	4
ttyS1, COM2	0x2F8-0x2FF	3
ttyS2, COM3	0x3E8-0x3FF	4
ttyS3, COM4	0x2E8-0x2FF	3

7.4 UNDERSTANDING UART REGISTERS

Understanding UART registers is very important for UART driver development. The registers are face of the UART and are used for controlling UART behavior.

Any 8250/16450/16550 compatible UART has 8 registers. However a register can behave differently depending upon DLAB bit, read or write. DLAB is bit 7 in LSR (More to come later).

An introduction to the UART registers is in order.

7.4.1 Receive Buffer Register (RBR)

RBR is a Read Only (RO) register at offset 0 with DLAB bit set to 0. As discussed earlier RBR contains the received byte. If FIFO is used; then RBR contains oldest unread byte. Each RBR read will return next byte until no more bytes are present.

The bit 0 in LSR (Line Status Register) goes to 0 when no more bytes are present in FIFO. Additionally UART can generate an interrupt when RBR has received a byte. In FIFO mode, interrupt is generated when UART has received data up to configured FIFO size or a timeout has occurred (no byte received since the last byte received).

Summary of RBR is shown in below table:

Table 7.3

Bit 7	Bit 6	Bit 5	Bit 4	Bit 3	Bit 2	Bit 1	Bit 0
Data bit 7	Data bit 6	Data bit 5	Data bit 4	Data bit 3	Data bit 2	Data bit 1	Data bit 0

7.4.2 Transmitter Holding Register (THR)

THR is a Write Only (WO) register at offset 0 with DLAB bit set to 0. If FIFO is not used, only one byte can be written. In FIFO mode, as many bytes as FIFO size can be written. If more bytes are written while FIFO is full, the data is lost.

Bit 5 in LSR (Line Status Register) can be used to check if THR is empty and therefore the UART driver can write more bytes to the THR. Additionally, UART can generate an interrupt when THR is empty.

Summary of THR is shown in below table:

Table 7.4

Bit 7	Bit 6	Bit 5	Bit 4	Bit 3	Bit 2	Bit 1	Bit 0
Data bit 7	Data bit 6	Data bit 5	Data bit 4	Data bit 3	Data bit 2	Data bit 1	Data bit 0

7.4.3 Interrupt Enable Register (IER)

As mentioned earlier, a UART can generate interrupt on various conditions or events. The interrupts can be configured selectively and only those interrupts are generated which UART is asked to. For enabling an interrupt, the corresponding bit in IER must be set to 1.

IER is a Read/Write (RW) register at offset 1 with DLAB set to 0. A summary of IER register is shown in below table:

Table 7.5

Bit 7	Bit 6	Bit 5	Bit 4	Bit 3	Bit 2	Bit 1	Bit 0
Always 0	Always 0	Always 0	Always 0	MODEM Status Interrupt	Receiver Line Status Change Interrupt	Transmit-ter Holding Register Empty Interrupt	Received Data Available Interrupt

7.4.4 Interrupt Identification Register (IIR)

IIR is a Read Only (RO) register at offset 2 with DLAB X (don't care). As mentioned earlier, UART can generate many kinds of interrupts. IER is used to identify the kind of interrupt generated. A summary of IER register is shown in below table:

Table 7.6

Bit 7	Bit 6	Bit 5	Bit 4	Bit 3	Bit 2	Bit 1	Bit 0
Always 0	Always 0	Always 0	Always 0	Interrupt ID Bit 2	Interrupt ID Bit 1	Interrupt ID Bit 0	Interrupt Pending

The following table lists bit values to identify their meaning.

Table 7.7

Bit	Value			Identification
0	0			Interrupt is pending. Bits 1, 2 and 3 are meaningful.
	1			No interrupt pending. Bits 1, 2 and 3 have no meaning.
1,2,3	Bit 3	Bit 2	Bit 1	
	0	0	0	Modem status change
	0	0	1	THR empty
	0	1	0	Received data available
	0	1	1	Line status change
	1	1	0	Character timeout

Every interrupt demands an action from the UART driver. For example, THR empty interrupt is an indication to the driver that the driver can transmit one more byte if FIFO mode is not enabled. In FIFO mode, driver can transmit as many bytes more as is FIFO size. Similarly, received data available and character timeout interrupts mean that driver can read data from RBR. Driver must read either one byte from RBR (FIFO mode disabled and received data available interrupt) or FIFO trigger level length data (FIFO mode enabled and received data available interrupt) or until bit 0 in LSR goes 0 (FIFO mode enabled and character timeout).

7.4.5 FIFO Control Register (FCR)

FCR is a write only (WO) register at offset 2 with DLAB X (don't care). FCR is used to control UART's FIFO behavior. A summary of FCR is shown in below table:

Table 7.8

Bit 7	Bit 6	Bit 5	Bit 4	Bit 3	Bit 2	Bit 1	Bit 0
Receive FIFO Trigger (MSB)	Receive FIFO Trigger (LSB)	Always 0	Always 0	DMA Mode Select	Transmit FIFO Reset	Receive FIFO Reset	FIFO Enable

FIFO mode can be enabled by setting bit 0 to logical 1. Bits 1 and 2 are used for resetting or flushing "receive FIFO" and "transmit FIFO" respectively. Bit 3 is set to 1 for selecting DMA mode.

UART FIFO can be configured to generate an interrupt after the FIFO is filled with preconfigured FIFO trigger level *i.e.*, UART can generate receive data available interrupt even before FIFO is completely filled. Following table lists bit values to identify FIFO trigger level size.

Table 7.9

Bit	Value		Receive FIFO trigger level
6,7	Bit 7	Bit 6	
	0	0	1 Byte
	0	1	4 Bytes
	1	0	8 Bytes
	1	1	14 Bytes

It is interesting to note that FIFO trigger level is always less than the maximum FIFO size (16). This is required in order to give some margin against FIFO overflow before the CPU acknowledges the interrupt and UART driver starts reading RBR *i.e.*, UART can still receive 2 more bytes before the driver starts reading RBR.

7.4.6 Line Control Register (LCR)

LCR is a read-write (RW) register at offset 3 with DLAB X (don't care). In fact, this is the register which has DLAB bit, and therefore LCR has important role in controlling UART register behavior. A summary of LCR is shown in below table:

Table 7.10

Bit 7	Bit 6	Bit 5	Bit 4	Bit 3	Bit 2	Bit 1	Bit 0
Divisor Latch Access Bit	Set Break	Stick Parity	Even Parity Select	Parity Enable	Number of Stop Bits	Word Length Select Bit 1	Word Length Select Bit 0

Following table lists bit values and their meaning:

Table 7.11

Bits	Value		Description
0,1	Bit 1	Bit 0	
	0	0	Data word length is 5 (rarely used)
	0	1	Data word length is 6
	1	0	Data word length is 7
	1	1	Data word length is 8
2	0		1 stop bit
	1		2 stop bits

3,4,5	Bit 5	Bit 4	Bit 3	
	X	X	0	No parity
	0	0	1	Odd parity
	0	1	1	Even parity
	1	0	1	High parity (stick) (rarely used)
	1	1	1	Low parity (stick) (rarely used)
6	0			Break signal disabled
	1			Break signal enabled
7	0			DLAB - RBR, THR and IER registers accessible
	1			DLAB - DL LSB and DL MSB registers accessible

7.4.7 MODEM Control Register (MCR)

MCR is a read-write (RW) register at offset 4 with DLAB X (don't care). This register is useful in modem control. A summary of MCR is shown in below table:

Table 7.12

Bit 7	Bit 6	Bit 5	Bit 4	Bit 3	Bit 2	Bit 1	Bit 0
Always 0	Always 0	Always 0	Loop	Out2	Out1	Request to Send (RTS)	Data Terminal Ready (DTR)

DTR and RTS bits are useful in modem communication. DTR is set to 1 when the UART is ready for data transmission while RTS is set to 1 when UART is ready to receive.

While bit Out1 is rarely used, bit Out2 is very important in generating interrupts. In many UARTs interrupts are not generated until bit Out2 is set to 1.

Another interesting bit is Loop bit. If this bit is set to 1, UART loops back outgoing (transmitted) data back to RBR. This bit can be very helpful in debugging UART driver.

7.4.8 Line Status Register (LSR)

LSR is a read-only (RO) register at offset 5 with DLAB X (don't care). This register is read by UART driver upon receiver line status interrupt arrival. Alternatively a polling UART driver shall use LSR to know receiving status and transmission status. A summary of LSR is shown in below table:

Table 7.13

Bit 7	Bit 6	Bit 5	Bit 4	Bit 3	Bit 2	Bit 1	Bit 0
Always 0	Transmit-ter Empty	THR Empty	Break Interrupt	Framing Error	Parity Error	Overrun Error	Data Ready

The data ready bit is set by UART whenever some data is available in RBR. This bit remains 1 as long as data is present in RBR (or FIFO) and goes to 0 when no data left in RBR.

Bit 1, Bit 2 and Bit 3 are set to 1 whenever UART detects overrun, parity and framing errors respectively.

Break interrupt (bit 4) is set to 1 when UART receives break signal from peer UART *i.e.*, when peer UART sets bit 6 of LCR register.

UART sets THR empty (bit 5) to 1 when THR register becomes empty. It means that UART driver can transmit more data.

Transmitter empty (bit 6) is set to 1 when the transmitter shift register also becomes empty.

7.4.9 MODEM Status Register (MSR)

MSR is a read-only (RO) register at offset 6 with DLAB X (don't care). This register is read by UART driver upon modem status interrupt arrival. A summary of MSR is shown in below table:

Table 7.14

Bit 7	Bit 6	Bit 5	Bit 4	Bit 3	Bit 2	Bit 1	Bit 0
Carrier Detect	Ring Indicator	Data Set Ready (DSR)	Clear to Send (CTS)	Change in Carrier Detect	Trailing Edge Ring Indicator	Change in DSR	Change in CTS

7.4.10 Scratch Register (SCR)

SCR is a read-write (RW) register at offset 7 with DLAB X (don't care). This is relatively less used register and can be used by UART driver to store one byte private information.

7.4.11 Divisor Latch LSB and Divisor Latch MSB

Divisor Latch LSB (DLL) and Divisor Latch MSB (DLM) are read-write (RW) registers at offset 0 and 1 respectively with DLAB 1. These registers are used to configure the UART baud rate. Following table lists DLL and DLM values and corresponding baud rate:

Table 7.15

DLL	DLM	Baud rate in bps
0x01	0x00	115200
0x02	0x00	57600
0x03	0x00	38400
0x06	0x00	19200
0x08	0x00	14400
0x0C	0x00	9600
0x10	0x00	7200
0x18	0x00	4200
0x30	0x00	2400
0xF6	0x00	1200

This concludes UART registers. As we discussed UART registers play different role based upon DLAB bit status and operating being performed. Following table briefs this:

Table 7.16

IO PORT Offset	DLAB = 0 READ	DLAB = 0 WRITE	DLAB = 1 READ	DLAB = 1 WRITE
0	RBR	THR	DLL	DLL
1	IER	IER	DLM	DLM
2	IIR	FCR	IIR	FCR
3	LCR	LCR	LCR	LCR
4	MCR	MCR	MCR	MCR
5	LSR	N/A	LSR	N/A
6	MSR	N/A	MSR	N/A
7	SCR	SCR	SCR	SCR

7.5 DEVELOPING 'POLLING BASED' UART DRIVER

After having understood UART registers, it's easy to start driver development. We shall develop UART driver as character device driver.

Let's start with a private structure to keep information of serial device. We define these in a header file say myserial.h

Table 7.17

```
/* FILE: myserial.h */
#ifndef __MY_SERIAL_
#define __MY_SERIAL_
struct serialDev
{
        unsigned int ioport;
        unsigned int ports;
};
#define TRACE(arg...) printk(arg)
#define SERIAL_MAJOR 124
#define SERIAL_DEVICE "myserial"
#define FIFO_SIZE 16
#endif
```

Next we prepare a file serialcore.c where actual driver code will be developed. We start the file with a small kernel module.

Table 7.18

```
/* FILE: serialcore.c */
#include <linux/kernel.h>
#include <linux/module.h>
#include <linux/fs.h>
```

```
#include "myserial.h"
struct serialDev *pDev = NULL;
int serialDev_init(struct serialDev *pDev)
{
        pDev->ioport = 0x3f8;
        pDev->ports = 8;
        return 0;
}
int init_module(void)
{
        pDev = kmalloc(sizeof(struct serialDev), GFP_KERNEL);
        if(!pDev) {
             printk("Memory allocation failed\n");
             return 0;
        }
        serialDev_init(pDev);
        printk("myserial inserted\n");
        return 0;
}
void cleanup_module(void)
{
        printk("myserial removed\n");
        if(pDev) {
             kfree(pDev);
        }
}
MODULE_LICENSE("GPL");
```

Above code shows a small kernel module which allocates memory for the serial device structure and initializes IO port base address and number of ports. As this driver shall only work for COM1 (ttyS0), we use base address 0x3f8 as explained in section 7.3.3.

We shall use following makefile to compile the kernel module.

Table 7.19

```
KDIR := /usr/src/linux-2.6.21.5
obj-m := serial.o
serial-objs := serialcore.o
default:
        make -C $(KDIR) SUBDIRS='pwd' modules
clean:
        make -C $(KDIR) SUBDIRS='pwd' clean
```

In the next step we introduce a character device driver with dummy and minimum functions.

Table 7.20

```
/* FILE: serialcore.c */
ssize_t serial_write(struct file* file, const char __user * buf,
size_t size, loff_t * boffset)
```

```
{
        TRACE("%s invoked\n", __FUNCTION__);
        return 0;
}
long serial_unlocked_ioctl(struct file* file, unsigned int cmd,
unsigned long arg)
{
        TRACE("%s invoked\n", __FUNCTION__);
        return 0;
}
int serial_open(struct inode * inode, struct file* file)
{
        TRACE("%s invoked\n", __FUNCTION__);
        return 0;
}
int serial_flush(struct file* file, fl_owner_t id)
{
        TRACE("%s invoked\n", __FUNCTION__);
        return 0;
}
int serial_release(struct inode * inode, struct file* file)
{
        TRACE("%s invoked\n", __FUNCTION__);
        return 0;
}
int serial_check_flags(int dummy)
{
        TRACE("%s invoked\n", __FUNCTION__);
        return 0;
}
struct file_operations serial_operations = {
        owner: THIS_MODULE,
        write: serial_write,
        unlocked_ioctl: serial_unlocked_ioctl,
        open: serial_open,
        flush: serial_flush,
        release: serial_release,
        check_flags: serial_check_flags,
};
int init_module(void)
{
        pDev = kmalloc(sizeof(struct serialDev), GFP_KERNEL);
        serialDev_init(pDev);
        if(register_chrdev(SERIAL_MAJOR, SERIAL_DEVICE,
 &serial_operations) < 0) {
                printk("could not register char dev with major %d\n",
 SERIAL_MAJOR);
```

```
                goto fail_chrdev;
        }
        printk("myserial inserted\n");
        return 0;
fail_chrdev:
        kfree(pDev);
        pDev = NULL;
        return 0;
}
void cleanup_module(void)
{
        printk("myserial removed\n");
        if(pDev) {
              unregister_chrdev(SERIAL_MAJOR, SERIAL_DEVICE);
              kfree(pDev);
        }
}
```

In the above table, we define only dummy functions for the character device driver and register the driver using register_chrdev function. The register_chrdev function takes major number, device name and file operations as arguments. The file operations define functions which are called whenever an application performs some action on the device. On module removal, we un-register the device using unregister_chrdev function which takes major number and device name as argument. In this module, we have defined major number to 124. On your system, you must ensure that this major number is not in use by any other device (/proc/devices). If it is in use, choose another major number of our UART driver.

Note that we have used unlocked_ioctl member function in the character driver file operations rather than ioctl. It is because during ioctl call big kernel lock is held. Therefore all new drivers are advised to use unlocked_ioctl unless they really need to hold the big kernel lock.

At this point of time, we can compile, insert and remove the dummy driver using following steps:

Table 7.21

```
root@localhost#
makeroot@localhost# insmod serial.ko
root@localhost# rmmod serial.ko
root@localhost# mknod /dev/ttyS0 c 124 0
```

The last entry in above table creates a device node for the UART. The 124 is this command is the major number we used for the serial driver. At this point of time an application can open the device /dev/ttyS0 using open system call. This shall invoke our dummy open function serial_open although it does nothing. Similarly a close system call shall invoke serial_release function.

Let's now start some real work. In next table, we prepare a new file serialio.h and serialio.c where we define and develop IO related functionalities.

Table 7.22

```
/* FILE: serialio.h */
#ifndef __SERIAL_IO_H__
#define __SERIAL_IO_H__
#define TRANSMITTER_HOLDING_REG     0x00
#define RECEIVER_BUFFER_REG         0x00
#define BAUD_RATE_DIVISOR_REG_LSB   0x00
#define BAUD_RATE_DIVISOR_REG_MSB   0x01
#define INTR_ENABLE_REG             0x01
#define INTR_IDENT_REG              0x02
#define FIFO_CTRL_REG               0x02
#define LINE_CTRL_REG               0x03
#define MODEM_CTRL_REG              0x04
#define LINE_STATUS_REG             0x05
#define MODEM_STATUS_REG            0x06
#endif
```

Above table defines UART register offset as discussed in section 7.4.

Following table defines some functions to perform read and write on IO ports. We shall use inb and outb functions defined in asm/io.h to read and write a byte respectively on the IO ports.

Table 7.23

```
/* FILE: serialio.c */
#include <linux/kernel.h>
#include <asm/io.h>
#include "myserial.h"
#include "serialio.h"
/* DLAB must remain to 0 default */
extern struct serialDev *pDev;
unsigned char read_line_control_reg(void)
{
        return inb(pDev->ioport + LINE_CTRL_REG);
}
void write_line_control_reg(unsigned char value)
{
        outb(value, pDev->ioport + LINE_CTRL_REG);
        return;
}
void set_baud_rate(unsigned int baudrate)
{
        unsigned char tmp, divisor_lsb=0, divisor_msb=0;
        TRACE("%s baudrate %d\n", __FUNCTION__, baudrate);
        switch(baudrate)
        {
              case 115200:
                    divisor_lsb = 1; divisor_msb = 0; break;
              case 57600:
                    divisor_lsb = 2; divisor_msb = 0; break;
```

```
                case 38400:
                        divisor_lsb = 3; divisor_msb = 0; break;
                case 19200:
                        divisor_lsb = 6; divisor_msb = 0; break;
                case 14400:
                        divisor_lsb = 8; divisor_msb = 0; break;
                case 9600:
                        divisor_lsb = 0xC; divisor_msb = 0; break;
                case 7200:
                        divisor_lsb = 0x10; divisor_msb = 0; break;
                case 4800:
                        divisor_lsb = 0x18; divisor_msb = 0; break;
                case 2400:
                        divisor_lsb = 0x30; divisor_msb = 0; break;
                case 1200:
                        divisor_lsb = 0xf6; divisor_msb = 0; break;
                default:
                        printk("Invalid baud rate %d\n", baudrate);
                        break;
        }
        /* set DLAB */
        tmp = read_line_control_reg();
        tmp = tmp | 0x80;
        write_line_control_reg(tmp);
        outb(divisor_lsb, pDev->ioport + BAUD_RATE_DIVISOR_REG_LSB);
        outb(divisor_msb, pDev->ioport + BAUD_RATE_DIVISOR_REG_MSB);
        /* clear DLAB */
        tmp = tmp & 0x7F;
        write_line_control_reg(tmp);
        return;
}
```

As shown in the code, function read_line_control_reg read LCR using function inb while write_line_control_register writes given byte to LCR using function outb. We chose to start with LCR read write functions because LCR gives us access to DLAB bit which controls other registers' behavior.

Next we define function set_baud_rate in above table. We select divisor_lsb and divisor_msb based on given baud rate and as defined in Table 7.15. Before writing to DLL and DLM registers, we make sure that DLAB bit is set to 1 and then we reset the DLAB bit to 0 (default value in this serial driver).

In next table, we define a function uart_init where we initialize the UART to a known state using already defined functions.

Table 7.24

```
/* FILE: serialio.c */
void uart_init(void)
{
        /* DLAB 0, Break Control 0, Stick Parity 0,
```

```
        /* Parity Disable, Stop Bits 1, Word length 8 bits */
        write_line_control_reg(0x03);
        /* disable all interrupts */
        outb(0, pDev->ioport + INTR_ENABLE_REG);
        /* enable FIFO, reset Rx Tx FIFO, FIFO trigger level 14 bytes */
        outb(0xC7, pDev->ioport + FIFO_CTRL_REG);
        outb(0x00, pDev->ioport + MODEM_CTRL_REG);
        outb(0x00, pDev->ioport + LINE_STATUS_REG);
        set_baud_rate(9600);
        return;
}
```

In UART initialization, we choose 8N1 configuration *i.e.*, word length is 8 bits, no parity and 1 stop bit. Also we set DLAB to 0.

Next we disable all interrupts because we are going to start with a polling based driver and therefore we don't need interrupts.

Next we enable FIFO, reset Tx and Rx FIFO and set receive FIFO trigger level to 14 (maximum).

The bit values used for such configuration are defined in section 7.4.

In next table, we complete UART initialization by augmenting init_module function in serialcore.c file.

Table 7.25

```
/* FILE: serialcore.c */
int init_module(void)
{
        pDev = kmalloc(sizeof(struct serialDev), GFP_ATOMIC);
        serialDev_init(pDev);
        register_chrdev(SERIAL_MAJOR,SERIAL_DEVICE,
        &serial_operations);
        if(!request_region(pDev->ioport, pDev->ports, SERIAL_DEVICE))
        {
              printk("port addr range 0x%04x-0x%04x not available\n",
              pDev->ioport, pDev->ioport+pDev->ports);
              goto fail_region;
        }
        uart_init();
        printk("myserial inserted\n");
        return 0;
fail_region:
        unregister_chrdev(SERIAL_MAJOR, SERIAL_DEVICE);
fail_chrdev:
        kfree(pDev);
        pDev = NULL;
        return 0;
}
```

Before we read and write to IO ports, we must request kernel to grant IO ports using request_region function. Although it is possible to read/write from IO ports without calling request_region, this is not advisable because it is possible that some other device is already using these IO ports. In such case, it may baffle the device using IO ports. After successful IO port grant, we should be able to see our device in /proc/ioports file. Finally we call uart_init function to initialize the UART.

Now modify the Makefile to include new source file serialio.c as follows:

Table 7.26

```
KDIR := /usr/src/linux-2.6.21.5
obj-m := serial.o
serial-objs := serialcore.o serialio.o
default:
        make -C $(KDIR) SUBDIRS='pwd' modules
clean:
        make -C $(KDIR) SUBDIRS='pwd' clean
```

At this point, we can again compile, insert and remove the UART driver which registers a character device and initializes the UART.

Before we start some real useful work with the UART driver, let's write some more IO functions which shall be used later in the driver.

Table 7.27

```
/* FILE: serialio.c */
void set_data_bits(unsigned char data_bits)
{
        unsigned char tmp, bit_conf=0;
        TRACE("%s databits %d\n", __FUNCTION__, data_bits);
        switch(data_bits)
        {
              case 8: bit_conf = 0x03; break;
              case 7: bit_conf = 0x02; break;
              case 6: bit_conf = 0x01; break;
              case 5: bit_conf = 0x00; break;
              default:
                    printk("invalid data_bits (%d)\n", data_bits);
                    return;
        }
        tmp = read_line_control_reg();
        tmp = tmp | bit_conf;
        write_line_control_reg(tmp);
        return;
}
void set_stop_bits(unsigned char stopbits)
{
        unsigned char tmp = read_line_control_reg();
        TRACE("%s stopbits %d\n", __FUNCTION__, stopbits);
        tmp = tmp | (stopbits & 0x04);
        write_line_control_reg(tmp);
        return;
}
```

```
void set_parity(unsigned int parity)
{
        unsigned char tmp = read_line_control_reg();
        TRACE("%s parity 0x%x\n", __FUNCTION__, parity);
        if(parity)
              tmp = tmp | 0x08;
        else  tmp = tmp & 0xF7;
        write_line_control_reg(tmp);
        return;
}
void transmit_data(unsigned char data)
{
        /* DLAB is 0 by default */
        outb(data, pDev->ioport + TRANSMITTER_HOLDING_REG);
        return;
}
unsigned char read_line_status_reg(void)
{
        return inb(pDev->ioport + LINE_STATUS_REG);
}
```

The function set_data_bits modifies LCR for appropriate word length. Function set_stop_bits modifies LCR for stop bits. Function set_parity modifies parity enable bit in LCR. Bit values for all these functions are defined in section 7.4.

Function transmit_data writes given byte to THR which shall be transmitted by UART, while function read_line_status_reg returns LSR status.

So far we have done UART initialization. But user applications (like minicom and the one we are using) configure the UART according to their requirements. User applications can do it through ioctl system call. The ioctl function takes device descriptor (returned by open system call), ioctl command and ioctl data pointer as arguments. The cmd and data pointer are passed to the device driver ioctl call as it is. Therefore, we receive those parameters in serial_unlocked_ioctl function. The ioctl commands are defined in user include file asm/ioctls.h.

Applications use a structure termios to control UART behavior. The structure termios is as follows:

Table 7.28

```
#define NCCS 19
struct termios {
        tcflag_t c_iflag;
        tcflag_t c_oflag;
        tcflag_t c_cflag;
        tcflag_t c_lflag;
        cc_t c_line;
        cc_t c_cc[NCCS];
};
```

A brief description of the structure members is as follows:

- c_iflag—contains input mode flags.
- c_oflag—contains output mode flags.

- c_cflag—contains control mode flags. This flag is used to pass UART control information.
- c_lflag—contains local mode flags.
- c_line—contains line discipline.
- c_cc—contains control characters.

As we see, c_cflag parameter is important to us because this parameter contains UART configuration information.

Next we augment serial_unlocked_ioctl function in serialcore.c to receive parameters from application and write a new function in serialio.c to configure those parameters.

Table 7.29

```
/* FILE: serialcore.c */
long serial_unlocked_ioctl(struct file* file, unsigned int cmd,
unsigned long arg)
{
        int i;
        struct termios options;
        TRACE("%s invoked\n", __FUNCTION__);
        copy_from_user(&options, (void*)arg, sizeof(struct termios));
        switch(cmd)
        {
              case 0x5401:
                    printk("TCGETS\n");
                    break;
              case 0x5402:
                    printk("TCSETS\n");
                    set_uart_options(&options);
                    break;
              case 0x5403:
                    printk("TCSETSW\n");
                    break;
              default:
                    printk("command = 0x%x(%u)\n", cmd, cmd);
        }
        return 0;
}
/* FILE: serialio.c */
#include <asm/termbits.h>
void set_uart_options(struct termios *p_options)
{
        unsigned int baudrate=0, data_bits=0;
        switch(p_options->c_cflag & CBAUD)
        {
              case B0: baudrate = 0; break;
              case B115200: baudrate = 115200; break;
              case B57600: baudrate = 57600; break;
              case B38400: baudrate = 38400; break;
              case B19200: baudrate = 19200; break;
              case B9600: baudrate = 9600; break;
```

```
            case B4800: baudrate = 4800; break;
            case B2400: baudrate = 2400; break;
            case B1200: baudrate = 1200; break;
        }
        set_baud_rate(baudrate);
        switch(p_options->c_cflag & CSIZE)
        {
            case CS5: data_bits = 5; break;
            case CS6: data_bits = 6; break;
            case CS7: data_bits = 7; break;
            case CS8: data_bits = 8; break;
        }
        set_data_bits(data_bits);
        set_parity(p_options->c_cflag & PARENB);
        set_stop_bits(p_options->c_cflag & CSTOPB);
        return;
}
```

In the serial_unlocked_ioctl function we copy data from user space to kernel space memory using copy_from_user. Then we take different action based upon the ioctl command. However, currently we are interested only in TCSETS (0x5402) which sets the UART options.

For setting the options, we defined another function set_uart_options which de-multiplexes control options. All de-multiplexing parameters and resultant parameters are defined in asm/termbits.h file. As we see in source code, logical AND with CBAUD returns baud rate constants. Similarly logical AND with CSIZE returns word length constants, PARENB returns parity enable and CSTOP returns stop bit length.

We use functions defined in Table 7.27 to configure received parameters.

At this point of time, we have a UART driver which registers itself as a character device driver, initializes UART and provides user control to configure baud rate, parity, word length, and stop bits.

Now we are ready to transmit data through UART. Let's enhance serial_write function to transmit data. As we discussed in section 7.4, we must not write more than FIFO size otherwise the data will be lost. Once FIFO is full, the driver must wait for FIFO to be empty. Since this is polling driver, the driver itself has to keep check of THR empty bit in LSR register.

Table 7.30

```
/* FILE: serialcore.c */
ssize_t serial_write(struct file* file, const char __user * buf,
size_t
size, loff_t * boffset)
{
        unsigned char tmp[1024] = {0}, status;
        int i, left=0, offset=0, can_send=0, cntr=0;
        TRACE("%s invoked\n", __FUNCTION__);
        copy_from_user(tmp, buf, size);
        left = size;
write_to_uart:
```

```
        if(left > FIFO_SIZE)
                can_send = FIFO_SIZE;
        else
                can_send = left;
/* debug */
for(i=0; i<can_send; i++)
        printk("%c", tmp[i+offset]);
printk("\n");
/* transmit */
        for(i=0; i<can_send; i++)
                transmit_data(tmp[i+offset]);
        left = left - can_send;
        if(left == 0) {
                printk("all data transmitted\n");
                return 0;
        }
        /* wait for THR empty bit */
        do
        {
                status = read_line_status_reg();
                if(status & 0x20) {
                        printk("Transmitter is empty now\n");
                        offset = offset + can_send;
                        goto write_to_uart;
        }
                else {
                        printk("FIFO is full\n");
                        schedule();
                        cntr++;
                        if(cntr > 100) {
                                printk("safty counter limit reached\n");
                                return 0;
                        }
                }
        }while(1);
        return 0; /* unreachable */
}
```

The first few lines below 'write_to_uart' label find the maximum data that can be sent over UART, and that much data is transmitted via UART by writing in THR. If all data has been transmitted, the serial_write returns. If there is data left to transmit, it has to wait for THR to be empty. For this purpose, it reads THR empty bit. If THR empty is set to 1 then driver transmits next data, otherwise it relinquish the CPU by calling schedule function. After schedule call, the driver process context is put to sleep and CPU schedules another process. Once the driver process context is reschedules, it again checks for THR empty bit.

We have polling based write register ready here. Connect remote host with null modem cable, run serial console on remote host, configure with the same parameters as in our application. Then insert the UART driver and run application. You should see the application data appearing on remote host console.

7.6 UPGRADING TO 'INTERRUPT BASED WRITE' UART DRIVER

In this section, we upgrade the existing polling based write driver to interrupt based write driver. For this, we need to the following:

- configure UART to deliver THR empty interrupt
- get an IRQ
- modify serial_write to stop polling and waiting for interrupt
- develop an IRQ handler

As discussed in section 7.4, we have to configure IER for enabling interrupts. And not to forget, Out2 bit in MCR as well. We modify uart_init function in serialio.c to do this:

Table 7.31

```
/* FILE: serialio.c */
void uart_init(void)
{
        write_line_control_reg(0x03);
        /* enable THR empty interrupt */
        outb(0x02, pDev->ioport + INTR_ENABLE_REG);
        outb(0xC7, pDev->ioport + FIFO_CTRL_REG);
        /* set OUT2 to receive interrupts */
        outb(0x08, pDev->ioport + MODEM_CTRL_REG);
        outb(0x00, pDev->ioport + LINE_STATUS_REG);
        set_baud_rate(9600);
        return;
}
```

Next is to get an IRQ from kernel. We do this by request_irq function. The request_irq function takes desired IRQ number, IRQ handler, IRQ flags, device name and device parameter pointer as arguments. We enhance init_module and cleanup_module for IRQ acquiring and releasing.

Table 7.32

```
/* FILE: myserial.h */
#define SERIAL_IRQ 4
/* FILE: serialcore.c */
#include <linux/interrupt.h>
int init_module(void)
{
        pDev = kmalloc(sizeof(struct serialDev), GFP_KERNEL);
        serialDev_init(pDev);
        register_chrdev(SERIAL_MAJOR,SERIAL_DEVICE,
        &serial_operations);
        request_region(pDev->ioport, pDev->ports, SERIAL_DEVICE);
        uart_init();
        if(request_irq(SERIAL_IRQ, serial_interrupt_handler, 0,
 SERIAL_DEVICE, NULL) < 0) {
                printk("could not get irq %d\n", SERIAL_IRQ);
                goto fail_irq;
        }
```

```
        printk("myserial inserted\n");
        return 0;
fail_irq:
        release_region(pDev->ioport, pDev->ports);
        unregister_chrdev(SERIAL_MAJOR, SERIAL_DEVICE);
        kfree(pDev);
        pDev = NULL;
        return 0;
}
void cleanup_module(void)
{
        printk("myserial removed\n");
        if(pDev)
        {
              free_irq(SERIAL_IRQ, NULL);
              release_region(pDev->ioport, pDev->ports);
              unregister_chrdev(SERIAL_MAJOR, SERIAL_DEVICE);
              kfree(pDev);
        }
}
```

The IRQ flags to the request_irq function can be one of following:

- IRQF_SHARED—Interrupt is shared among more than one device. With this flag, the last parameter must be non-NULL, so that device driver can identify if the interrupt is generated by its device.
- IRQF_DISABLED—Local interrupts remain disabled during interrupt handler call.
- 0—If none of them is required.

In next paragraphs, we will develop an IRQ handler and modify serial_write function. Our earlier serial_write was a polling based function. To make it interrupt based, we introduce a sleep and wakeup mechanism. When serial_write function has more data to send but FIFO is full, it will sleep and wait for interrupt to arrive. The interrupt handler shall wakeup the serial_write function to inform about THR empty.

For sleep and wakeup mechanism, we use completion structure. Therefore we add one more member to our serial device structure and initialize it in serialDev_init function.

Table 7.33

```
/* FILE: myserial.h */
#include <linux/completion.h>
struct serialDev
{
        unsigned int ioport;
        unsigned int ports;
        struct completion write_possible;
};
/* FILE: serialcore.c */
int serialDev_init(struct serialDev *pDev)
{
        pDev->ioport = 0x3f8;
```

```
        pDev->ports = 8;
        init_completion(&pDev->write_possible);
        return 0;
}
```

Next we modify the serial_write function to sleep and wait rather than poll. We change the polling code by following code:

Table 7.34

```
/* FILE: serialcore.c */
        for(i=0; i<can_send; i++)
              transmit_data(tmp[i]);
        t = wait_for_completion_interruptible_timeout(&pDev-
>write_possible, 10*HZ);
        if(signal_pending(current)) {
              printk("interrupt received\n");
              return -EINTR;
        }
        if(!t) {
              printk("no interrupt received for 10 seconds\n");
              return -EIO;
        }
        left = left - can_send;
        if(left == 0) {
              printk("all data transmitted\n");
              return size;
        }
        offset = offset + can_send;
        goto write_to_uart;
        return 0; /* not reachable */
```

We use wait_for_completion_interruptible_timeout function. This function has following properties:

- It waits for completion
- It changes task state to TASK_INTERRUPTIBLE. It means, if the application receives a signal (SIGTERM, SIGKILL etc), this function returns.
- It returns after a time limit even if completion is not done and signal is not received.

Therefore, this function can return in several events. The next function call to signal_pending returns non-zero value if a signal was delivered to the application. If the return value of this function is zero, it implies that timeout has occurred.

If both of above conditions are not true, that means the function has been waked-up by completion.

Now the work left is to develop an IRQ handler. We do this in following table:

Table 7.35

```
/* FILE: serialcore.c */
irqreturn_t serial_interrupt_handler(int irq, void *dev_id)
```

```
{
        unsigned char status, status2;
        status = read_interrupt_ident_reg();
        if(status & 0x01) {
                printk("No interrupt pending\n");
                return IRQ_HANDLED;
        }
        switch(status & 0x0E)
        {               case 0x02:
                        /* Transmitter Holding Register Empty */
                        complete(&pDev->write_possible);
                        break;
                case 0x0C:
                        /* character timeout indication */
                        /* fall through */
                case 0x04:
                        /* Received data available */
                        printk("Received data available interrupt\n");
                        break;
                case 0x06:
                        /* Receiver Line Status */
                        status2 = read_line_status_reg();
                        if(status2 & 0x02)
                                printk("Overrun Error\n");
                        if(status2 & 0x04)
                                printk("Parity Error\n");
                        if(status2 & 0x08)
                                printk("Framing Error\n");
                        if(status2 & 0x0A)
                                printk("Break Interrupt\n");
                        break;
                case 0x00:
                        /* MODEM status */
                        printk("MODEM status interrupt\n");
                        break;
                default:
                        return IRQ_NONE;
        }
        return IRQ_HANDLED;
}
```

As discussed earlier, 0th bit of IIR must be 0 if any interrupt is pending. If it is set to 1, the IRQ handler returns without doing any thing. If this bit is set to 0, then we read bit 1, 2, and 3 of IIR to decode the kind of interrupt as explained in Table 7.7. Since, we are interested only in THR empty interrupt; we signal it by doing a complete call on the completion parameter. For rest of the interrupts, as of now, we simply print a message.

The return value of an interrupt handler must be IRQ_HANDLED if the interrupt handler handled the interrupt, else it must return IRQ_NONE. These return values are used for statistics purpose by kernel.

Let's compile the UART driver and insert again. Make the setup ready, if it is not and run the application again. You should see the application data appearing on remote host console pretty much similar to the previous case. But the difference lies in the driver and we know that difference!!

7.7 UPGRADING TO 'INTERRUPT BASED READ' UART DRIVER

In this section, we add read capability to the UART driver which is by far only able to send data out.

To enable the UART driver to read data, we need to make following change:

- Modify IER so that UART generate interrupt for data receiving as well.
- Upgrade IRQ handler to process new interrupts and receive data.
- Develop serial_read function to deliver data to application.

For serial_read, we implement following strategy:

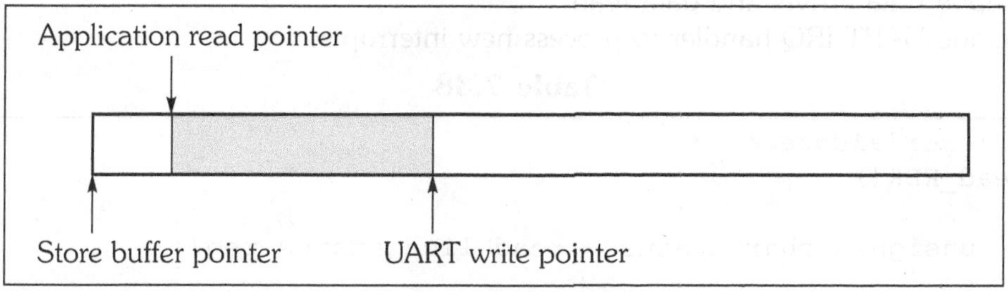

Figure 7.2

Data received by IRQ is stored in a buffer pointed by "store buffer pointer". The UART writes data at "UART write pointer" which keeps moving as data is received. Application reads data from "application read pointer". The shaded part of the buffer shows the data available in buffer which has not been read by application yet.

Let's start upgrading the UART driver by first upgrading serialDev structure to accommodate members for above mentioned strategy.

Table 7.36

```
/* FILE: myserial.h */
#include <linux/spinlock.h>
#define MAX_STORE 1024
struct serialDev
{
        struct completion read_possible;
        unsigned char buf_store[MAX_STORE];
        unsigned char *app_read;
        unsigned char *uart_write;
        int avble_data;
        spinlock_t lock;
};
```

We introduce a lock here to prevent data corruption between IRQ handler and serial_read function, since both of them operate on the same buffer as we will see shortly.

Next we upgrade serialDev_init function to initialize all new members as follows:

Table 7.37

```
/* FILE: serialcore.c */
int serialDev_init(struct serialDev *pDev)
{
        init_completion(&pDev->read_possible);
        pDev->app_read = pDev->buf_store;
        pDev->uart_write = pDev->buf_store;
        pDev->avble_data = 0;
        spin_lock_init(&pDev->lock);
        return 0;
}
```

Both app_read pointer and uart_write pointer initialized to buf_store, and shall be modified depending upon data arrival and data read.

Let's upgrade UART IRQ handler to process new interrupts:

Table 7.38

```
/* FILE: serialcore.c */
void read_RBR()
{
        unsigned char status = read_line_status_reg();
        do {
              if(pDev->avble_data < MAX_STORE) {
              *pDev->uart_write++ = read_receiver_buffer_reg();
              pDev->avble_data++;
        }
              else { /* overflow */
                    unsigned char discard;
                    discard = read_receiver_buffer_reg();
              }
                    status = read_line_status_reg();
              }while(status & 0x01);
        return;
}
irqreturn_t serial_interrupt_handler(int irq, void *dev_id)
{
        unsigned char status, status2;
        TRACE("%s\n", __FUNCTION__);
        status = read_interrupt_ident_reg();
        if(status & 0x01){
              printk("No interrupt pending\n");
              return IRQ_HANDLED;
        }
        switch(status & 0x0E)
        {           case 0x02:
                    /* Transmitter Holding Register Empty */
              printk("THR empty interrupt\n");
```

```
                    complete(&pDev->write_possible);
                    break;
            case 0x0C:
                    /* character timeout indication */
                    /* fall through */
            case 0x04:
                    /* Received data available */
                    printk("Received data available interrupt\n");
                    read_RBR();
                    complete(&pDev->read_possible);
                    break;
            case 0x06:
                    /* Receiver Line Status */
                    printk("Receiver Line Status interrupt\n");
                    status2 = read_line_status_reg();
                    if(status2 & 0x02)
                          printk("Overrun Error\n");
                    if(status2 & 0x04)
                          printk("Parity Error\n");
                    if(status2 & 0x08)
                          printk("Framing Error\n");
                    if(status2 & 0x0A)
                          printk("Break Interrupt\n");
                    break;
            case 0x00:
                    /* MODEM status */
                    printk("MODEM status interrupt\n");
                    break;
            default:
                    printk("unknown interrupt: 0x%02x\n", status &
0x0E);
                    return IRQ_NONE;
        }
        return IRQ_HANDLED;
}
```

We have introduced a new function read_RBR. This function reads all the data from receiver FIFO and transfers it in buf_store at uart_write location and increments avble_data as long as buf_store overflow does not occur.

Function read_RBR is invoked from IRQ handler when "receiver data available" interrupt is received or when "character timeout interrupt" is received. It returns when 0th bit in LSR turns 0.

The IRQ handler then performs a wakeup operation if serial_read is waiting for the data to come.

Let's introduce serial_read function which delivers received data to application. The application buffer size may be less than, equal to or greater than available size. In serial_read function, we do different things based on application buffer size.

Table 7.39

```
/* FILE: serialcore.c */
ssize_t serial_read(struct file* file, char __user * buf, size_t size,
loff_t * offset)
{
        unsigned char tmp[MAX_STORE] = {0};
        unsigned long flags;
        int t=0, ret=0;
        TRACE("%s invoked\n", __FUNCTION__);
read_again:
        spin_lock_irqsave(&pDev->lock, flags);
        if(pDev->avble_data == 0) {
              spin_unlock_irqrestore(&pDev->lock, flags);
              t = wait_for_completion_interruptible(&pDev-
>read_possible);
        }
        else if(pDev->avble_data <= size) {
              memcpy(tmp, pDev->app_read, pDev->avble_data);
              ret = pDev->avble_data;
              pDev->app_read = pDev->buf_store;
              pDev->uart_write = pDev->buf_store;
              pDev->avble_data = 0;
              spin_unlock_irqrestore(&pDev->lock, flags);
              copy_to_user(buf, tmp, ret);
              return ret;
        }
        else
        {
              /* more data available than required */
              memcpy(tmp, pDev->app_read, size);
              ret = size;
              pDev->app_read += size;
              pDev->avble_data -= size;
              spin_unlock_irqrestore(&pDev->lock, flags);
              copy_to_user(buf, tmp, ret);
              return ret;
        }
        if(t < 0)
              return t; /* signal received */
        goto read_again;
        return -1; /* unreachable */
}
```

The first important thing is holding spinlock while dealing with shared buffer. Since an interrupt can stop execution flow of serial_read, we must first disable the interrupts and hold a spinlock to protect from same code executing on other CPU in SMP case.

If there is no data available, serial_read releases the spinlock, enables the interrupts and waits for data arrival (which is signaled by IRQ hander after read_RBR call).

If available data is less than application buffer size, we return all available data and reset app_read and uart_write pointers to buf_store base address, and set avble_data to 0.

However if available data is greater than application buffer size, we return only up to application buffer size and do not touch uart_write. We increment app_read by the data read length.

At this point, the UART driver is ready to send and receive data on serial port ttyS0 (COM1). Finally modify the serial_app.c application to read some data as follows:

Table 7.40

```
/* FILE: serial_app.c */
ret = read(fd, data, sizeof(data));
printf("read returns %d\n", ret);
for(i=0; i<ret; i++)
        printf("%c", data[i]);
printf("\n");
```

Compile the modified application and then press some keys at the serial console of remote host. Although you will not see those keys appearing on serial console window, all those data will be received and displayed by your application.

7.8 SUMMARY

We stop the UART (serial port) device driver development here. Although this driver is far behind from a real UART driver which does lot more things than one we developed, yet this driver is capable of doing basic things and paves path for developing a real driver.

7.9 ASSIGNMENTS

This section lists some assignments which enhances our naïve driver. Readers can do following enhancements to increase their code understanding about the UART driver.

- Make setserial utility to work with this driver.
  - o Hint—Implement TIOCGSERIAL (0x541E) ioctl call and return parameters in serial_struct structure.
- Make minicom utility to work with this driver
  - o Hint—Write dummy character driver functions with a trace. Implement the functions and ioctls as and when needed.
- This driver works only for COM1 (ttyS0). Rewrite it to work for both COM1 and COM2 *i.e.*, one driver should work for both serial ports.
- This driver lets any number of applications to simultaneously read/write on serial port. Change the driver so that only one application does it at a time.

7.10 REFERENCES

- termios manual page

8 Developing USB Mass Storage Block Device Driver

In this chapter we learn to develop a USB mass storage block device driver in incremental order. This chapter shall cover following topics:

- Developing a USB device driver
- Developing a mass storage device driver
- USB specifications and protocol
- Developing a block device driver
- Additionally, the driver can be mapped to learn SCSI drivers.

The chapter is divided in following sections:

- Introduction
- Driver development setup
- Understanding USB devices
- Developing USB driver
- Understanding mass storage device control commands
- Adding mass storage device control commands to USB driver
- Understanding USB specifications and protocol
- Understanding URB
- Developing CBW and device communication functions
- Talking to USB device
- Adding block device driver interface to USB driver
- Troubleshooting
- Assignments
- References

8.1 INTRODUCTION

USB pen drives, also known as USB flash drives, are becoming increasing popular in day to day life for carrying data. Similarly, other memory cards like SD cards, MMC cards, CF cards, micro SD cards are used in consumer electronics devices like camera, mobiles etc., which can be used on a PC using a USB card reader (in case PC does not have a slot for them). We will refer to all such devices as USB memory devices in this chapter.

In this chapter, we shall develop a device driver for such a device. If you have not used USB memory devices on Linux before, it is advisable to first learn using them on Linux so that you can map user space operations in device driver.

(Ref: http://www.cs.sfu.ca/~ggbaker/personal/cf-linux)

The following diagram displays functional layers involved in USB memory device read or write operations. The "USB Memory Card" represents actual memory device which interacts with UHCI controller layer through USB interface. Out of functional layers shown in Figure 8.1, we shall implement "Block Device Driver" and "USB Device Driver" layers.

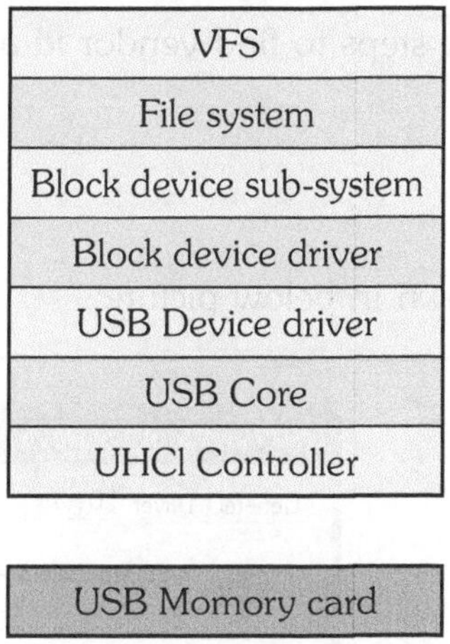

Figure 8.1

Whenever any application makes a read or write request to the USB memory device, the application call is diverted to VFS (Virtual File System) using system call table and file inode. The VFS, then, directs to actual file system on the USB memory devices *i.e.,* if you are using a VFAT file system, the control goes to VFAT file system code. The file system directs the call flow to block device sub-system which takes care of I/O scheduling and organizing requests to increase operation efficiency.

Next is the block device driver which shall execute read and write calls to the device using USB device driver. We shall develop both of these layers in this chapter.

The USB device driver does not interact to USB memory device directly, but it uses API and data structures provided by USB core to perform operations. USB core in turn uses UHCI controller which does actual communication with USB memory device.

8.2 DRIVER DEVELOPMENT SETUP

Every USB memory device is uniquely identified by its vendor id and product id. Therefore it is essential to know the vendor id and product id of the memory device before developing device driver for the same. Itís worth noting that, although these devices have different vendor id and product id, yet their behavior is more or less same, because each of these devices is USB compliant. There are several ways of finding vendor id and product id; like checking device specification or using the device in already working OS.

In Linux, you can use lsusb command to list all USB devices which also displays vendor id and product id. Following example shows some USB devices on a development host. The first number in ID field is vendor id while the second number is product id. These id numbers are in hexadecimal.

Table 8.1

```
guest@localhost:~$ lsusb
Bus 004 Device 004: ID 0951:1607 Kingston Technology
Bus 004 Device 001: ID 0000:0000
Bus 003 Device 001: ID 0000:0000
Bus 002 Device 002: ID 046d:08af Logitech, Inc.
Bus 002 Device 001: ID 0000:0000
Bus 001 Device 001: ID 0000:0000
```

On Windows™ OS, follow below steps to find vendor id and product id

- Go to My Computer
- Properties
- Hardware
- Device Managers

Here you can find the ids as shown in below picture:

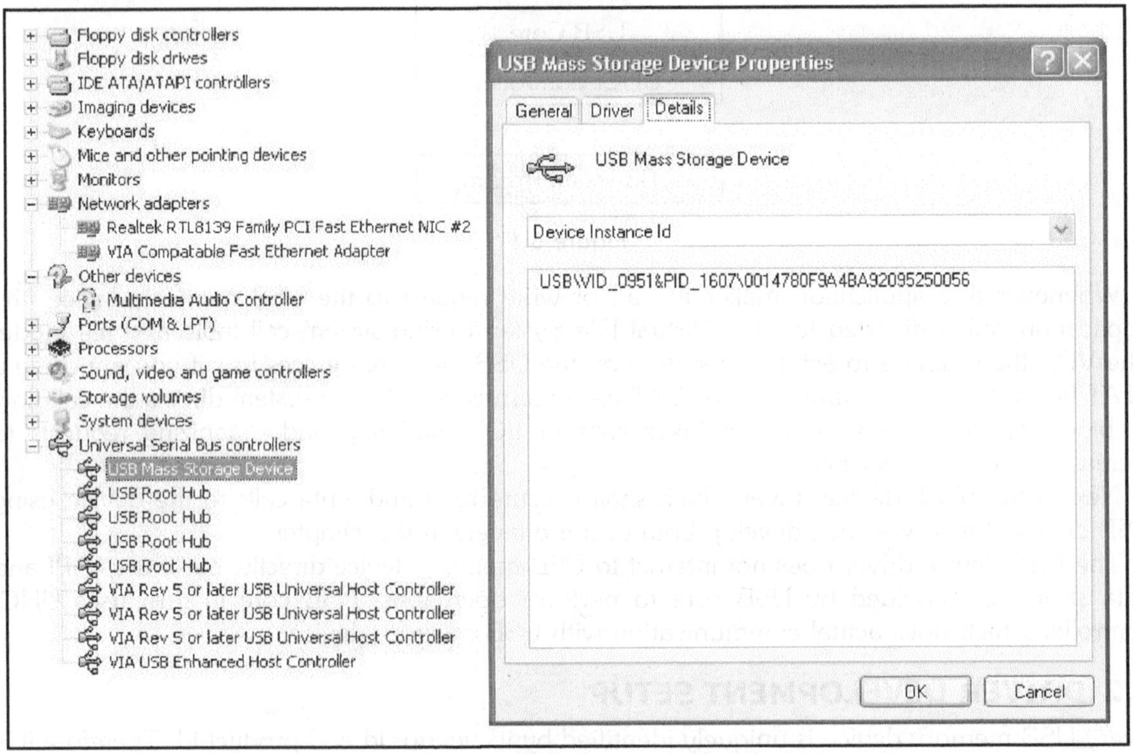

Figure 8.2

As you can see, the id numbers are present with VID and PID prefixes.

After getting vendor and product id, we shall recompile the kernel as Linux 2.6 kernel already has a USB mass storage driver and we have to remove it so that the new driver communicates with the device exclusively.

For excluding existing mass storage driver from Linux kernel, uncheck 'mass-storage support' from the USB drivers. However keep 'UHCI controller' and 'usbmon' option checked. You must have at least following in your kernel configuration.

Table 8.2

```
#
# USB support
#
CONFIG_USB=y
CONFIG_USB_DEVICEFS=y
CONFIG_USB_EHCI_HCD=y
CONFIG_USB_OHCI_HCD=y
CONFIG_USB_UHCI_HCD=y
# CONFIG_USB_STORAGE is not set
CONFIG_USB_MON=y
#
# DOS/FAT/NT Filesystems
#
CONFIG_FAT_FS=y
CONFIG_MSDOS_FS=y
CONFIG_VFAT_FS=y
#
# Native Language Support
#
CONFIG_NLS=y
CONFIG_NLS_ISO8859_1=y
#
# Kernel hacking
#
CONFIG_DEBUG_FS=y
```

Build the kernel and boot the development host with new kernel.

Note:

- Make sure, you are not using a USB multiple card readers as it would be difficult to handle such device initially and will create unnecessary confusion. Therefore, use either a USB pen drive or a single card reader.
- Throughout the driver development, plug-in the USB memory device, before you insert the driver module.

8.3 UNDERSTANDING USB DEVICES

The USB devices are a little complex having a hierarchy of logical units. This section describes them in same order. Figure 8.3 depicts schematic view of a USB device.

A USB device consists of one or more configurations, to work in different modes. At a time only one configuration can be activated. However, there are few devices which support multiple configurations.

A configuration contains one or more interfaces. For example, a USB to serial converter device providing multiple serial ports can have multiple interfaces. The Linux USB sub system treats one interface as one device, and therefore it is possible that a USB device having more than one interface is controlled by multiple device drivers.

An interface contains one or more endpoints. The endpoints are like unidirectional pipes which carry commands or data from host to device and vice-versa.

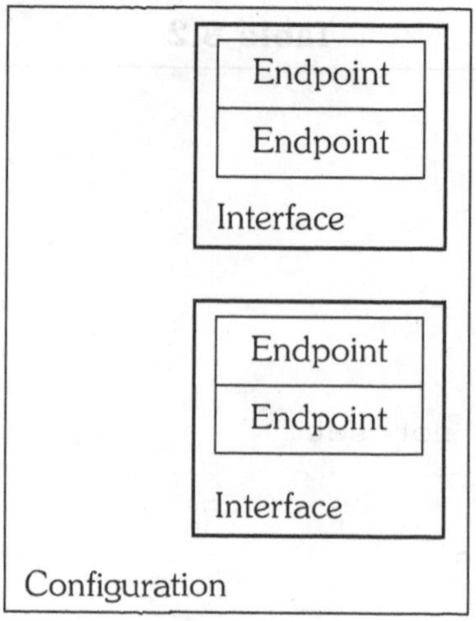

Figure 8.3

An endpoint can be one of following types:

- Control endpoint – These endpoints are used to configure and control the device. Every USB device has at least one control endpoint.
- Bulk endpoint – These endpoints are used to carry large data to/from the device reliably. For example, USB pen drives have two bulk endpoints for IN and OUT directions respectively.
- Interrupt endpoint – These endpoints can be used to carry small data with higher priority. For example, USB keyboards and mouse have such endpoints.
- Isochronous endpoint – These endpoints are used to carry large data without reliability. For example, USB webcam have such endpoints.

Coming back to the interface, an interface can posses different settings referred as alternate settings or descriptors. The first setting is always the default setting.

Fortunately, the USB memory devices are not so complex and most of them have one configuration, one interface (which has only one setting) and 3 endpoints (1 control, 1 bulk-in and 1 bulk-out). As we will see a little later, these parameters are actually derived by reading device descriptors.

8.4 DEVELOPING USB DRIVER

In this section, we develop a dummy USB driver which we shall continue to evolve as we progress. Let's start with a structure to hold information about the USB driver.

Table 8.3

```
/* FILE: usb_core.h */
#ifndef _USB_CORE_H_
#define _USB_CORE_H_
struct usbdev_private {
        struct usb_device *udev;
};
#define TRACE(arg...) printk(arg)
#define LOG_MSG(arg...) printk(arg)
#endif
```

As we are starting with a dummy driver, we do not need many parameters in the device private structure. The only member in the structure shall hold struct usb_device pointer, which will be provided to the USB driver by usbcore as we'll see shortly.

Next, we write the dummy USB driver source. Any USB driver has to register a table of USB devices it supports and a probe function. Whenever a USB device matching vendor id and product id provided by the driver is inserted, the usbcore invokes driver's probe function.

Table 8.4

```
/* FILE: usb_core.c */
#include <linux/kernel.h>
#include <linux/module.h>
#include <linux/usb.h>
#include <linux/slab.h>
#include "usb_core.h"
#define USB_PEN_DRIVE_VID 0x0f5f
#define USB_PEN_DRIVE_PID 0x1325
#define USB_KINGSTON_VID 0x0951
#define USB_KINGSTON_DT_PID 0x1602
#define USB_KINGSTON_4G_PID 0x1607
struct usbdev_private *p_usb_dev_info;
static int usbdev_probe(
        struct usb_interface *interface, const struct usb_device_id
        *id)
{
        TRACE("<1>usbdev_probe ENTRY\n");
        p_usb_dev_info = kmalloc(sizeof(struct usbdev_private),
        GFP_KERNEL);
        if(!p_usb_dev_info)
            return -1;
        memset(p_usb_dev_info, 0, sizeof(struct usbdev_private));
        p_usb_dev_info->udev = interface_to_usbdev(interface);
        usb_get_dev(p_usb_dev_info->udev);
        return 0;
}
static void usbdev_disconnect(struct usb_interface *interface)
{
        TRACE("usbdev_disconnect called\n");
        usb_put_dev(p_usb_dev_info->udev);
        return;
}
/* table of devices that work with this driver */
static struct usb_device_id usbdev_table [] = {
        { USB_DEVICE(USB_PEN_DRIVE_VID, USB_PEN_DRIVE_PID) },
        { USB_DEVICE(USB_KINGSTON_VID, USB_KINGSTON_DT_PID) },
        { USB_DEVICE(USB_KINGSTON_VID, USB_KINGSTON_4G_PID) },
        { }                             /* Terminating entry */
};
static struct usb_driver usbdev_driver = {
        name: "usbdev",
        probe: usbdev_probe,
```

```
        disconnect: usbdev_disconnect,
        id_table: usbdev_table
};
int init_module(void)
{
        usb_register(&usbdev_driver);
        return 0;
}
void cleanup_module(void)
 {
        usb_deregister(&usbdev_driver);
        return;
}
MODULE_LICENSE("GPL");
```

The array usbdev_table of struct usb_device_id defines the vendor id and product id of all the USB memory devices, this driver supports. You must create an entry for your device here, so that the driver recognizes your devices as well. Note that the last entry of the table must always be NULL to mark end of the table. The macro USB_DEVICE create appropriate device entries for structure usb_device_id.

Next we define a static instance of struct usb_driver. Here we assign the probe function for the driver, disconnect function (which shall be called whenever any USB device mentioned in usb_device_id table is removed from the system) and the usb_device_id table. Also we give a name to this driver.

In the init_module and cleanup_module functions, we use functions usb_register and usb_deregister to add and remove the driver from system respectively.

Letís give a little insight to the probe function. As mentioned earlier, this function shall be invoked as and when a USB device mentioned in usb_device_id table is connected to the system. In this function, we allocate memory for the driver private data structure usbdev_private.

As mentioned earlier, the Linux USB sub-system treats each interface as a separate functional device. Therefore, it is expected to receive pointer to usb_interface structure in the probe function. The second parameter of type struct usb_device_id holds the vendor id and product id of the device connected to the system. We extract usb_device pointer from the usb_interface using the macro interface_to_usbdev. The function usb_get_dev increments usage count for the device to mark it busy.

The usb_disconnect function is invoked when the USB device is ejected from the system. We call usb_put_dev to decrement the usage count.

The dummy driver is ready to be compiled. Following table lists a small Makefile for the driver.

Table 8.5

```
KERNEL_DIR := /usr/src/linux-2.6.21.5
obj-m := usb.o
usb-objs := usb_core.o
default:
        make -C $(KERNEL_DIR) SUBDIRS='pwd' modules
clean:
        make -C $(KERNEL_DIR) SUBDIRS='pwd' clean
```

Use following command sequences to compile, insert and remove the USB driver module.

Table 8-6

```
root@localhost#make
root@localhost#insmod usb.ko
root@localhost#rmmod usb
```

You must see trace prints of function usbdev_probe and usbdev_disconnect during module insert time and module removal time. If you do not see those prints, possibly your device is not listed in usb_device_id table. Before you proceed further, make sure that usbdev_probe and usbdev_disconnect are invoked for your device.

Let's enhance the dummy driver to do some useful work and gather some more information about the device by reading descriptors. As mentioned earlier, usb_probe function receives pointer to usb_interface structure which has all required information. Following table defines a new function to gather the device information.

Table 8.7

```
/* FILE: usb_core.c */
static int device_info(struct usb_interface* interface)
{
        struct usb_host_interface *iface_desc;
        struct usb_endpoint_descriptor *endpoint;
        int i;
        unsigned char epAddr, epAttr;
        /* set up the endpoint information */
        /* check out the endpoints */
        iface_desc = &interface->altsetting[0]; /* XXX */
        printk("No. of altsetting = %d\n", interface->num_altsetting);
        printk("No. of endpoints = %d\n", iface_desc-
>desc.bNumEndpoints);
        for (i = 0; i < iface_desc->desc.bNumEndpoints; ++i) {
               endpoint = &iface_desc->endpoint[i].desc;
               epAddr = endpoint->bEndpointAddress;
               epAttr = endpoint->bmAttributes;
               if((epAttr & USB_ENDPOINT_XFERTYPE_MASK) ==
 USB_ENDPOINT_XFER_BULK)
               {
                      if ((epAddr & 0x80) == USB_DIR_IN)
                      {
                             LOG_MSG("found a bulk in endpoint: %d\n", i);

                      p_usb_dev_info->ep_in = endpoint-
>bEndpointAddress;
                      }
                      if ((epAddr & 0x80) == USB_DIR_OUT)
                      {
                             LOG_MSG("found a bulk out endpoint: %d\n",
                             i);
```

```
                        p_usb_dev_info->ep_out = endpoint-
>bEndpointAddress;
                    }
                }
            }
            /* setup device information */
            p_usb_dev_info->class = iface_desc->desc.bInterfaceClass;
            p_usb_dev_info->subclass = iface_desc-
>desc.bInterfaceSubClass;
            p_usb_dev_info->protocol = iface_desc-
>desc.bInterfaceProtocol;
            LOG_MSG("class: %d\n", p_usb_dev_info->class);
            LOG_MSG("subclass: %d\n", p_usb_dev_info->subclass);
            LOG_MSG("protocol: %d\n", p_usb_dev_info->protocol);
            return 0;
}
```

As mentioned earlier, an interface can have multiple alternate settings or descriptors. However, this driver always chooses the default one. We can get the number of total endpoints of the interface by bNumEndpoints member in the interface descriptor.

Next we iterate through all the endpoints to determine their direction and type. The direction of an endpoint can be determined by its address bEndpointAddress in endpoint descriptor. The most significant bit (7th bit) of the endpoint address indicates its direction. Macro USB_DIR_IN and USB_DIR_OUT should be used for greater portability and readability.

The type of endpoint can be determined by bmAttributes field in endpoint descriptor. The 0th and 1st bit of bmAttributes indicates the type of endpoint as shown below:

Table 8.8

Bit 1	Bit 0	Type of endpoint
0	0	Control
0	1	Isochronous
1	0	Bulk
1	1	Interrupt

The macro USB_ENDPOINT_XFERTYPE_MASK can be used to mask off all other bits except 0 and 1. We must find out all other endpoints here but since USB memory devices do not have them, we omit the code here.

However, we must observe that the default control endpoint is not included in bNumEndpoints. As we will see later, we can get the default control endpoint by some functions provided by Linux USB sub-system.

Next we retrieve some more information about the device; class, subclass and protocol. These numbers are assigned by USB organization.

Let's modify usbdev_private structure to accommodate the device information retrieved by device_info function.

Table 8.9

```
/* FILE: usb_core.h */
struct usbdev_private {
        struct usb_device *udev;
        unsigned char class;
        unsigned char subclass;
        unsigned char protocol;
        unsigned char ep_in; /* in endpoint */
        unsigned char ep_out; /* out endpoint */
};
```

Finally call the function device_info from usbdev_prob as shown below.

Table 8.10

```
/* FILE: usb_core.c */
        if(device_info(interface)) {
              kfree(p_usb_dev_info);
              return -1;
        }
```

The usbdev_probe function returns a negative number if it is either not the right driver for the device or is not able to handle the device for some reason. If the driver is all ready to handle the device, it must return 0 in usbdev_probe.

Let's compile the module again and insert it. You must see some device details about endpoints, their type, class, subclass and protocol.

So far we have used information given by USB sub-system in the struct usb_interface descriptor. Next we discover way to talk to the USB device.

8.5 UNDERSTANDING MASS STORAGE DEVICE CONTROL COMMANDS

This section describes control commands for mass storage devices, and then examines two control messages.

The USB control messages have following message format.

Table 8.11

bmRequestType	bRequest	wValue	wIndex	wLength	Data
1 byte	1 byte	2 bytes	2 bytes	2 bytes	Variable

The message element bmRequestType is a bit map as shown in below table.

Table 8.12

Bits	Value	Remark
7	0	Direction is from host to device
6, 5	00	Standard request
6, 5	01	Class request
6, 5	10	Vendor request

6, 5	11	Reserved
4, 3, 2, 1, 0	00000	Recipient is device
4, 3, 2, 1, 0	00001	Recipient is interface
4, 3, 2, 1, 0	00010	Recipient is endpoint
4, 3, 2, 1, 0	00011	Recipient is other
4, 3, 2, 1, 0	Rest	Reserved

8.5.1 Bulk-Only Mass Storage Reset

This command is sent to a USB device to reset it. The command has following parameters.

- bmRequestType – 0x21
- bRequest – 0xFF
- wValue – 0x0000
- wIndex – Interface number (0x0000)
- wLength – 0x00 (No extra data)
- Data – None

8.5.2 Get max LUN

LUN is logical unit number. Linux USB sub-system uses this number to identify different disks. For example, if you are using a USB multiple card reader, you shall have more than 1 LUN while in a single USB card reader or USB memory device, you have 1 LUN.

The term max LUN is a little confusing in the sense it is not number of LUN(s) but it is highest number of LUN starting from 0. This means if max LUN in your system is 0, you have 1 LUN. If max LUN is 3, you have 4 LUNs.

This command has following parameters.

- bmRequestType – 0xA1
- bRequest – 0xFE
- wValue – 0x0000
- wIndex – Interface number (0x0000)
- wLength – 0x0001
- Data – 1 byte (To receive max LUN from the device)

8.6 ADDING MASS STORAGE DEVICE CONTROL COMMANDS TO USB DRIVER

In this section, we add Reset and max LUN commands to the USB driver. Since these are control commands, these must be sent on control endpoint (also known as control pipe). We shall use usb_sndctrlpipe and usb_rcvctrlpipe functions to get outbound control pipe and inbound control pipe respectively, and then shall use usb_contrl_msg function to send the message to the device.

Let's first implement reset_device function.

Table 8.13

```
/* FILE: usb_core.c */
static int reset_device(struct usb_device *udev)
```

```
{
        int result = 0, pipe = usb_sndctrlpipe(udev, 0);
        result = usb_control_msg(udev, pipe, 0xff,
                    USB_DIR_OUT|USB_TYPE_CLASS|USB_RECIP_INTERFACE,
              0, 0, NULL, 0, 2*HZ);
        if(result < 0) {
              printk("Device Reset Failed (%d)\n", result);
              return -1;
        }
        printk("Device Reset Successfully\n");
        return 0;
}
```

The usb_control_msg functions forms a control message in the format discussed earlier using the parameters and sends it to the USB device (via usbcore). The first parameter to the usb_control_msg is usb_device pointer which we have stored in usbdev_private structure. The second parameter is the pipe which we get from either usb_rcvctrlpipe or usb_sndctrlpipe depending upon whether data is to be received or not. Third parameter to the function is bRequest. Fourth parameter is bmRequestType. Fifth parameter is wValue. Sixth parameter is wIndex. Seventh parameter is pointer to data. Since we do not expect any data to be received the pointer is NULL. Eighth parameter is wLength. The last parameter is timeout after which usb_control_msg shall return regardless of command status (*i.e.*, completed or not). Therefore, the USB device must respond within timeout time.

Next we implement get_max_lun function. We add a new member to usbdev_private structure to store value returned by get_max_lun function.

Table 8.14

```
/* FILE: usb_core.h */
struct usbdev_private {
        unsigned char ep_out; /* out endpoint */
        unsigned char max_lun;
};
/* FILE: usb_core.c */
static int get_max_lun(struct usb_device *udev)
{
        int pipe, result=0;
        unsigned char data=0;
        pipe = usb_rcvctrlpipe(udev, 0);
        result = usb_control_msg(udev, pipe, 0xfe,
                    USB_DIR_IN|USB_TYPE_CLASS|USB_RECIP_INTERFACE,
              0, 0, &data, sizeof(data), HZ);
        if(result == 1)
              return data;
        printk("get_max_lun failed.. result = %d\n", result);
        return -1;
}
```

Let's call these functions in usbdev_probe and see the things happening!

Table 8.15

```
/* FILE: usb_core.c */
        reset_device(p_usb_dev_info->udev);
        p_usb_dev_info->max_lun = get_max_lun(p_usb_dev_info->udev);
```

Recompile the USB driver and insert it. The module shall reset the USB device and will print maximum LUN supported by device.

8.7 UNDERSTANDING USB SPECIFICATIONS AND PROTOCOL

So far we have communicated to a USB device using control messages. Besides the control messages, USB specifications describes many other ATAPI mass storage commands just like for SCSI devices. We shall describe and implement some ATAPI commands later in this chapter, however, first let's understand how these commands work.

ATAPI commands follow a state machine as shown below.

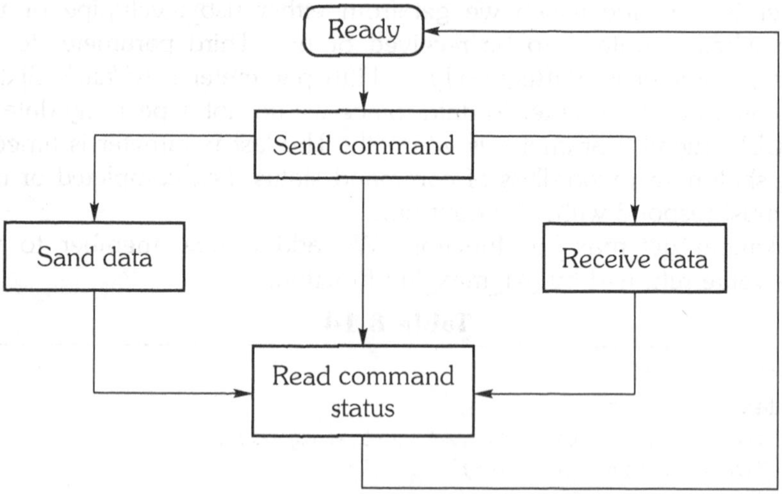

Figure 8.4

As shown in the state machine, an ATAPI command may optionally be followed by sending or receiving data. Then status must be read from the device. After reading the status, next ATAPI command can be send to the device.

As we'll see later, every ATAPI command has its own message format. However, these commands to the USB mass storage devices are wrapped in another message called Command Block Wrapper (CBW). The command status is always read in Command Status Wrapper (CSW). The ATAPI command is called CBWCB (CBW Command Block).

8.7.1 Command Block Wrapper (CBW)

Every ATAPI command is preceded by CBW. As defined in USB specifications, CBW has following message format.

Byte \ Bit	7	6	5	4	3	2	1	0
0-3	dCBW Signature							
0-7	dCBW Tag							
8-11	dCBW Data transfer length							
12	bmCBW Flags							
13	Reserved (0)				bCBWLUN			
14	Reserved (0)			bCBWCB Length				
15-30	CBWCB							

Figure 8.5

The CBW details are as follows:

- dCBWSignature—It is the signature that helps identifying CBW messages. The value of this signature for USB mass storage devices is 0x55534243 (big endian) which translates to string "USBC".
- dCBWTag—It is a tag or number assigned to the CBW. The CSW shall echo same tag number when status for the CBW is read. Therefore, the tag associates CSW with CBW.
- dCBWDataTransferLength—This field holds the data length which shall be transferred between host and device during the command execution (*i.e.*, during 'Send Data' and 'Receive Data' state). If this field contains 0 then no data transfer shall take place and 'Read Command Status' state follows 'Send Command' state directly.
- bmCBWFlags—The 7th bit of this field indicates data transfer direction. If this bit is 0 then after 'Send Command' state, 'Send Data' state occurs. If this bit is 1 then after 'Send Command' state, 'Receive Data' state occurs. However, if dCBWDataTransferLength is 0, this bit is meaningless. Rest all bits are reserved.
- bCBWLUN—This field contains the LUN number. If the USB driver is handling a multiple USB card reader, appropriate LUN number corresponding to the disk must be specified. However, for single USB card reader or USB memory devices, this field shall contain 0 as they support only 1 LUN.
- bCBWCBLength—This field holds length of Command Block (CB) *i.e.*, length of actual ATAPI command.
- CBWCB—This contains the ATAPI command.

8.7.2 Command Status Wrapper (CSW)

The CSW has following message format.

Byte \ Bit	7	6	5	4	3	2	1	0
0-3	dCBWSignature							
4-7	dCBWTag							
8-11	dCSWDataResidue							
12	bCSWStatus							

Figure 8.6

The CSW details are as follows:

- dCSWSignature—This is signature to identify CSW messages. The value of this signature for USB mass storage devices is 0x55534253 (big endian) which translates to string "USBS".
- dCSWTag—The device shall use this value from associated CBW.
- dCSWDataResidue—If the 'Read Status' state followed 'Send Data' state, this field contains difference between dCBWDataTransferLength and actual amount of data processed by the device. If the 'Read Status' state followed 'Receive Data' state, this field contains difference between dCBWDataTransferLength and actual amount of data sent by the device.
- bCSWStatus—This field holds the execution status of the command. A non-zero value indicates failure while zero indicates success.

8.8 UNDERSTANDING URB

While we have understood the message format which the USB device driver shall use to talk to USB device, we must not forget that USB device driver does not actually talk to the USB device, but to the usbcore. The interaction between USB device driver and usbcore is not these messages but a structure known as URB. The messages we discussed are embedded in the URB.

URB stands for "USB Request Block". This structure contains all parameters to perform any kind of USB transfer. All transfer requests are asynchronously sent to usbcore and their completion is notified by a call back function (by the usbcore to the USB device driver). The Linux USB sub-system provides many API(s) to work with URB as we'll see shortly.

8.9 IMPLEMENTING WRAPPER AND USB DEVICE COMMUNICATION FUNCTIONS

8.9.1 Command Block Wrapper (CBW)

As we discussed, every ATAPI command is wrapped in CBW message. Therefore it is imperative to develop a generic function to encode CBW message. We create a new file usb_transport.c where we defined functions related to USB device communication.

Table 8.16

```
/* FILE: usb_core.h */
#define CBW_LEN 15
#define CBWCB_LEN 31
#define CSW_LEN 13
struct usb_cmd_info {
        unsigned char cmd;
        unsigned char lun;
        int cbw_data_xfer_len;
        int lba;
};
/* FILE: usb_transport.c */
#include <linux/kernel.h>
#include <linux/module.h>
#include <linux/slab.h>
#include <linux/highmem.h>
```

```
static int usb_cmd_num = 0;
int usbdev_prepare_cmd_request(
              unsigned char *buff, int len, struct usb_cmd_info
 *cmd_info)
{
        int command_len = 0;
        if(len < CBWCB_LEN) {
              LOG_MSG("Request buffer too short\n");
              return -1;
        }
        else
              memset(buff, 0, len);
        /* dCBWSignature */
        buff[0]='U';
        buff[1]='S';
        buff[2]='B';
        buff[3]='C';
        /* dCBWTag */
        memcpy(buff+4, &usb_cmd_num, 4);
        usb_cmd_num++;
        /* dCBWDataTransferLength */
        memcpy(buff+8, &cmd_info->cbw_data_xfer_len, 4);
        /* bmCBWFlags will be filled later depending upon request */
        buff[13] = cmd_info->lun & 0x0f;
        /* encode CB */
        switch(cmd_info->cmd) {
              default:
                    command_len = -1;
                    LOG_MSG("Command not supported\n");
                    return -1;
        }
        return command_len;
}
```

The function usbdev_prepare_cmd_request receives pointer to usb_cmd_info structure, which shall be filled by every ATAPI command implementation. The function usbdev_prepare_cmd_request shall prepare a CBW for every command.

8.9.2 Command Status Wrapper (CSW)

In this section, we develop a decoding function for CSW which shall be useful later. We create another new file usb_debug.c where we implement all informational functions.

Table 8.17

```
/* FILE: usb_debug.c */
#include <linux/kernel.h>
#include <linux/module.h>
#include "usb_core.h"
void decode_csw(unsigned char *data, unsigned int len)
```

```
{
        if(len != CSW_LEN) {
              printk("Invalide CSW length\n");
              return;
        }
        printk("#########  DECODING CSW  ########\n");
        printk("%c", data[0]);
        printk("%c", data[1]);
        printk("%c", data[2]);
        printk("%c", data[3]);
        printk("Tag: %d\n", *(int*)(data+4));
        printk("Data Residue: %d\n", *(int*)(data+8));
        switch(data[12]) {
              case 0x00:
                    printk("Command Passed\n");
                    break;
              case 0x01:
                    printk("Command Failed\n");
                    break;
              case 0x02:
                    printk("Phase Error\n");
                    break;
              default:
                    printk("Unknown status: %d\n", data[12]);
        }
        return;
}
```

This function simply follows CSW message format and prints command execution status.

8.9.3 USB Device Communication Functions

Next, we add a few functions to communicate with the USB device. These functions shall be frequently used by ATAPI commands which we'll implement in next section. These functions shall send or receive given data to/from the USB device.

Table 8.18

```
/* FILE: usb_core.c */
#define DIR_WRITE 1
#define DIR_READ  2
int usbdev_bulk_data_out(
              struct usbdev_private* p_usbdev,
              unsigned char *src, unsigned int len)
 {
        int status;
        TRACE("ENTER: usbdev_bulk_data_out\n");
        if(len == 0)
              return 0;
```

```
        status = usbdev_bulk_raw(DIR_WRITE, p_usbdev, src, len);
        TRACE("EXIT: usbdev_bulk_data_out\n");
        return status;
}
int usbdev_bulk_data_in(
              struct usbdev_private* p_usbdev,
              unsigned char *dest, unsigned int len)
{
        int status;
        TRACE("ENTER: usbdev_bulk_data_in\n");
        if(len == 0)
              return 0;
        status = usbdev_bulk_raw(DIR_READ, p_usbdev, dest, len);
        TRACE("EXIT: usbdev_bulk_data_in\n");
        return status;
}
static int usbdev_bulk_raw(
              int dir, struct usbdev_private *p_usbdev,
              unsigned char *data, unsigned int len)
 {
        int pipe, result, len_done, halt_clearing=0;
        struct completion *urb_done = NULL;
        struct urb *p_urb_request;
        unsigned char *dma_buf;
        urb_done = kmalloc(sizeof(struct completion), GFP_KERNEL);
        if(urb_done)
              init_completion(urb_done);
        else {
              printk("urb_done is NULL\n");
              return -1;
        }
        if(dir == DIR_READ)
              pipe=usb_rcvbulkpipe(p_usbdev->udev, p_usbdev->ep_in);
        else if(dir == DIR_WRITE)
              pipe=usb_sndbulkpipe(p_usbdev->udev, p_usbdev->ep_out);
        else {
              printk("USB_INVALID_REQ\n");
              return -1;
        }
        p_urb_request = usb_alloc_urb(0, GFP_KERNEL);
        if(p_urb_request == NULL) {
              printk("usb_alloc_urb failed\n");
              kfree(urb_done);
              return -1;
        }
/* allocating usb dma memory */
dma_buf = usb_buffer_alloc(p_usbdev->udev,
                          len, GFP_KERNEL, &p_urb_request->transfer_dma);
```

```
        if(dma_buf == NULL) {
              printk("DMA buffer allocation failed\n");
              usb_free_urb(p_urb_request);
              kfree(urb_done);
              return -1;
        }
        else
              memset(dma_buf, 0, len);
        if(dir == DIR_WRITE)
              memcpy(dma_buf, data, len);
        usb_fill_bulk_urb(p_urb_request,
                    p_usbdev->udev, pipe, dma_buf, len,
                    usbdev_wakeup_on_completion, urb_done);
        p_urb_request->transfer_flags |= URB_NO_TRANSFER_DMA_MAP;
        result = usb_submit_urb(p_urb_request, GFP_KERNEL);
        if(result) {
              LOG_MSG("usb_submit_urb failed\n");
              usb_free_urb(p_urb_request);
              kfree(urb_done);
              return result;
        }
        /* wait for request completion */
        wait_for_completion(urb_done);
        kfree(urb_done);
        len_done = p_urb_request->actual_length;
        result = p_urb_request->status;
        if(dir == DIR_READ)
              memcpy(data, dma_buf, len_done);
        /* free usb dma memory */
        usb_buffer_free(p_urb_request->dev,
              p_urb_request->transfer_buffer_length,
              p_urb_request->transfer_buffer,
              p_urb_request->transfer_dma);
        usb_free_urb(p_urb_request);
        /* error handling */
        if(result) {
              if(result == -ETIMEDOUT)
                    LOG_MSG("usbdev_bulk_raw: time out\n");
              else if(result == -ENOENT)
                    LOG_MSG("usbdev_bulk_raw: transfer aborted\n");
              else if(result == -EPIPE) {
                    LOG_MSG("usbdev_bulk_raw: pipe stalled\n");
              if(usb_clear_halt(p_usbdev->udev, pipe) < 0)
                    LOG_MSG("halt could not be cleared\n");
              }
        return -1;
        }
        if(len_done != len) /* this is not really an error */
```

```
                return -1;
        return 0;
}
static void usbdev_wakeup_on_completion(struct urb *urb)
{
        struct completion *urb_done_ptr;
        TRACE("ENTER: usbdev_wakeup_on_completion\n");
        urb_done_ptr = (struct completion *)urb->context;
        complete(urb_done_ptr);
        return;
}
```

In above table, we develop two functions named usbdev_bulk_data_out and other usbdev_bulk_data_in. The function usbdev_bulk_data_out transfers data from host to device while usbdev_bulk_data_in transfers data from device to host. As we see both these functions call usbdev_data_raw which does the real work.

The following paragraph explains functionality of usbdev_data_raw.

1. It first allocates a completion structure (we will explain it later).
2. Based on data transfer direction, it receives corresponding pipe.
3. Initializes completion structure.
4. Allocates a URB using usb_alloc_urb API. The first argument is useful for ISO packets. Since we do not use them, we pass it as zero. The second argument is memory allocation flag. As we'll see later, we invoke these functions through a work queue, and therefore it is perfectly fine for this function to sleep. Therefore, we use GFP_KERNEL.
5. Allocates DMA buffer using usb_buffer_alloc API. This API allocates a DMA buffer and returns virtual address of the buffer. The physical address of the DMA buffer is returned in the third argument of usb_buffer_alloc.
6. If the data is to be transferred from host to device (DIR_WRITE), it copies the data to buffer allocated by usb_buffer_alloc.
7. Fills the URB structure using usb_fill_bulk_urb API. The last two arguments of usb_fill_bulk_urb are a call back function and parameter to the call back function. As we mentioned earlier, the completion of URB is notified by invoking this call back function.
8. Submits the URB using usb_submit_urb API.
9. Waits for the URB completion using urb_done_ptr variable (completion structure allocated in step 1).
10. Whenever the URB is completed, the usbcore shall invoke the call back function usbdev_wakeup_on_completion. This function signals completion on urb_done_ptr therefore usbdev_bulk_raw wakes-up and resumes execution.
11. If data transfer direction is from device to host (DIR_READ), it copies data from dma_buf.
12. Frees allocated memories in this function before URB submission.
13. Checks if any error has occurred during URB execution. If pipe has halted, clears halt using usb_clear_halt.
14. Returns data transfer status.

At this point, the driver is ready to transfer data with device. As we will see in next section, these transfer function shall be used by ATAPI commands. Before this, let's modify Makefile to include new source file usb_transport.c.

Table 8.19

```
KERNEL_DIR := /usr/src/linux-2.6.21.5
obj-m := usb.o
usb-objs := usb_core.o usb_transport.o usb_debug.o
default:
        make -C $(KERNEL_DIR) SUBDIRS='pwd' modules
clean:
        make -C $(KERNEL_DIR) SUBDIRS='pwd' clean
```

8.10 TALKING TO USB DEVICE

In this section, we understand and develop some ATAPI commands.

8.10.1 INQUIRY Command

The INQUIRY requests the device that device parameters information is sent to the host. It has following message format.

Byte \ Bit	7	6	5	4	3	2	1	0
0	Operation code (0x12)							
1	LUN			Reserved (0)				
2	Reserved (0)							
3	Reserved (0)							
4	Allocation length (0x24)							
5	Reserved (0)							
6-11	PAD							

Figure 8.7

The operation code for INQUIRY is 0x12. LUN is logical unit number. Allocation Length indicates maximum number of bytes; host has allowed the device to return. The standard value is 36 (0x24) as we see in INQUIRY response.

The INQUIRY RESPONSE has following message format.

Byte \ Bit	7	6	5	4	3	2	1	0
0	Reserved			Peripheral Device Type				
1	RMB	Reserved						
2	Reserved							
3	Reserved							
4	Additional length							
5-7	Reserved							
8-15	Vendor identification							
16-31	Product identification							
32-35	Product revision level							

Figure 8.8

The Peripheral Device Type (PDT) indicates the kind of device connected. It has following values.

Table 8.20

Value	Description
0x00	SBC direct access device
0x05	CDROM device
0x07	Optical memory device
0x0E	RBC direct access device
Rest	Reserved

The RMB (Removal Media Bit) specifies if the device is removable. If RMB is 1, it implies that device is removable. If RMB is 0, it means device is not removable.

Additional Length implies if the response message has more length than standard length 36.

The Vendor Identification, Product Identification and Product Revision Level are device information in form of ASCII characters.

Equipped with all information about INQUIRY command, lets implement this function in the device driver. We shall upgrade usbdev_prepare_cmd_request function to implement Command Block (CB) for INQUIRY command, and then implement a function to send INQUIRY command. Finally implement a function to decode INQUIRY response.

Table 8.21

```
/* FILE: usb_core.h */
#define LUN 0
#define INQUIRY 0x12
#define INQUIRY_CMD_LEN 6
#define INQUIRY_RSP_LEN 36
/* FILE: usb_transport.c */
        switch(req_info->cmd) {
              case INQUIRY:
                    buff[12] = 0x80; /* direction */
                    buff[14] = INQUIRY_CMD_LEN & 0x1f;
                    /* cb */
                    buff[CBW_LEN+0] = INQUIRY;
                    buff[CBW_LEN+1] = (req_info->lun << 5) & 0xe0;
                    buff[CBW_LEN+4] = req_info->cbw_data_xfer_len;
                    command_len = CBWCB_LEN;
                    break;
              default:
                    command_len = -1;
                    LOG_MSG("Command not supported\n");
                    return -1;
        }
        return command_len;
}
/* FILE: usb_transport.c */
```

```
int usbdev_send_inquiry(void)
{
        struct usbdev_private *p_usbdev = p_usb_dev_info;
        unsigned char cbw_buf[CBWCB_LEN] = {0}, csw_buf[0x24] = {0};
        int result;
        struct usb_cmd_info req_info;
        memset(&req_info,0, sizeof(req_info));
        req_info.cmd = INQUIRY;
        req_info.lun = LUN;
        req_info.cbw_data_xfer_len = INQUIRY_RSP_LEN;
        if(usbdev_prepare_cmd_request(
              cbw_buf, CBWCB_LEN, &req_info) < 0)
        {
              LOG_MSG("usbdev_prepare_cmd_request failed\n");
              return -1;
}
        /* send command */
        result = usbdev_bulk_data_out(p_usbdev, cbw_buf, CBWCB_LEN);
        if(result != 0) {
              LOG_MSG("usbdev_bulk_data_out failed\n");
              return -1;
        }
        /* read command response */
        result = usbdev_bulk_data_in(
              p_usbdev, csw_buf, req_info.cbw_data_xfer_len);
if(result != 0) {
              LOG_MSG("usbdev_bulk_data_in failed\n");
              return -1;
        }
        else
              decode_inquiry_response(
              (csw_buf, req_info.cbw_data_xfer_len);
        /* read command status */
        result = usbdev_bulk_data_in(p_usbdev, csw_buf, CSW_LEN);
        if(result != 0) {
              LOG_MSG("usbdev_bulk_data_in failed\n");
              return -1;
        }
        else
              decode_csw(csw_buf, CSW_LEN);
        result = csw_buf[12] ? -1 : 0;
        if(result)
              printk("INQUIRY_STATUS : %d\n", csw_buf[12]);
        return result;
        }
/* FILE: usb_debug.c */
void decode_inquiry_response(unsigned char *data, unsigned int len)
{
```

```
        unsigned char peripheral_dev_type;
        unsigned char rmb;
        unsigned char additional_len;
        int i;
        if(len != INQUIRY_RESPONSE_LEN) {
                printk("Invalid INQUIRY response length\n");
                return;
        }
        peripheral_dev_type = data[0] & 0x1f;
        switch(peripheral_dev_type) {
                case 0:
                        printk("SBC Direct-access device\n");
                        break;
                case 0x05:
                        printk("CD-ROM device\n");
                        break;
                case 0x07:
                        printk("Optical memory device\n");
                        break;
                case 0x0e:
                        printk("RBC Direct-access device\n");
                        break;
                default:
                        printk("Out of scope\n");
        }
        rmb = data[1];
        if(rmb == 0x80)
                printk("Medium is removable\n");
        else if(rmb == 0)
                printk("Medium is not removable\n");
        else
                printk("Erroneous RMB\n");
        additional_len = data[4];
        printk("Additional Length: %d\n", additional_len);
        printk("Vendor: ");
        for(i=8; i<16; i++)
                printk("%c", data[i]);
        printk("\n");
        printk("Product: ");
        for(i=16; i<32; i++)
                printk("%c", data[i]);
        printk("\n");
        printk("Product Revision Level: ");
        for(i=32; i<36; i++)
                printk("%c", data[i]);
        printk("\n");
        return;
}
```

For INQUIRY CBW, in the usbdev_prepare_cmd_request function, we set bmCBWFlags to 0x80 as this command is meant to transfer data from device to host. Since we are not going to send any PAD data in INQUIRY command, we set bCBWCBLength to 6 (which is INQUIRY command length without padding).

For INQUIRY CB, we fill operation code as 0x12, while LUN and Allocation Length are filled as given by usbdev_send_enquiry function.

In function usbdev_send_enquiry, we implement INQUIRY ATAPI command. The function details are as follows:

1. Fills usb_cmd_info structure. The usbdev_send_enquiry sets LUN to 0 as we are working with single USB card reader or USB memory device. If you have a multiple USB card reader, set the LUN accordingly. The cbw_data_xfer_len is set to 36 which is INQUIRY response length.
2. Calls usbdev_prepare_cmd_request function to prepare CBWCB (Every ATAPI command in our device driver shall fill usb_cmd_info structure and call usbdev_prepare_cmd_request function).
3. Sends the command to USB device using usbdev_bulk_data_out function as described in previous section.
4. Reads INQUIRY response using usbdev_bulk_data_in function.
5. If INQUIRY response received successfully, decodes INQUIRY response using decode_inquiry_response function.
6. Reads commands status using usbdev_bulk_data_in function and calls decode_csw function as described in previous section.
7. Returns command execution status from CSW.

The function decode_inquiry_response decodes received data from device in the format mentioned earlier. It prints PDT, RMB, Additional Length, Vendor Identification, Product Identification and Product Revision Level.

8.10.2 TEST UNIT READY Command

The TEST UNIT READY command provides a way to check if device is ready to receive medium-access ATAPI commands. No data transfer happens for this command, and driver must read CSW directly after sending CBWCB.

The command has following message format.

Byte \ Bit	7	6	5	4	3	2	1	0
0	Operation code (0x00)							
1	LUN			Reserved				
2	Reserved							
3	Reserved							
4	Reserved							
5	Reserved							
6-11	PAD							

Figure 8.9

The command has operation code 0x00. LUN is logical unit number.

Let's implement this command now by enhancing usbdev_prepared_cmd_request and implementing usbdev_send_test_unit_ready function.

Table 8.22

```
/* FILE: usb_core.h */
#define TEST_UNIT_READY 0x00
#define TEST_UNIT_READY_CMD_LEN 6
/* FILE: usb_transport.c */
        switch(req_info->cmd) {
              case TEST_UNIT_READY:
                    buff[14] = TEST_UNIT_READY_CMD_LEN & 0x1f;
                    /* cb */
                    buff[CBW_LEN+0] = TEST_UNIT_READY;
                    buff[CBW_LEN+1] = (req_info->lun << 5) & 0xe0;
                    command_len = CBWCB_LEN;
                    break;
        }
        return command_len;
}
int usbdev_send_test_unit_ready(void)
{
        struct usbdev_private *p_usbdev = p_usb_dev_info;
        unsigned char cbw_buf[CBWCB_LEN] = {0}, csw_buf[CSW_LEN] = {0};
        int result;
        struct usb_cmd_info req_info;
        memset(&req_info, 0, sizeof(req_info));
        req_info.cmd = TEST_UNIT_READY;
        req_info.lun = LUN;
        if(usbdev_prepare_cmd_request(
                    cbw_buf, CBWCB_LEN, &req_info) < 0)
        {           LOG_MSG("usbdev_prepare_cmd_request failed\n");
              return -1;
        }
/* send command */
result = usbdev_bulk_data_out(p_usbdev, cbw_buf, CBWCB_LEN);
        if(result != 0) {
              LOG_MSG("usbdev_bulk_data_out failed\n");
              return -1;
        }
        /* read command status */
        result = usbdev_bulk_data_in(p_usbdev, csw_buf, CSW_LEN);
        if(result != 0) {
              LOG_MSG("usbdev_bulk_data_in failed\n");
              return -1;
        }
        result = csw_buf[12] ? -1 : 0;
        if(result)
              printk("TEST_UNIT_READY_STATUS : %d\n", csw_buf[12]);
        return result;
}
```

In usbdev_prepare_cmd_request function, we fill CB for command TEST UNIT READY. This code is very similar to INQUIRY command CB filling except that we do not set bmCBWFlags since no data transfer takes place in this command execution.

The usbdev_send_test_unit_ready function is pretty similar to usbdev_send_inquiry except that it does not send/receive any data between sending CBWCB and receiving CSW. Finally it returns command execution status from CSW.

8.10.3 READ CAPACITY Command

The READ CAPACITY command provides a mechanism for host computer to request information regarding USB device capacity *i.e.*, using this command the USB driver knows if the USB device is 512MB or 1GB or something else.

The READ CAPACITY command has following message format.

Byte \ Bit	7	6	5	4	3	2	1	0
0	Operation code (0x25)							
1	LUN				Reserved			
2	Reserved							
3	Reserved							
4	Reserved							
5	Reserved							
6	Reserved							
7	Reserved							
8	Reserved							
9	Reserved							
10-11	PAD							

Figure 8.10

The command has operation command 0x25. LUN is logical unit number.

The READ CAPACITY response has following message format.

Byte \ Bit	7	6	5	4	3	2	1	0
0	(MSB) Last logical block address							
1								
2								
3								(LSB)
4	(MSB) Block length in Bytes							
5								
6								
7								(LSB)

Figure 8.11

The response returns Last Logical Block Address (LLBA). Therefore, the media size is LLBA+1. The response also returns Block Length in bytes.

Let's implement this command for USB device driver. We add another member in usbdev_private structure to store device capacity.

Table 8.23

```
/* FILE: usb_core.h */
#define READ_CAPACITY 0x25
#define READ_CAPACITY_CMD_LEN 6
#define READ_CAPACITY_RSP_LEN 8
struct usbdev_private {
        unsigned char ep_in; /* in endpoint */
        unsigned char ep_out; /* out endpoint */
        unsigned int capacity;
};
/* FILE: usb_transport.c */
        switch(req_info->cmd) {
              case READ_CAPACITY:
                    buff[12] = 0x80; /* direction */
                    buff[14] = READ_CAPACITY_CMD_LEN & 0x1f;
                    /* cb */
                    buff[CBW_LEN+0] = READ_CAPACITY;
                    buff[CBW_LEN+1] = (req_info->lun << 5) & 0xe0;
                    command_len = CBWCB_LEN;
                    break;
        }
        return command_len;
}
int usbdev_read_capacity(void)
{
        struct usbdev_private *p_usbdev = p_usb_dev_info;
        unsigned char cbw_buf[CBWCB_LEN] = {0}, csw_buf[CSW_LEN] = {0};
        int result;
        struct usb_cmd_info req_info;
        unsigned int llba, block_len;
        memset(&req_info, 0, sizeof(req_info));
        req_info.cmd = READ_CAPACITY;
        req_info.lun = LUN;
        req_info.cbw_data_xfer_len = READ_CAPACITY_RSP_LEN;
        if(usbdev_prepare_cmd_request(
                          cbw_buf, CBWCB_LEN, &req_info) < 0)
        {
              LOG_MSG("usbdev_prepare_cmd_request failed\n");
              return -1;
        }
        /* send command */
        result = usbdev_bulk_data_out(p_usbdev, cbw_buf, CBWCB_LEN);
        if(result != 0) {
```

```
                LOG_MSG("usbdev_bulk_data_out failed\n");
                return -1;
        }
        /* read command response */
        result = usbdev_bulk_data_in(
                        p_usbdev, csw_buf, req_info.cbw_data_xfer_len);
        if(result != 0) {
                LOG_MSG("usbdev_bulk_data_in failed\n");
                return -1;
        }
        llba = (csw_buf[0] << 24) |
                (csw_buf[1] << 16) | (csw_buf[2] << 8) | csw_buf[3];
        block_len = (csw_buf[4] << 24) |
                (csw_buf[5] << 16) | (csw_buf[6] << 8) | csw_buf[7];
        /* read command status */
        result = usbdev_bulk_data_in(p_usbdev, csw_buf, CSW_LEN);
        if(result != 0) {
                LOG_MSG("usbdev_bulk_data_in failed\n");
                return -1;
        }
        result = csw_buf[12] ? -1 : 0;
        if(result)
                printk("READ_CAPACITY_STATUS : %d\n", csw_buf[12]);
        else {
                printk("Last Logical Block Address: %#x\n", llba);
                printk("Blcok Length in Bytes: %d\n", block_len);
                p_usbdev->capacity = llba + 1;
        }
        return result;
}
```

CB filling of READ CAPACITY is pretty similar to INQUIRY since both commands expect data transfer from the USB device. On the same lines, the function usbdev_read_capacity also follows same order of sending CBWCB, receiving data and then receiving CSW. On successful CSW read, the device capacity is stored in capacity member of usbdev_private structure.

Let's make use of all ATAPI commands in usbdev_probe function to actually send them to the USB device.

Table 8.24

```
/* FILE: usb_core.c */
#define MAX_TRY 3
static int usbdev_probe(
struct usb_interface *interface, const struct usb_device_id *id)
{
        int try = 0;
        p_usb_dev_info = kmalloc(sizeof(struct usbdev_private),
GFP_KERNEL);
        memset(p_usb_dev_info, 0, sizeof(struct usbdev_private));
        p_usb_dev_info->udev = interface_to_usbdev(interface);
        usb_get_dev(p_usb_dev_info->udev);
        device_info(interface);
```

```
        reset_device(p_usb_dev_info->udev);
        p_usb_dev_info->max_lun = get_max_lun(p_usb_dev_info->udev);
        if(usbdev_send_inquiry() < 0) {
              LOG_MSG("USB_SEND_INQUIRY FAILED\n");
              return -1;
        }
        else
              LOG_MSG("USB_SEND_INQUIRY OK\n");
        do {
              if(usbdev_send_test_unit_ready() < 0) {
                    LOG_MSG("USB_SEND_TEST_UNIT_READY FAILED\n");
        }
        else {
                    LOG_MSG("USB_SEND_TEST_UNIT_READY OK\n");
                    break;
        }
              try++;
              }while(try < MAX_TRY);
              if(try == MAX_TRY} {
              LOG_MSG("Device not ready.. giving up\n");
              return -1;
        }
        if(usbdev_read_capacity() < 0) {
              LOG_MSG("USB_READ_CAPACITY FAILED\n");
              return -1;
        }
        else
              LOG_MSG("USB_READ_CAPACITY OK\n");
        return 0;
}
```

Let's compile the USB driver and insert it. You must see lot of information about the USB device on screen which possibly you already know!

So far all the ATAPI commands are used either to control the device or get some information about the device. We shall finish this section with two more ATAPI commands which does actual contents read/write to the media. As expected, these functions shall not be invoked by USB driver, but by the block device driver interface which shall be implemented at the end of chapter.

8.10.4 READ(10) Command

The READ_10 command requests the USB device to transfer data to the host computer from specified block and up to specified length. The command has message format as shown in Figure 8.12.

The command has operation code 0x28. As usual, LUN is logical unit number. The Logical Block Address specifies the block number at which read operation begins. The Transfer Length specifies number of contiguous blocks to read. Note that the unit of Transfer Length is number of blocks and not bytes.

How about READ_10 response format! Well there is no format in this case, because in response we read direct data from the media. Since driver has no interest in the media contents, it simply returns this to block device driver interface as we'll see later.

Byte \ Bit	7	6	5	4	3	2	1	0
0	Operation code (0x28)							
1	LUN			Reserved				
2	(MSB)							
3	Logical block address							
4								
5								(LSB)
6	Reserved							
7	(MSB) Transfer length							
8								(LSB)
9	Reserved							
10-11	PAD							

Figure 8.12

Let's implement READ_10 command for the driver.

Table 8.25

```
/* FILE: usb_core.h */
#define READ_10 0x28
#define READ_10_CMD_LEN 10
#define USBDEV_SECTOR_SIZE 512
/* FILE: usb_transport.c */
switch(req_info->cmd) {
        case READ_10:
                buff[12] = 0x80; /* direction */
                buff[14] = READ_10_CMD_LEN & 0x1f;
                /* cb */
                buff[CBW_LEN+0] = READ_10;
                buff[CBW_LEN+1] = (req_info->lun << 5) & 0xe0;
                buff[CBW_LEN+2] = (unsigned char)(req_info->lba >> 24);
                buff[CBW_LEN+3] = (unsigned char)(req_info->lba >> 16);
                buff[CBW_LEN+4] = (unsigned char)(req_info->lba >> 8);
                buff[CBW_LEN+5] = (unsigned char)(req_info->lba);
                buff[CBW_LEN+7] = (unsigned char)
                  ((req_info->cbw_data_xfer_len/USB_SECTOR_SIZE) >> 8);
                buff[CBW_LEN+8] = (unsigned char)
                    (req_info->cbw_data_xfer_len/USB_SECTOR_SIZE);
                command_len = CBWCB_LEN;
                break;
}
int usbdev_send_read_10(int lba, int xfer_len, unsigned char *buffer)
```

```
{
        struct usbdev_private *p_usbdev = p_usb_dev_info;
        unsigned char cbw_buf[CBWCB_LEN] = {0}, csw_buf[CSW_LEN] = {0};
        int result;
        struct usb_cmd_info req_info;
        LOG_MSG("READ10: sector: 0x%x, xfer_len: %d(0x%x sectors)\n",
                lba, xfer_len, xfer_len/512);
        memset(&req_info, 0, sizeof(req_info));
        req_info.cmd = READ_10;
        req_info.lun = LUN;
        req_info.cbw_data_xfer_len = xfer_len;
        req_info.lba = lba;
        if(usbdev_prepare_cmd_request(
                cbw_buf, CBWCB_LEN, &req_info) < 0)
        {
              LOG_MSG("usbdev_prepare_cmd_request failed\n");
              return -1;
        }
        /* send command */
        result = usbdev_bulk_data_out(p_usbdev, cbw_buf, CBWCB_LEN);
        if(result != 0) {
              LOG_MSG("usbdev_bulk_data_out failed\n");
              return -1;
        }
        /* read command response */
        result = usbdev_bulk_data_in(
                p_usbdev, buffer, req_info.cbw_data_xfer_len);
        if(result != 0) {
              LOG_MSG("usbdev_bulk_data_in failed\n");
              return -1;
        }
        /* read command status */
        result = usbdev_bulk_data_in(p_usbdev, csw_buf, CSW_LEN);
        if(result != 0) {
              LOG_MSG("usbdev_bulk_data_in failed\n");
              return -1;
        }
        result = csw_buf[12] ? -1 : 0;
        if(result)
              printk("READ_10_STATUS : %d\n", csw_buf[12]);
        return result;
}
```

The CB for READ_10 operations has more fields than other ATAPI commands. As lba member in usb_cmd_info structure is specified in number of blocks, we directly assign this variable in READ_10 CB. However, cbw_data_xfer_len is in number of bytes. Therefore, we convert it to block number by dividing by USBDEV_SECTOR_SIZE.

The usbdev_send_read_10 functions shall receive read block address and length from block device driver interface. The USB driver simply passes those values to the device in form of

READ_10 CB. Rest of the function is pretty similar to previous ones except that after sending CBWCB, data is read in buffer provided by block device driver. The function terminates with status reading from CSW.

8.10.5 WRITE(10) Command

The WRITE_10 command requests the USB device to transfer data from the host computer to the USB device, to specified block and up to specified length. The command has following message format.

<table>
<tr><td>Byte \ Bit</td><td>7</td><td>6</td><td>5</td><td>4</td><td>3</td><td>2</td><td>1</td><td>0</td></tr>
<tr><td>0</td><td colspan="8">Operation code (0x2A)</td></tr>
<tr><td>1</td><td colspan="3">LUN</td><td colspan="5">Reserved</td></tr>
<tr><td>2</td><td colspan="8" rowspan="4">(MSB)
Logical block address
(LSB)</td></tr>
<tr><td>3</td></tr>
<tr><td>4</td></tr>
<tr><td>5</td></tr>
<tr><td>6</td><td colspan="8">Reserved</td></tr>
<tr><td>7</td><td colspan="8" rowspan="2">(MSB)
Transfer length
(LSB)</td></tr>
<tr><td>8</td></tr>
<tr><td>9</td><td colspan="8">Reserved</td></tr>
<tr><td>10-11</td><td colspan="8">PAD</td></tr>
</table>

Figure 8.13

As we see, the WRITE_10 message format is pretty much similar to READ_10. The only difference lies in data transfer direction, this time from host computer to the USB device.

Let's implement WRITE_10 for USB device driver.

Table 8.26

```
/* FILE: usb_core.h */
#define WRITE_10 0x2A
#define WRITE_10_CMD_LEN 10
/* FILE: usb_transport.c */
switch(req_info->cmd) {
        case WRITE_10:
              buff[12]  = 0x00; /* direction */
              buff[14]  = WRITE_10_LEN & 0x1f;
              /* cb */
              buff[CBW_LEN+0]  = WRITE_10;
              buff[CBW_LEN+1]  = (req_info->lun << 5) & 0xe0;
              buff[CBW_LEN+2]  = (unsigned char)(req_info->lba >> 24);
              buff[CBW_LEN+3]  = (unsigned char)(req_info->lba >> 16);
              buff[CBW_LEN+4]  = (unsigned char)(req_info->lba >> 8);
```

```
            buff[CBW_LEN+5] = (unsigned char)(req_info->lba);
            buff[CBW_LEN+7] = (unsigned char)((req_info-
>cbw_data_xfer_len/USB_SECTOR_SIZE) >> 8);
            buff[CBW_LEN+8] = (unsigned char)(req_info-
>cbw_data_xfer_len/USB_SECTOR_SIZE);
            command_len = CBWCB_LEN;
            break;
}
int usbdev_send_write_10(int lba, int xfer_len, unsigned char *buffer)
{
        struct usbdev_private *p_usbdev = p_usb_dev_info;
        unsigned char cbw_buf[CBWCB_LEN] = {0}, csw_buf[CSW_LEN] = {0};
        int result;
        struct usb_cmd_info req_info;
        memset(&req_info, 0, sizeof(req_info));
        req_info.cmd = WRITE_10;
        req_info.lun = LUN;
        req_info.cbw_data_xfer_len = xfer_len;
        req_info.lba = lba;
        if(usbdev_prepare_cmd_request(cbw_buf, CBWCB_LEN, &req_info)
<0){
            LOG_MSG("usbdev_prepare_cmd_request failed\n");
            return 1;
        }
        /* send command */
        result = usbdev_bulk_data_out(p_usbdev, cbw_buf, CBWCB_LEN);
        if(result != 0) {
            LOG_MSG("usbdev_bulk_data_out failed\n");
            return -1;
        }
        /* write data */
        result = usbdev_bulk_data_out(p_usbdev, buffer,
 req_info.cbw_data_xfer_len);
        if(result != 0) {
            LOG_MSG("usbdev_bulk_data_in failed\n");
            return -1;
        }
        /* read command status */
        result = usbdev_bulk_data_in(p_usbdev, csw_buf, CSW_LEN);
        if(result != 0) {
            LOG_MSG("usbdev_bulk_data_in failed\n");
            return -1;
        }
        result = csw_buf[12] ? -1 : 0;
        if(result)
            printk("WRITE_10_STATUS : %d\n", csw_buf[12]);
        return result;
}
```

The CB filling of WRITE_10 is exactly same to READ_10 except the difference in bmCBWFlags which has direction from host to device.

Similarly, the function usbdev_send_write_10 is similar to usbdev_send_read_10 except that after sending CBWCB it sends data out to the device from the block device driver supplied buffer. The function terminates with status reading from CSW.

We finish ATAPI command implementation here. Although there are many more ATAPI commands which USB mass storage devices support, but for this naïve driver these implemented commands are sufficient. Let's compile again and insert module. Well, if you expecting any difference from last insertion, you got to wait. Because READ_10 and WRITE_10 commands are not invoked until we associate this USB device driver to a block device driver.

This finishes USB device driver development and USB specification & protocol development. In next section, we develop a block device driver and use already developed USB device driver, so that the drive can actually be used by an application or a user.

8.11 DEVELOPING BLOCK DEVICE DRIVER

The block device drivers provide an interface to the devices that transfer randomly accessible data in fixed size blocks. Typical such devices are hard disk, floppy disk, CDROM etc. Since USB memory devices posses similar features, we choose to provide a block device driver interface to the USB device driver developed so far.

As shown in Figure 8.14, Linux block sub-system interacts with block device driver to access the block device. However, this interaction is not through direct function calls, but through a queuing mechanism. This queue is known as 'request queue'. This interaction can be shown as below diagram.

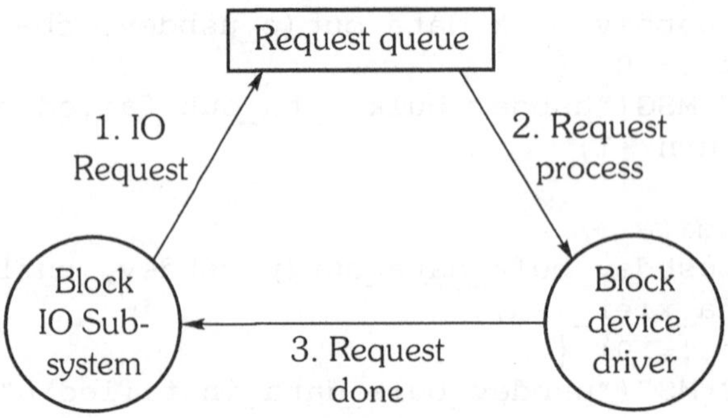

Figure 8.14

Every block device driver has at least one such request queue. The Linux block sub-system adds IO requests received from file system to this queue. The block device driver takes these IO requests from the request queue and process them. The block device driver signals to Block IO sub-system once the de-queued request is completed.

Every block device driver has to provide a function (known as 'request function') to process requests from 'request queue'. This function is invoked by Block IO sub-system whenever it adds any IO request to the 'request queue'. The Block IO sub-system invokes the 'request function' in softirq context; therefore 'request function' must not sleep. Since usbdev_send_read_10 and usbdev_send_write_10 functions developed in the USB device driver has sleep nature (memory allocation using GFP_KERNEL and call to wait_for_completion), the block device driver design must satisfy both constraints.

The following diagram shows block device driver design.

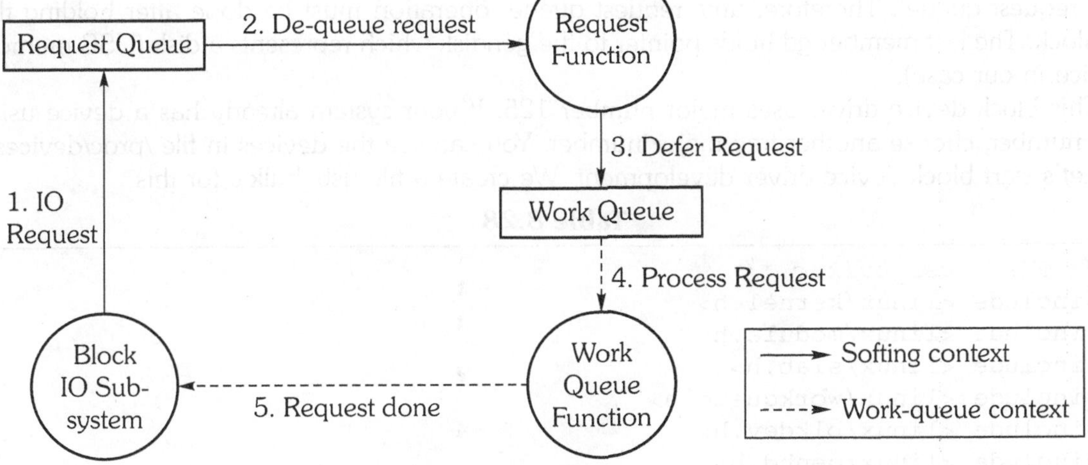

Figure 8.15

As shown in the diagram, the 'request function' only removes the request from 'request queue' and defers its execution by posting it to a work queue. Therefore, the 'request function' returns immediately meeting softirq requirement. At later point of time, kernel invokes the 'work queue function' which does real processing of the request. Since work queue functions are allowed to sleep, USB driver functions like usbdev_send_read_10 and usbdev_send_write_10 can be invoked from work queue function context.

Let's start block device driver development by defining a private data structure for the driver and another structure to defer the request to work-queue.

Table 8.27

```
/* FILE: usb_bulk.h */
#ifndef __USB_BULK_H__
define __USB_BULK_H__
#include <linux/spinlock.h>
#include <linux/workqueue.h>
#define DEVICE_NAME "USB_CARD_READER"
#define MAJOR_NR 125
struct blkdev_private {
        struct workqueue_struct *usbdevQ;
        spinlock_t lock;
        struct request_queue *queue;
        struct gendisk *gd;
};
struct usbdev_work {
        struct work_struct work;
        struct request *req;
};
#endif
```

The usbdevQ member in blkdev_private structure holds pointer to the 'work queue' which driver will use to defer IO requests. The queue member holds pointer to the 'request queue'. The lock spinlock is used to protect race conditions while adding and removing IO requests from the 'request queue'. Therefore, any 'request queue' operation must be done after holding this spinlock. The last member gd holds pointer to the gendisk which represents a disk (USB memory device in our case).

This block device driver uses major number 125. If your system already has a device using this number, choose another free major number. You can see the devices in file /proc/devices.

Let's start block device driver development. We create a file usb_bulk.c for this.

Table 8.28

```
/* FILE: usb_bulk.c */
#include <linux/kernel.h>
#include <linux/module.h>
#include <linux/slab.h>
#include <linux/workqueue.h>
#include <linux/blkdev.h>
#include <linux/genhd.h>
#include "usb_core.h"
#include "usb_bulk.h"
static int blkdev_open(struct inode *inode, struct file *filep)
{
        TRACE("blkdev_open called\n");
        return 0;
}
static int blkdev_release(struct inode *inode, struct file *filep)
{
        TRACE("blkdev_release called\n");
        return 0;
}
static struct block_device_operations blkdev_ops =
{
        owner: THIS_MODULE,
        open: blkdev_open,
        release: blkdev_release
};
static struct blkdev_private *p_blkdev = NULL;
int init_usb_bulk(unsigned int capacity)
{
        struct gendisk *usb_disk = NULL;
        p_blkdev = kmalloc(sizeof(struct blkdev_private), GFP_KERNEL);
        if(!p_blkdev) {
              printk("ENOMEM in %s at %d\n", __FUNCTION__, __LINE__);
              return 0;
        }
        memset(p_blkdev, 0, sizeof(struct blkdev_private));
        p_blkdev->usbdevQ = create_workqueue("usbdevQ");
        if(!p_blkdev->usbdevQ) {
              printk("create work queue failed\n");
```

```
        goto err;
    }
    spin_lock_init(&p_blkdev->lock);
    p_blkdev->queue = blk_init_queue(
                    usbdev_request, &p_blkdev->lock);
    usb_disk = p_blkdev->gd = alloc_disk(2);
    if(!usb_disk)
        goto err2;
    usb_disk->major = MAJOR_NR;
    usb_disk->first_minor = 0;
    usb_disk->fops = &blkdev_ops;
    usb_disk->queue = p_blkdev->queue;
    usb_disk->private_data = p_blkdev;
    strcpy(usb_disk->disk_name, DEVICE_NAME);
    set_capacity(usb_disk, capacity);
    add_disk(usb_disk);
    LOG_MSG("registered block device\n");
    return 0;
err2:
    destroy_workqueue(p_blkdev->usbdevQ);
err:
    kfree(p_blkdev);
    LOG_MSG("could not register block device\n");
    return 0;
}
void cleanup_usb_bulk(void)
{
    struct gendisk *usb_disk = p_blkdev->gd;
    del_gendisk(usb_disk);
    blk_cleanup_queue(p_blkdev->queue);
    destroy_workqueue(p_blkdev->usbdevQ);
    kfree(p_blkdev);
    return;
}
```

Above code listing shows some functions for block device driver. Let's start with block device initialization function init_usb_bulk. The function details are as follows:

1. Allocates memory for blkdev_private structure.
2. Creates a work queue using create_workqueue kernel function.
3. Initializes 'request queue' spinlock lock. As mentioned earlier, this lock must be held before doing any operation on the 'request queue'.
4. Creates a 'request queue' using blk_init_queue kernel function. This function takes two parameters. The first parameter is 'request function' which shall be invoked whenever any IO request is pending on the 'request queue'. The second parameter is request queue lock which must be held while operating on the request queue.
5. Allocates a gendisk using alloc_disk kernel function. This function takes one parameter which specifies minor numbers supported by the device. Roughly, this means number of

partitions supported by the device. Since most OS uses USB memory devices as partitioned devices, you must specify at least 2.

6. Assigns major number to the gendisk structure.
7. Assigns first minor number to the gendisk. Therefore, this driver shall support minor number starting from first minor number to first minor number plus alloc_disk parameter.
8. Assigns block_device_operations to gendisk. The block_device_operations structure contains operation which can be performed directly on block device. In this simple block driver, we only use open and release member and define dummy functions blkdev_open and blkdev_release respectively. It is worth mentioning that data read and write to the block device is done through 'request queue' and 'request function', still there are some applications (for example fdisk, mkfs.XX, mount, umount etc) which uses open and release functions of block device directly.
9. Assigns 'request queue' pointer and private data and disk_name to gendisk.
10. Sets block device capacity. As we saw during USB driver development, this value is retrieved by usbdev_read_capacity function, and is stored in capacity member of usbdev_private structure. We shall use that retrieved value here.
11. Registers the disk with kernel using add_disk function. It must be noted, that the block device must be completely ready before calling add_disk function because many data read calls shall be made as soon as add_disk is called (Infact even before add_disk returns). Note that we are yet to invoke function init_usb_bulk from main execution usbdev_probe function, which we'll do after defining 'request function'.

The cleanup_usb_bulk frees everything allocated in init_usb_bulk function.

Let's implement usbdev_request which we used in blk_init_queue as 'request function'.

Table 8.29

```
/* FILE: usb_bulk.c */
void usbdev_request(request_queue_t *q)
{
        struct request *req;
        struct usbdev_work *usb_work = NULL;
        while((req = elv_next_request(q)) != NULL)
        {
              if(! blk_fs_request(req)) {
                    end_request(req, 0);
                    continue;
              }
              usb_work = kmalloc(
                          sizeof(struct usbdev_work), GFP_ATOMIC);
              if(!usb_work) {
                    printk("Memory allocation failed\n");
                    end_request(req, 0);
                    continue;
              }
              LOG_MSG("deferring req=%p\n", req);
              usb_work->req = req;
              INIT_WORK(&usb_work->work, do_usbdev_data_transfer);
              queue_work(p_blkdev->usbdevQ, &usb_work->work);
```

```
            blkdev_dequeue_request(req);
        }
        return;
}
```

As we discussed in block device driver design, this function has responsibility of removing IO request from the 'request queue' and offload it to the work queue. The details of this function are as follows:

1. It gets IO request from 'request queue' using elv_next_request function (more about this function later).
   Note: The elv_next_request only returns pointer to next IO request on the queue. It does not remove it from 'request queue'.
2. It checks if the request is a file system request using blk_fs_request. If it is not a file system request, the driver signals request completion by calling end_request function with second parameter as 0 which means failure.
   Note: Call to end_request function can be mapped to step 5 in Figure 8.15 (block device driver design diagram). The end_request function also removes the IO request from 'request queue'.
3. It allocates a usbdev_work structure to pass the request to work queue.
   Note: The memory allocation flag is GFP_ATOMIC because 'request function' is called in softirq context.
4. Embeds current IO request 'req' in usbdev_work structure.
5. Initializes work structure. The second parameter to INIT_WORK is the 'work queue function' which shall be invoked to complete the deferred work.
6. Queues it to block device driver's work queue.
7. Removes the IO request from 'request queue' using blkdev_dequeue_request function.

Note: It should be noted that this function does many operations on 'request queue' without holding queue's lock. It is because Linux block IO sub-systems holds queue's lock before invoking 'request queue function'. Therefore, if you need to do something extra here, you must release the lock and reacquire before doing other operations on queue or before returning.

Next we implement the 'work queue function' which removes the request from work queue. This function removes the request, processes it and signals completion.

Table 8.30

```
/* FILE: usb_bulk.c */
void do_usbdev_data_transfer(struct work_struct *work)
{
        struct usbdev_work *usb_work;
        struct request *current_request;
        int sectors_xferred=1;
        unsigned long flags;
        usb_work = container_of(work, struct usbdev_work, work);
        current_request = usb_work->req;
        LOG_MSG("do_usbdev_data_transfer req = %p\n",
                current_request);
        sectors_xferred = __do_usbdev_data_transfer(current_request);
        spin_lock_irqsave(&p_blkdev->lock, flags);
```

```
        if(!end_that_request_first (
                                   current_request, 1, sectors_xferred))
        {
                LOG_MSG("req %p finished\n", current_request);
                end_that_request_last(current_request, 1);
        }
        spin_unlock_irqrestore(&p_blkdev->lock, flags);
        kfree(usb_work);
        return;}
```

Details of do_usbdev_data_transfer are as follows:

1. Retrieves usb_work pointer using container_of macro, and then retrieves the request pointer.
2. Invokes __do_usbdev_data_transfer which does actual request processing.
3. Signals request completion. Note that here we do not use end_request to signal request completion because end_request also removes the request from 'request queue'. But we have already removed the request from queue using blkdev_dequeue_request in usbdev_request function. Therefore, here we do all the things end_request does except removing the request from the queue. And as mentioned earlier, any operation on the 'request queue' must be done by holding request queue's lock.

Next we'll implement the __do_usbdev_data_transfer function which does actual processing to the IO requests. Before this, we need to understand the 'request queue' and IO request internals so that it would be easy to implement the request processing function.

The details of IO requests can be understood by following diagram.

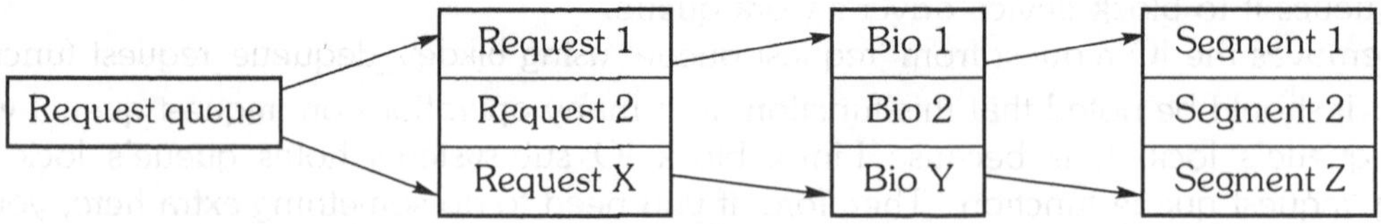

Figure 8.16

As shown in above diagram, every 'request queue' contains one or more IO requests. Every IO request contains one or more bio structures. Every bio structure contains one or more segments. Every segment corresponds to a page in physical memory (RAM) with an offset and length where data transfer shall take place.

Although each of them is maintained in linked lists, Linux kernel provides macros to iterate through these link lists. These macros increase code readability as well as ensure greater portability.

- To iterate through all requests in the 'request queue', we use elv_next_request function (Of course, as mentioned earlier, request must be removed by blkdev_dequeue_request function).
- To iterate through all bio(s) in the request, we use rq_for_each_bio macro. This macro takes two parameters. The first parameter is un-initialized pointer to bio structure. This parameter is assigned to the current bio while iterating. The second parameter is pointer to the request to be iterated.

- To iterate through all segments in the bio, we use bio_for_each_segment macro. This parameter takes three parameters. The first parameter is un-initialized pointer to bio_vec structure. The bio_vec structure represents a segment. This parameter shall be assigned to the current segment while iterating. The second parameter is pointer to the bio structure being iterated. The third parameter is an un-initialized integer which is assigned current segment number while iterating.

Equipped with this information, let's implement __do_usbdev_data_transfer function.

Table 8.31

```
/* FILE: usb_bulk.c */
int __do_usbdev_data_transfer(struct request *current_request)
{
        int result=-1, num_sect=0;
        unsigned int direction = rq_data_dir(current_request);
        struct bio *bio;
        rq_for_each_bio(bio, current_request)
        {
        int i;
        struct bio_vec *bvec;
        sector_t sector = bio->bi_sector;
        bio_for_each_segment(bvec, bio, i)
        {
            char *buffer = NULL;
            int total_len = bio_cur_sectors(bio)*USB_SECTOR_SIZE;
           unsigned char *tmp_buffer = kmalloc(total_len, GFP_ATOMIC);
            if(!tmp_buffer)
            {
                printk("buffer allocation failed\n");
                return 0;
            }
            if(direction == READ) {
                result = usbdev_send_read_10(
                                      sector, total_len, tmp_buffer);
                buffer = __bio_kmap_atomic(bio, i, KM_USER0);
                memcpy(buffer, tmp_buffer, total_len);
                __bio_kunmap_atomic(bio, KM_USER0);
            }
            if(direction == WRITE) {
                buffer = __bio_kmap_atomic(bio, i, KM_USER0);
                memcpy(tmp_buffer, buffer, total_len);
                __bio_kunmap_atomic(bio, KM_USER0);
                result = usbdev_send_write_10(
                                      sector, total_len, tmp_buffer);
            }
            kfree(tmp_buffer);
            if(result < 0) {
                LOG_MSG("USBDEV_SEND_%s_10 FAILED\n",
                direction == READ ? "READ":"WRITE");
```

```
            }
            else {
                LOG_MSG("USBDEV_SEND_%s_10 OK\n",
                direction == READ ? "READ":"WRITE");
            }
            sector += bio_cur_sectors(bio);
        }
        num_sect += bio->bi_size/USB_SECTOR_SIZE;
    }
    return num_sect;
}
```

The function details are as follows:

1. It retrieves data transfer direction using rq_data_dir macro.
2. Iterates through each bio structure in the request.
   Note: Further steps shall be executed for each bio.
3. Retrieves sector number for current bio.
4. Iterates through each segment in the bio structure.
   Note: Further steps shall be executed for each segment.
5. Determines data transfer length in total_len variable using macro bio_cur_sectors.
   Note: bio_cur_sectors returns data transfer length in terms of sectors. To convert it in number of bytes, we multiply it by USB_SECTOR_SIZE.
6. Depending upon data transfer direction, it invokes usbdev_send_read_10 or usbdev_send_write_10. However, it must be noted that in each of these function we do not pass page (corresponding to the segment) buffer. Because, it is possible that those pages have been swapped out of main memory (RAM) and therefore we may end up using pointer to the pages which are no longer in RAM. To make sure, those pages are in RAM, we invoke __bio_kmap_atomic function. However, sleep is not allowed between __bio_kmap_atomic and __bio_kunmap_atomic while both usbdev_send_read_10 and usbdev_send_write_10 do sleep. To get away from this problem, we do data transfer in a temporary buffer and then transfer data from temporary buffer to page buffer with __bio_kmap_atomic in force.
7. Increments sector number at the end of each bio_for_each_segment loop, so that next data transfer happens on next sector. The bio_for_each_segment loops terminates here.
8. Increments number of sectors transferred at the end of every rq_for_each_bio loop. The rq_for_each_bio loop terminates here.
9. Returns total number of sectors transferred.

This ends block device driver implementation. Let's modify functions usbdev_probe and usbdev_disconnect in usb_core.c to include block device driver code.

Table 8.32

```
/* FILE: usb_core.c */
static void usbdev_disconnect(struct usb_interface *interface)
{
        TRACE("usbdev_disconnect called\n");
```

```
        usb_put_dev(p_usb_dev_info->udev);
        cleanup_usb_bulk();
        return;
}
static int usbdev_probe(
        struct usb_interface *interface, const struct usb_device_id
        *id)
{
        /* Other initialization code */
        if(usbdev_read_capacity() < 0) {
              LOG_MSG("USB_READ_CAPACITY FAILED\n");
              usbdev_do_sense(TEST_UNIT_READY);
              return -1;
}
        else
              LOG_MSG("USB_READ_CAPACITY OK\n");
        init_usb_bulk(p_usb_dev_info->capacity);
        return 0;
}
```

We invoke init_usb_bulk from usbdev_probe to finally register the block device driver interface. Similarly, we invoke cleanup_usb_bulk from usbdev_disconnect to do cleanup job.

Finally let's modify the Makefile.

Table 8.33

```
KERNEL_DIR := /usr/src/linux-2.6.21.5
obj-m := usb.o
usb-objs := usb_core.o usb_transport.o usb_debug.o usb_bulk.o
default:
        make -C $(KERNEL_DIR) SUBDIRS='pwd' modules
clean:
        make -C $(KERNEL_DIR) SUBDIRS='pwd' clean
```

Recompile the USB driver and insert it. Assuming the USB memory device has been already in use on Windows or Linux (or any OS), the device has file system and data already. Let's create device nodes and mount the file system as follows.

Table 8.34

```
root@localhost# insmod usb.ko
root@localhost# mknod /dev/my_usb  b 125 0
root@localhost# mknod /dev/my_usb1  b 125 1
root@localhost# mount -t vfat /dev/my_usb1 /mnt
```

Note that, we create two devices with same major number but different minor number. The minor number match to what we specified during init_usb_bulk

For mounting the file system, following assumptions are made.

- USB memory device is using VFAT file system. All OS uses this file system for USB device by default unless created another file system exclusively. If the USB memory device is using some other file system, specify that file system with –t option.

- The USB memory device is a partitioned device. All OS generally partition the USB memory devices. However, if your device is not partitioned, use /dev/my_usb instead of /dev/my_usb1
- The mount point /mnt exists. If you already have data in /mnt directory, those data will be hidden after mount operation and will show contents of USB memory device. The original contents shall be visible after you umount the /dev/my_usb1.

To remove USB driver from kernel, use following commands (make sure no application is using /mnt directory otherwise umount will fail).

Table 8.35

```
root@localhost# umount /mnt
root@localhost# rmmod usb
```

After mounting the USB device, you must be able to see the file listed in /mnt directory. Of course, you can read and write files to /mnt directory which in-effect reads and writers to USB memory device.

This completes USB mass storage block device driver development. Happy hacking!

8.12 TROUBLESHOOTING

The real block device drivers and USB drivers are much more complex than the one we developed. Moreover, the devices are even more complex. The driver developed in this chapter implements basic features and does not do a very good error handling, therefore you may face problems. But don't worry, they are solvable. Remember, some very high grade device drivers are already running in Linux kernel for all such devices.

8.12.1 REQUEST SENSE Command

USB devices support one ATAPI command REQUEST SENSE. Host computers can use this command to retrieve sense data from USB devise. The sense data contains error condition information. Therefore, this command is send to the USB device whenever any error occurs.

The REQUEST SENSE command has following message format.

Byte \ Bit	7	6	5	4	3	2	1	0
0	Operation code (0x03)							
1	LUN			Reserved (0)				
2	Reserved (0)							
3	Reserved (0)							
4	Allocation length							
5-11	Reserved (0)							

Figure 8.17

The REQUEST SENSE response has following message format.

Byte \ Bit	7	6	5	4	3	2	1	0
0	Valid	Error code (0x70)						
1	Reserved							
2	Vender specific			Reserved		Sense key		
3-6	Information (Vendor specific)							
7	Additional sense length							
8-11	Vender specific							
12	Additional sense code							
13	Additional sense code qualifier							
14	Field replaceable unit							
15-17	SKSV	Sense key specific						
18...	Additional sense bytes							

Figure 8.18

Out of this response message, the Sense key, Additional sense code (ASC) and Additional sense code qualifier (ASCQ) are useful in debugging USB device state. The following table shows different combinations of above parameters and their meaning. Values in table are in hexadecimal format.

Table 8.36

Sense key	ASC	ASCQ	Error description
01	17	01	Recovered data with retries
01	18	00	Recovered data with ECC
02	3A	00	Medium not present
02	04	01	Logical drive not ready - becoming ready
02	04	04	Logical drive not ready - format in progress
02	06	00	No reference position found
03	02	00	No seek complete
03	03	00	Write fault
03	10	00	ID CRC error
03	11	00	Un-recovered read error
03	12	00	Address mask not found for ID field
03	14	00	Recorded entity not found
03	30	00	Incompatible medium installed

03	30	01	Cannot read medium – unknown format
03	30	02	Cannot read medium – incompatible format
03	31	01	Format command failed
05	20	00	Invalid command operation code
05	21	00	Logical block address out of range
05	24	00	Invalid field in command packet
05	25	00	Logical unit not supported
05	26	00	Invalid field in parameter list
05	53	02	Medium removal prevented
06	28	00	Not ready to ready transition – media changed
06	29	00	Power on reset or bus device reset occurred
07	27	00	Write protected media
0B	4E	00	Overlapped command attempted

8.12.2 USBMON

Linux kernel has an inbuilt USB monitor USBMON which can be used to monitor messages flowing between host computer and USB device just like the tcpdump for capturing packets on network. As mentioned in setup section earlier, to use this feature, you must have USBMON enabled in your kernel.

Use following commands to prepare USBMON.

Table 8.37

```
root@localhost# mount -t debugfs / /sys/kernel/debug
root@localhost# cd /sys/kernel/debug/usbmon
root@localhost# ls
0s  0t  1s  1t  2s  2t  3s  3t  4s  4t
root@localhost# cat 4t
```

There are two files "s" and "t" for each USB bus. If your device is on bus 4, you should check for 4s and 4t. The 'cat 4t' command shall continue to display all messages being exchanged between host computer and USB device. Command 'lsusb' can be used to check which bus the device is attached to.

Files 0s and 0t represents wildcard *i.e.,* 'cat 0t' shall display USB messages being exchanged on all buses. The message display is in a very raw format as of now. Refer to Documentation/usb/usbmon.txt for decoding message formats.

8.13 SUMMARY

Mass storage drivers' performance is a very crucial aspect of entire system performance. Although this driver does design does not care much about performance for sake of brevity and simplicity; a commercial driver must always take care of. For example, it would always be suitable to implement this driver using tasklet in place of work queue but then the design must be modified because tasklet are not allowed to sleep.

8.14 ASSIGNMENTS

1. Implement REQUEST SENSE command.
2. Submit URB with a time limit *i.e.,* if a URB completion is not done in certain time limit cancel the URB.
   Hint: Use *usb_kill_urb* or *usb_unlink_urb* functions.
3. This driver has a constraint that USB device must be connected before inserting module. Fix this constraint.
   Hint: Implement media revalidation function.
4. Upgrade this driver for USB multiple card readers.
   Hint: Treat each LUN as separate device.

8.15 REFERENCES

- Linux documentation
- USB specification

9 PCI Based Network Device Driver

In this chapter, we develop a PCI based network device driver. The PCI part of this driver can be used for any PCI based device, while the network part of this driver can be used for any other network card (NIC). This chapter assumes reader's familiarity with chapter "LINUX NETWORKING SUBSYSTEM".

Unlike USB and UART, the NICs do not have a well defined interface or protocol. Every NIC has its own register set; therefore it is essential to have NIC specification (also referred as datasheet) available for driver development. This chapter chooses Realtek™ 8139 (also referred as RTL8139™) as the development device. The specification for this device can be obtained from

- http://www.realtek.com.tw/
- http://www.alldatasheet.com/datasheet-pdf/pdf/84677/ETC/RTL8139.html

This chapter has been divided in following sections:

- Setting up kernel
- Detecting a PCI device
- Understanding the PCI configuration space
- Accessing a PCI device
- Initializing net_device
- Understanding RealTek8139's transmission mechanism
- Making the device ready to transmit packets
- Understanding RealTek8139's receiving mechanism
- Making the device ready to receive packets

9.1 SETTING UP THE KERNEL

Linux kernel has device driver for RTL8139 from very long time, and therefore you are likely to have the driver in your kernel too. To insert your driver safely, you must first remove the existing driver in the kernel.

Open your favorite kernel configuration tool, and make sure .config has following configuration:

Table 9.1

```
# CONFIG_8139CP is not set
# CONFIG_8139TOO is not set
```

9.2 DETECTING A PCI DEVICE

New kernels support probe based device detection. This means, every PCI device driver registers the kinds of devices it supports with the kernel. If any of those devices is present, kernel invokes probe function of the device driver.

Table 9.2 illustrates a simple kernel module to detect a PCI device.

Table 9.2

```
/* rtl8139.c */
#include <linux/module.h>
#include <linux/pci.h>
#define DRIVER "rtl8139"
static int rtl8139_probe(struct pci_dev *pdev, const struct
pci_device_id *ent)
{
        printk("rtl8139_probe invoked\n");
        return 0;
}
static void rtl8139_remove(struct pci_dev *pdev)
{
        printk("rtl8139_remove invoked\n");
}
#define RTL_VENDER_ID  0x10EC
#define RTL_DEVICE_ID  0x8139
static struct pci_device_id rtl8139_table[] = {
{RTL_VENDER_ID, RTL_DEVICE_ID, PCI_ANY_ID, PCI_ANY_ID, 0,0,0},
{0}
};
static struct pci_driver rtl8139_driver ={
        .name = RTL_DRIVER,
        .id_table = rtl8139_table,
        .probe = rtl8139_probe,
        .remove = rtl8139_remove
};
int init_module(void)
{
        int ret;
        ret = pci_register_driver(&rtl8139_driver);
        if(ret < 0)
              printk("could not register pci driver\n");
        else
              printk("Registered PCI driver\n");
        return 0;
}
```

```
void cleanup_module(void)
{
        pci_unregister_driver(&rtl8139_driver);
        return;
}
MODULE_LICENSE("GPL");
```

The structure pci_driver is used to hold probe and remove functions of devices listed in id_table. The id_table has following format:

Table 9.3

```
struct pci_device_id {
    __u32 vendor, device;
                        /* Vendor and device ID or PCI_ANY_ID*/
    __u32 subvendor, subdevice;
                        /* Subsystem ID's or PCI_ANY_ID */
    __u32 class, class_mask;
                        /* (class,subclass,prog-if) triplet */
    kernel_ulong_t driver_data;
                        /* Data private to the driver */
};
```

Every PCI vendor and every device from each vendor has can be uniquely identified by the vendor id and device id. The list is available at http://www.pcidatabase.com/. The vendor and device members of id_table must be initialized to corresponding vendor and device. For RTL8139 case, these values are 0x10EC and 0x8139 respectively. The subvendor and subdevice members can be initialized to generic value PCI_ANY_ID. Rest of the members can be initialized to NULL. Last entry of id_table must always be NULL.

Therefore the pci_driver structure holds information about all the devices it supports, and probe and remove function for those devices. The kernel will call these functions when one of the supported devices is found on the PCI bus.

Function pci_register_driver is used for introducing the device driver capabilities to the kernel. Similarly, pci_unregister_driver is used to remove the driver from kernel. Let's use following Makefile to compile this driver.

Table 9.4

```
KTREE := /usr/src/linux-2.6.21.5m
obj-m := rtl8139.o
default:
        make -C $(KTREE) SUBDIRS='pwd' modules
clean:
        make -C $(KTREE) SUBDIRS='pwd' clean
```

If you have a RTL8139 NIC plugged into your system; you will see rtl8139_probe being invoked when you insert above driver.

Old PCI drivers did not use probe method but used pci_find_device function themselves to discover the device they support. However, this old method is deprecated now and you should not use this in new drivers. Table 9-5 illustrates how old PCI drivers discovered the device:

Table 9.5

```
#include <linux/module.h>
#include <linux/stddef.h>
#include <linux/pci.h>
int init_module(void)
{
    struct pci_dev *pdev;
    pdev = pci_find_device(RTL_VENDER_ID, RTL_DEVICE_ID, NULL);
    if(!pdev)
        printk("Device not found\n");
    else
        printk("Device found\n");
    return 0;
}
```

The third parameter in pci_device_function can point to previous PCI device found in search. If it is new search, it must be NULL.

9.3 UNDERSTANDING PCI CONFIGURATION SPACE

Although different NIC from different vendors have different set of registers, yet every PCI compliant device has a certain common registers, called PCI configuration space. PCI configuration space is 256 byte long. Out of this 256 bytes space, first 64 bytes space is standardized while rest is device dependent. Figure 9.1 illustrates the first 64 byte space.

Offset				
0x00	Vendor ID		Device ID	
0x04	Command register		Status register	
0x08	Revision ID	Class code		
0x0c	Cache line	Latency timer	Header type	BIST
0x10	Base address register 0			
0x14	Base address register 1			
0x18	Base address register 2			
0x1c	Base address register 3			
0x20	Base address register 4			
0x24	Base address register 5			
0x28	CardBus CIS pointer			
0x2c	Sub-system vendor ID		Sub-system device ID	
0x30	Expansion ROM base address			
0x34	Cap pointer	Reserved		
0x38	Reserved			
0x3c	IRQ Line	IRQ Pin	Min. Gnt	Max. Latency

Figure 9.1. PCI Configuration Space

The Vendor ID and Device ID are two bytes registers which hold unique identification values of the device. The Base Address Registers (also known as BAR) contain addresses assigned to the device (described shortly in detail).

It must be noted that PCI specification follows little endian format. Therefore, while writing registers of size two bytes or more, you must write in little endian format.

9.4 ACCESSING THE PCI DEVICE

At system boot time, a PCI device is inactive and it can not function. The PCI initialization code (which can be either in BIOS or in kernel initialization part) enumerates all PCI devices present in system *i.e.,* every PCI devices' geographical information is found (bus number, slot number etc). Based on the geographical information, every device is assigned an address. These addresses are written in BAR.

The address can be either in I/O mapped space or can be in memory mapped space. I/O mapped address must be written only in I/O BAR, and memory mapped must be written only in memory BAR. To determine type of BAR, PCI initialization code reads 0th bit of each BAR. If the bit is 0 the BAR is memory type else it is I/O type. Then PCI initialization code writes I/O and memory mapped addresses to corresponding BAR. Later device drivers can read these registers and access the device on those addresses.

If you see, RealTek8139 specifications, you will find that the first BAR (numbered as 0) is I/OAR, while second BAR (numbered as 1) is MEMAR.

9.5 INITIALIZING NET-DEVICE

Now let's use PCI functions to initialize the PCI NIC. A network device is represented by net_device structure. To access the network device, we must have PCI addresses described previously mapped to memory space.

Now it's time to revert back to driver development. Before that I remind you about the priv field of the structure net_device. We will declare a structure which holds private data to our device and that structure shall be pointed to by member priv. The structure has the following members (We will update structure members as we progress).

Table 9.6

```
struct rtl8139_private
{
        struct pci_dev *pci_dev;  /* PCI device */
        void *mmio_addr; /* memory mapped IO addr */
        unsigned long regs_len; /* length of IO or MMIO region */
        struct net_device_stats stats;
};
```

Next we develop two functions for allocating and initializing net_device, and for initializing PCI related part of the net_device. Table 9.7 illustrates function rtl8139_init function which allocates memory for global pointer rtl8139_dev, which we shall be using as net_device. Additionally, this function sets the member pci_dev of rtl8139_private to the detected device.

Table 9.7

```
static int rtl8139_init(struct pci_dev *pdev, struct net_device
 **dev_out)
```

```
{
        struct net_device *dev;
        struct rtl8139_private *priv;
        /*
         * alloc_etherdev allocates memory for dev and dev->priv.
         * dev->priv shall have sizeof(struct rtl8139_private) memory
         * allocated.
         */
        dev = alloc_etherdev(sizeof(struct rtl8139_private));
        if(!dev) {
              LOG_MSG("Could not allocate etherdev\n");
              return -1;
        }
        priv = dev->priv;
        priv->pci_dev = pdev;
        *dev_out = dev;
        return 0;
}
```

Table 9.8 illustrates function rtl8139_pci_init which does PCI related initialization.

Table 9.8

```
static int rtl8139_pci_init(struct pci_dev *pdev)
{
        unsigned long mmio_start, mmio_end, mmio_len, mmio_flags;
        void *ioaddr;
        struct rtl8139_private *priv = rtl8139_dev->priv;
        if(pci_enable_device(pdev)) {
              LOG_MSG("Could not enable the device\n");
              return -1;
        }
        else
              LOG_MSG("Device enabled\n");
        /* get PCI memory mapped I/O space base address from BAR1 */
        mmio_start = pci_resource_start(pdev, 1);
        mmio_end = pci_resource_end(pdev, 1);
        mmio_len = pci_resource_len(pdev, 1);
        mmio_flags = pci_resource_flags(pdev, 1);
        /* make sure above region is MMIO region */
        if(!(mmio_flags & IORESOURCE_MEM)) {
              LOG_MSG("region not MMIO region\n");
              goto cleanup1;
        }
        /* get PCI memory space */
        if(pci_request_regions(pdev, DRIVER)) {
              LOG_MSG("Could not get PCI region\n");
              goto cleanup1;
}
```

```
        pci_set_master(pdev);
        /* ioremap MMIO region */
        ioaddr = ioremap(mmio_start, mmio_len);
        if(!ioaddr) {
              LOG_MSG("Could not ioremap\n");
              goto cleanup2;
        }
        rtl8139_dev->base_addr = (long)ioaddr;
        priv->mmio_addr = ioaddr;
        priv->regs_len = mmio_len;
        return 0;
cleanup2:
        pci_release_regions(priv->pci_dev);
cleanup1:
        free_netdev(rtl8139_dev);
        pci_disable_device(priv->pci_dev);
        return -1;
}
```

Function rtl8139_pci_init's objective is to get the base_addr field of the net_device. This is the starting memory location of device registers. This driver has been written for memory-mapped I/O only. To get the memory-mapped I/O base address, we use PCI APIs like pci_resource_start, pci_resource_end, pci_resource_len, pci_resource_flags etc. These APIs let us read the PCI configuration space without knowing internal details. The second argument to these APIs is the BAR number. As mentioned earlier, RTL8139 has first BAR (numbered as 0) as I/OAR; while second BAR (numbered as 1) as MEMAR. Since this driver is using memory-mapped I/O, we pass the second argument as 1. Before accessing the addresses returned by the above APIs, we have to do two things. First is to reserve the above resources (memory space) by driver; this is done by calling the function pci_request_regions. This will make sure that no other device driver is allowed to access this region until our driver frees it. The second thing is to remap I/O addresses, because the address returned by pci_resource_start is bus address. To map this bus address into CPU space, we need to call ioremap function. The remapped io_addr is assigned to the base_addr member of the net_device, and this is the point where we can start to read/write the device registers.

With help of these two functions and some dummy functions, we complete rtl8139_probe function. Table 9.9 illustrates modified rtl8139_probe function.

Table 9.9

```
static struct net_device *rtl8139_dev;
static int rtl8139_start_xmit(struct sk_buff *skb, struct net_device
*dev)
{
        LOG_MSG("rtl8139_start_xmit is called\n");
        return 0;
}
static int rtl8139_open(struct net_device *dev)
{
        LOG_MSG("rtl8139_open is called\n");
```

```
        return 0;
}
int rtl8139_stop(struct net_device *dev)
{
        LOG_MSG("rtl8139_open is called\n");
        return 0;
}
static struct net_device_stats* rtl8139_get_stats(struct net_device
*dev)
{
        struct rtl8139_private *priv = dev->priv;
        LOG_MSG("ENTER: %s\n", __FUNCTION__);
        return &(priv->stats);
}
static int rtl8139_probe(struct pci_dev *pdev, const struct
pci_device_id *ent)
{
        struct rtl8139_private *priv;
        int i;
        printk("%s\n", __FUNCTION__);
        if(rtl8139_init(pdev, &rtl8139_dev)) {
              LOG_MSG("Could not initialize device\n");
              return -1;
}
        priv = rtl8139_dev->priv; /* rtl8139 private information */
        rtl8139_pci_init(pdev);
        /* UPDATE NET_DEVICE */
        for(i = 0; i < 6; i++) {  /* Hardware Address */
              rtl8139_dev->dev_addr[i] = readb((void*)(rtl8139_dev-
>base_addr+i));
              rtl8139_dev->broadcast[i] = 0xff;
}
        rtl8139_dev->hard_header_len = 14;
        memcpy(rtl8139_dev->name, DRIVER, sizeof(DRIVER)); /* Device
Name */
        rtl8139_dev->irq = pdev->irq;  /* Interrupt Number */
        rtl8139_dev->open = rtl8139_open;
        rtl8139_dev->stop = rtl8139_stop;
        rtl8139_dev->hard_start_xmit = rtl8139_start_xmit;
        rtl8139_dev->get_stats = rtl8139_get_stats;
        /* register the device */
        if(register_netdev(rtl8139_dev)) {
              LOG_MSG("Could not register netdevice\n");
              iounmap(priv->mmio_addr);
              pci_release_regions(priv->pci_dev);
              free_netdev(rtl8139_dev);
              pci_disable_device(priv->pci_dev);
        }
```

```
        return 0;
}
static void rtl8139_remove(struct pci_dev *pdev)
{
        struct rtl8139_private *priv;
        printk("%s\n", __FUNCTION__);
        priv = rtl8139_dev->priv;
        iounmap(priv->mmio_addr);
        pci_release_regions(priv->pci_dev);
        unregister_netdev(rtl8139_dev);
        pci_disable_device(priv->pci_dev);
        return;
}
```

As shown above, rtl8139_probe does device initializing using rtl8139_init and rtl8139_pci_init function. Then it reads device hardware address (also called MAC address) and assign to dev_addr member of net_device. If you see "Register Descriptions" in RealTek8139 specification, the first 6 bytes are the hardware address of the device. Finally this function assigns all required net_device functions although most of them are dummy functions.

Now we have a dummy or template driver ready. Compile the module and insert it. Now execute a series of commands; "*ifconfig*", "*ifconfig - a*", "*ifconfig rtl8139 up*", "*ifconfig*" and "*ifconfig rtl8139 down*", and observe their output. These debug logs show you when each function is called. If everything goes fine, you should see device rtl8139 when you issue "ifconfig - a" and should get message "function rtl8139_get_stat" called. You should get message "function rtl8139_open called" when you issue command "ifconfig rtl8139 up". Similarly you should get "function rtl8139_stop called" when you issue command "ifconfig rtl8139 down".

Although we have registered a network device with the kernel, the device can neither transmit nor receive packets, since we have not defined those functions. Every NIC has proprietary mechanism for transmitting and receiving packets. Therefore, we must first understand those mechanisms for writing functions.

9.6 UNDERSTANDING REALTEK8139'S TRANSMISSION MECHANISM

In this section, I describe RealTek8139 transmission mechanism; however, I recommend to download "RTL8139 (A/B) Programming Guide", which provides exact details. RealTek8139 has 4 Transmission Descriptors; each descriptor has a fixed I/O address offset. The 4 descriptors are used in round-robin order. This means that for transmitting four packets, the driver will use descriptor 0, descriptor 1, descriptor 2 and descriptor 3 in round-robin order. For transmitting next packet, driver will use descriptor 0 again (provided that is available). If you read the RealTek8139 specification, the section "Register Description" has TSAD0, TSAD1, TSAD2 and TSAD3 registers at offset 0x20, 0x24, 0x28, 0x2C, respectively. These registers store "Transmit Start Address of Descriptors" *i.e.*, they store starting address (in memory) of packets to be transmitted. Later RTL8139 reads packet contents from these addresses, DMA to its own FIFO, and transmits on wire.

Packet transmission involves one more register TSD (Transmission Status Descriptor). There is one TSD for each TSAD. After writing packet's memory address in TSAD, driver writes instruction in TSD register to start transmission. As soon as TSD in written (RTL8139 is instructed), NIC starts packet transmission. We will shortly see that this driver allocates DMAable memory for packet contents, and stores the address of that memory in TSAD registers.

9.7 MAKING THE DEVICE READY TO TRANSMIT PACKETS

In this section, we discuss driver source used to make the device ready for transmission. We defer discussion of the receiving source to further sections. We will discuss functions rtl8139_open and rtl8139_stop, in this section. Before that, we enhance our rtl8139_private structure, to accommodate members to hold data related to packet transmission.

Table 9.10

```
#define NUM_TX_DESC 4
struct rtl8139_private
{
        struct pci_dev *pci_dev;  /* PCI device */
        void *mmio_addr; /* memory mapped I/O addr */
        unsigned long regs_len; /* length of I/O or MMI/O region */
        struct net_device_stats stats;
        unsigned int tx_flag;
        unsigned int cur_tx;
        unsigned int dirty_tx;
        unsigned char *tx_buf[NUM_TX_DESC];    /* Tx bounce buffers */
        unsigned char *tx_bufs;        /* Tx bounce buffer region. */
        dma_addr_t tx_bufs_dma;
};
```

Member tx_flag shall contain transmission flags to notify the device about some parameters described shortly. Field cur_tx shall hold current transmission descriptor, while dirty_tx denotes the first of transmission descriptors, which have not completed transmission. (This also means that, we can't use dirty descriptor for further packet transmission until previous packet is transmitted completely.) Array tx_buf holds addresses of 4 “transmission descriptors”. Field tx_bufs is also used in same context, as we will see shortly. Both tx_buf and tx_bufs do hold kernel virtual address, which can be used by the driver, but the device cannot use these addresses. The device need to access physical addresses, which are stored in field tx_bufs_dma.

Next comes, the RTL8139 registers which will be needed to operate the NIC. Here is a list of register offsets, used in code. You can get more details about these values from the RealTek8139 specifications. Table 9.11 illustrated below is nothing but RTL8139 specifications.

Table 9.11

```
#define TX_BUF_SIZE  1536  /* should be at least MTU + 14 + 4 */
#define TOTAL_TX_BUF_SIZE  (TX_BUF_SIZE * NUM_TX_SIZE)
/* 8139 register offsets */
#define TSD0     0x10
#define TSAD0    0x20
#define RBSTART  0x30
#define CR       0x37
#define CAPR     0x38
#define IMR      0x3c
#define ISR      0x3e
```

```
#define TCR                 0x40
#define RCR                 0x44
#define MPC                 0x4c
#define MULINT              0x5c
/* TSD register commands */
#define TxHostOwns          0x2000
#define TxUnderrun          0x4000
#define TxStatOK            0x8000
#define TxOutOfWindow       0x20000000
#define TxAborted           0x40000000
#define TxCarrierLost       0x80000000
/* CR register commands */
#define RxBufEmpty          0x01
#define CmdTxEnb            0x04
#define CmdRxEnb            0x08
#define CmdReset            0x10
/* ISR Bits */
#define RxOK                0x01
#define RxErr               0x02
#define TxOK                0x04
#define TxErr               0x08
#define RxOverFlow          0x10
#define RxUnderrun          0x20
#define RxFIFOOver          0x40
#define CableLen            0x2000
#define TimeOut             0x4000
#define SysErr              0x8000
#define INT_MASK (RxOK | RxErr | TxOK | TxErr | \
               RxOverFlow | RxUnderrun | RxFIFOOver | \
               CableLen | TimeOut | SysErr)
```

As you observed before, when a network device is brought up (ifconfig up); kernel calls open function of the device; rtl8139_open in this case. This function has responsibility to allocate necessary resources required for device operation. Similarly rtl8139_stop function has responsibility of freeing those resources when device is brought down (ifconfig down).

Table 9.12 illustrates modified rtl8139_open function to allocate such resources.

Table 9.12

```
static int rtl8139_open(struct net_device *dev)
{
        int retval;
        struct rtl8139_private *priv = dev->priv;
        LOG_MSG("ENTER: %s\n", __FUNCTION__);
        /* get the IRQ
         * second arg is interrupt handler
         * third is flags, 0 means no IRQ sharing
         */
        retval = request_irq(
```

```
                  dev->irq, rtl8139_interrupt, 0, dev->name, dev);
        if(retval)
              return retval;
        /* get memory for Tx buffers
         * memory must be DMA`ble
         */
        priv->tx_bufs = pci_alloc_consistent(
              priv->pci_dev, TOTAL_TX_BUF_SIZE, &priv-
>tx_bufs_dma);
        if(!priv->tx_bufs) {
              free_irq(dev->irq, dev);
              return -ENOMEM;
}
        priv->tx_flag = 0;
        rtl8139_init_ring(dev);
        rtl8139_hw_start(dev);
        return 0;
}
static void rtl8139_init_ring (struct net_device *dev)
{
        struct rtl8139_private *priv = dev->priv;
        int i;
        priv->cur_tx = 0;
        priv->dirty_tx = 0;
        for (i = 0; i < NUM_TX_DESC; i++)
              priv->tx_buf[i] = & priv->tx_bufs[i * TX_BUF_SIZE];
        return;
}
static void rtl8139_hw_start (struct net_device *dev)
{
        struct rtl8139_private *priv = dev->priv;
        void *ioaddr = priv->mmio_addr;
        u32 i;
        LOG_MSG("<1>rtl8139_hw_start called\n");
        rtl8139_chip_reset(ioaddr);
        /* Must enable Tx before setting transfer thresholds! */
        writeb(CmdTxEnb, ioaddr + CR);
        /* tx config */
        writel(0x00000600, ioaddr + TCR); /* DMA burst size 1024 */
        /* init Tx buffer DMA addresses */
        for (i = 0; i < NUM_TX_DESC; i++) {
              writel(priv->tx_bufs_dma + (priv->tx_buf[i] - priv-
>tx_bufs), ioaddr + TSAD0 + (i * 4));
        }
        /* initialise missed packet counter */
        writel(0, ioaddr + MPC);
        /* no early-rx interrupts */
        writew((readw(ioaddr + MULINT) & 0xF000), ioaddr + MULINT);
```

```
        /* Enable all known interrupts by setting the interrupt mask */
        writew(INT_MASK, ioaddr + IMR);
        netif_start_queue (dev);
        return;
}
```

The function rtl8139_open starts with requesting the IRQ by calling API request_irq. In this function, we register the interrupt handler rtl8139_interrupt. This function shall be called by kernel, whenever the device generates an interrupt. Now, we allocate memory, where outgoing packets reside before being sent on wire. Note that API pci_allocate_consistant returns kernel virtual address. The physical address is returned in third argument, which is later used by driver. Also observe that we have allocated memory needed for all four descriptors. Function rtl8139_init_ring distributes this memory to four descriptors. Here, we call function rtl8139_hw_start to make the device ready for transmitting packets. At first, we reset the device, so that device shall be in a predictable and known state. This is done by writing reset value (described in specification) in CR (Command Register). We wait until the written value is read back, which means device has reset. The next function, barrier ( ), is called to force the kernel to do required memory I/O immediately without doing any optimization. Once the device is reset, we enable transmission mode of the device by writing transmission enable value in CR. Next, we configure TCR (Transmission Configuration Register). The only thing we are specifying to TCR register is “Max DMA Burst Size per Tx DMA Burst”. The rest we leave at default values. (See specification for more details.) Now we write the DMAable address of all four descriptors to TSAD (Transmission Start Address Descriptor) registers. Next, we enable the interrupt, by writing in IMR (Interrupt Mask Register). This register lets us configure the interrupts; the device will be generating. Last, we call netif_start_queue to tell the kernel that device is ready. The only thing remaining is writing the rtl8139_interrupt function. For the time being, let’s skip this. At this time, the device is ready to send packets, but the function to send packets out is missing. (Remember hard_start_xmit.) So, let’s do it.

Table 9.13

```
static int rtl8139_start_xmit(struct sk_buff *skb, struct net_device
*dev)
{
        struct rtl8139_private *priv = dev->priv;
        void *ioaddr = priv->mmio_addr;
        unsigned int entry = priv->cur_tx;
        unsigned int len = skb->len;
        LOG_MSG("rtl8139_start_xmit called\n");
#define ETH_MIN_LEN 60  /* minimum ethernet frame size */
        if (len < TX_BUF_SIZE) {
              if(len < ETH_MIN_LEN)
                    memset(priv->tx_buf[entry], 0, ETH_MIN_LEN);
              skb_copy_and_csum_dev(skb, priv->tx_buf[entry]);
              dev_kfree_skb(skb);
} else {
              dev_kfree_skb(skb);
              LOG_MSG("packet dropped... length more than tx buf\n");
```

```
                return 0;
        }
        writel(priv->tx_flag | max(len, (unsigned int)ETH_MIN_LEN),
                        ioaddr + TSD0 + (entry * sizeof (u32)));
        entry++;
        priv->cur_tx = entry % NUM_TX_DESC;
        if(priv->cur_tx == priv->dirty_tx) {
                LOG_MSG("Current Tx queue overwriting dirty Tx
 queue\n");
                netif_stop_queue(dev);
        }
        return 0;
}
```

The function rtl8139_start_xmit, explained in Table 9.13, is very trivial. First, it finds the available transmission descriptor and then checks that the packet size is at least 60 bytes (as Ethernet packet size can't be less than 60 bytes). Once this is ensured, the function skb_copy_and_csum_dev is called, which copies the packet contents to the DMA capable memory. In the next writel, we inform the device about the packet length. At this time, the packet is transmitted on the wire. Next, we determine the next available transmission descriptors, and, if this happens to be equal to a dirty descriptor, we stop the device; otherwise we simply return.

After every packet transmission, the RTL8139 device informs about transmission status via an interrupt. Therefore, the driver must read interrupt from device. In Table 9.12, we registered an interrupt handler to receive interrupts from the device. Let's modify the interrupt handler to read transmission status.

Table 9.14

```
static irqreturn_t rtl8139_interrupt(int irq, void *dev_instance)
{
        struct net_device *dev = (struct net_device*)dev_instance;
        struct rtl8139_private *priv = dev->priv;
        void *ioaddr = priv->mmio_addr;
        unsigned short isr = readw(ioaddr + ISR);
        /* clear all interrupt.
         * Specs says reading ISR clears all interrupts and writing
         * has no effect. But this does not seem to be case. Sometimes
         * interrupt keeps on arriving unless cleared forcibly.
         */
        writew(0xffff, ioaddr + ISR);
        if((isr & TxOK) || (isr & TxErr))
                rtl8139_tx_interrupt(isr, dev);
        if(isr & CableLen)
                LOG_MSG("cable length change interrupt\n");
        if(isr & TimeOut)
                LOG_MSG("time interrupt\n");
        if(isr & SysErr)
                LOG_MSG("system err interrupt\n");
```

```
        return IRQ_HANDLED;
}
static void rtl8139_tx_interrupt(unsigned short isr, struct
net_device *dev)
{
        struct rtl8139_private *priv = dev->priv;
        void *ioaddr = priv->mmio_addr;
        while((priv->dirty_tx != priv->cur_tx) ||
 netif_queue_stopped(dev))
              {
              unsigned int txstatus =
                    readl(ioaddr + TSD0 + priv->dirty_tx *
 sizeof(int));
              if(!(txstatus & (TxStatOK | TxAborted | TxUnderrun)))
                    break; /* yet not transmitted */
              if(txstatus & TxStatOK) {
                    LOG_MSG("Transmit OK interrupt\n");
                    priv->stats.tx_bytes += (txstatus & 0x1fff);
                    priv->stats.tx_packets++;
              }
              else {
                    LOG_MSG("Transmit Error interrupt\n");
                    priv->stats.tx_errors++;
              }
              priv->dirty_tx++;
              priv->dirty_tx = priv->dirty_tx % NUM_TX_DESC;
              if((priv->dirty_tx == priv->cur_tx) &&
 netif_queue_stopped(dev))
              {
                    LOG_MSG("waking up queue\n");
                    netif_wake_queue(dev);
              }
        }
        return;
}
```

Since there is only one IRQ the device generates, rtl8139_interrupt will be called for all kinds of interrupts. Therefore the interrupt handler must de-multiplex using masks to know exact interrupt type. As show in Table 9-14, the interrupt handler reads ISR status and then calls function rtl8139_tx_interrupt only if the interrupt is either TxOK or TxErr.

When driver receives a transmission interrupt, it increments dirty_tx so that during next transmission next TSAD is used.

Our device is now ready to send packets out. (Remember, we can't receive packets, yet.) Compile the driver, and try sending ping packets out of the host. At other end, you should see some ARP packets. Even remote hosts reply to ARP packets; they are useless for us, as we are not ready to receive packets.

9.8 UNDERSTANDING REALTEK8139'S RECEIVING MECHANISM

The receive path of RTL8139 is designed as a ring buffer (A liner memory, managed as ring memory). Whenever the device receives a packet, packet contents are stored in ring buffer memory, and the location of the next packet to store is updated (to first packet starting address + first packet length). The device keeps on storing packets in this fashion until linear memory is exhausted. In that case, the device starts again writing at the starting address of linear memory, thus making it a ring buffer.

9.9 MAKING THE DEVICE READY TO RECEIVE PACKETS

Now, we will make the device ready to receive packets. For this, we will look into some of already discussed functions, and then the interrupt handler. First, we extend the structure rtl8139_private to accommodate variables needed to receive packets.

Table 9.15

```
/* Size of the in-memory receive ring. */
#define RX_BUF_LEN_IDX    2      /* 0==8K, 1==16K, 2==32K, 3==64K */
#define RX_BUF_LEN  (8192 << RX_BUF_LEN_IDX)
#define RX_BUF_PAD  16  /* see 11th and 12th bit of RCR: 0x44 */
#define RX_BUF_WRAP_PAD 2048 /* spare padding to handle pkt wrap */
#define RX_BUF_TOT_LEN     (RX_BUF_LEN + RX_BUF_PAD + RX_BUF_WRAP_PAD)
struct rtl8139_private
{
        struct pci_dev *pci_dev;  /* PCI device */
        void *mmio_addr; /* memory mapped IO addr */
        unsigned long regs_len; /* length of IO or MMIO region */
        unsigned int tx_flag;
        unsigned int cur_tx;
        unsigned int dirty_tx;
        unsigned char *tx_buf[NUM_TX_DESC]; /* Tx bounce buffers */
        unsigned char *tx_bufs; /* Tx bounce buffer region. */
        dma_addr_t tx_bufs_dma;
        struct net_device_stats stats;
        unsigned char *rx_ring;
        dma_addr_t rx_ring_dma;
        unsigned int cur_rx;
};
```

Now we re-look into rtl8139_open function, where we allocated memory for transmission side only. Now, we allocate memory for packet receiving also.

Table 9.16

```
        /* get memory for Tx/Rx buffers
         * memory must be DMA'ble
         */
        priv->tx_bufs = pci_alloc_consistent(
                    priv->pci_dev, TOTAL_TX_BUF_SIZE, &priv-
>tx_bufs_dma);
```

```
        priv->rx_ring = pci_alloc_consistent(
                        priv->pci_dev, RX_BUF_TOT_LEN, &priv-
>rx_ring_dma);
        if(!priv->tx_bufs || !priv->rx_ring) {
                free_irq(dev->irq, dev);
                if(priv->tx_bufs) {
                        pci_free_consistent(priv->pci_dev,
                                TOTAL_TX_BUF_SIZE, priv-
>tx_bufs, priv->tx_bufs_dma);
                        priv->tx_bufs = NULL;
                }
                if(priv->rx_ring) {
                        pci_free_consistent(priv->pci_dev,
                                RX_BUF_TOT_LEN, priv->rx_ring,
priv->rx_ring_dma);
                        priv->rx_ring = NULL;
                }
                return -ENOMEM;
        }
```

The code in Table 9.16 calculates the memory required for ring buffer. The calculation of RX_BUF_TOT_LEN depends upon some device configuration parameters. As we see shortly in rtl8139_hw_start, we configure Bits 12-11 of RCR register as 10, which configures a 32K+16 receive buffer length. Therefore, we allocate that much memory for the receive buffer. Also, we configure bits 7 to 1, which means RTL8139 will keep moving the rest of the packet data into the memory, immediately after the end of Rx buffer. Therefore, we allocate 2048 bytes of buffer extra to cope up with such situations.

Now that we've looked into function rtl8139_open, we look into rtl8139_hw_start, where we configure the device for receiving packets.

Table 9.17

```
        /* Must enable Tx/Rx before setting transfer thresholds! */
        writeb(CmdTxEnb | CmdRxEnb, ioaddr + CR);
       /* tx config */
        writel(0x00000600, ioaddr + TCR); /* DMA burst size 1024 */
        /* rx config */
        writel(((1 << 12) | (7 << 8) | (1 << 7) |
                        (1 << 3) | (1 << 2) | (1 << 1)), ioaddr+ RCR);
        /* init Tx buffer DMA addresses */
        for (i = 0; i < NUM_TX_DESC; i++) {
                writel(priv->tx_bufs_dma + (priv->tx_buf[i] - priv-
>tx_bufs), ioaddr + TSAD0 + (i * 4));
        }
        /* init RBSTART */
        writel(priv->rx_ring_dma, ioaddr + RBSTART);
        /* initialise missed packet counter */
        writel(0, ioaddr + MPC);
```

And then we modify rtl8139_init_ring function to initialize receive buffer counter.

Table 9.18

```
        priv->cur_tx = 0;
        priv->dirty_tx = 0;
        priv->cur_rx = 0;
```

As shown in Table 9.17, the first change in rtl8139_hw_start function is that we are writing CmdTxEnb | CmdRxEnb to CR register, which means the device will be transmitting as well as receiving packets. The next change is device receive configuration. I have not used macros in code, but they are quite obvious, if you see the rtl8139 specification. The bits used in this statement are as follows:

- Bit 1 - Accept physical match packets
- Bit 2 - Accept multicast packets
- Bit 3 - Accept broadcast packets
- Bit 7 - WRAP. When set to 1, RTL8139 will keep moving the rest of packet data into the memory immediately after the end of Rx buffer.
- Bit 8-10 - Max DMA burst size per Rx DMA burst. We are configuring this to 111, which means unlimited.
- Bit 11-12 - Rx buffer length. We are configuring to 10 which means 32K+16 bytes.

The next major change is configuring RBSTART register. This register contains starting address of receive buffer. Later, we initialize MPC (Missed Packet Counter) register to zero and configure the device for not generating early interrupts.

This completes receive path initialization. However, the most important work yet to do is to receive packets. This is done in interrupt handler. As we discussed before, the common interrupt handler is called for all device interrupts. Therefore, the interrupt handler has to check if the interrupt is for a packet arrival. In that case, interrupt handler has to allocate a skb buffer and receive the packet. We write function rtl8139_rx_interrupt for this and modify rtl8139_interrupt to call rt8139_rx_interrupt when packet arrival interrupt occurs.

Table 9.19

```
/* rtl8139_interrupt modification */
        if((isr & TxOK) || (isr & TxErr))
              rtl8139_tx_interrupt(isr, dev);
        if((isr & RxOK) || (isr & RxErr))
              rtl8139_rx_interrupt(isr, dev);
        if(isr & CableLen)
              LOG_MSG("cable length change interrupt\n");
static void rtl8139_rx_interrupt(unsigned short isr, struct
net_device *dev)
{
        struct rtl8139_private *priv = dev->priv;
        void *ioaddr = priv->mmio_addr;
        if(isr & RxErr) {
              /* TODO: Need detailed analysis of error status */
              LOG_MSG("receive err interrupt\n");
              priv->stats.rx_errors++;
              return;
```

```
}
        LOG_MSG("RxOK receive interrupt received\n");
        while((readb(ioaddr + CR) & RxBufEmpty) == 0)
        {
              unsigned int rx_status;
              unsigned short rx_size;
              unsigned short pkt_size;
              struct sk_buff *skb;
              if(priv->cur_rx > RX_BUF_LEN)
                    priv->cur_rx = priv->cur_rx % RX_BUF_LEN;
              /* TODO: need to convert rx_status from little to host
               * endian. I ignore because my CPU is little endian.
               * A portable driver must do it.
               */
              rx_status = *(unsigned int*)(priv->rx_ring + priv-
>cur_rx);
              rx_size = rx_status >> 16;
              /* first two bytes are receive status register
              * and next two bytes are pkt len
              */
              pkt_size = rx_size - 4;
              /* hand over packet to system */
              skb = dev_alloc_skb (pkt_size + 2);
              if (skb) {
                    skb->dev = dev;
                    skb_reserve (skb, 2); /* 16 byte align the IP
fields */
                    eth_copy_and_sum(
                                skb, priv->rx_ring + priv-
>cur_rx + 4, pkt_size, 0);
                    skb_put (skb, pkt_size);
                    skb->protocol = eth_type_trans (skb, dev);
                    netif_rx (skb);
                    dev->last_rx = jiffies;
                    priv->stats.rx_bytes += pkt_size;
                    priv->stats.rx_packets++;
        }
        else {
                    LOG_MSG("Memory squeeze, dropping packet.\n");
                    priv->stats.rx_dropped++;
        }
              /* increment priv->cur_rx and keep it aligned */
              priv->cur_rx = (priv->cur_rx + rx_size + 4 + 3) & ~3;
              /* update CAPR */
              writew(priv->cur_rx, ioaddr + CAPR);
        }
        return;
}
```

As shown in Table 9.14, the ISR register is read in variable isr. Any further de-multiplexing of interrupts is the interrupt handler's job. If we receive TxOK, TxErr, or RxErr, we update necessary statistics. Receiving an RxOK interrupt means we have received a frame successfully, and the driver has to process it. We read from the receiver buffer until we have read all data. (loop while ((readb (ioaddr + CR) & RxBufEmpty) == 0) does this job.) First, we check if tp->cur_rx has gone beyond RX_BUF_LEN. If that is the case, we wrap it. The received frame contains 4 extra bytes at the start of frame (appended by RTL8139), apart from packet contents and other headers. The first two bytes indicate frame status and next two bytes indicate frame length. (The length includes first 4 bytes, also.) These values are always in little-endian order, and must be converted to host order. Then, we allocate a skb for received packet, copy the frame contents into skb, and queue the skb for later processing. Then, we update CAPR (Current Address of Packet Read), to let the RTL8139 know about the next write location.

This finishes the network device driver development. Compile all code together, and insert new driver. Configure some IP address to the device and send ping packets to another destination, and you would be happy to see ping application receiving reply packets.

9.10 SUMMARY

PCI devices are very popular till date and most of the network adaptor support PCI bus. These PCI devices support much more features than implemented in this driver. This driver design is kept to support basic features for sake of brevity. You can experiment with this driver by porting to other devices or by adding more features.

9.11 ASSIGNMENTS

- Understand difference between NAPI and non-NAPI drivers, and discuss performance aspect of each.
- Upgrade the driver explained in this chapter to support promiscuous mode and configure multicast L2 address.
  Hint: IFF_PROMISC, IFF_MULTICAST, dev->mc_list

9.12 REFERENCES

- Kernel networking documents-http://www.kernel.org/doc/Documentation/networking/

10 Memory Allocation and Miscellaneous Topics

10.1 MEMORY ALLOCATION

Memory allocation and management is a very crucial part of kernel programming or device driver development. Memory allocation is more involved in kernel space than user space. This chapter explains various methods of memory allocation in kernel space, and explains their suitability to different scenarios.

10.1.1 Kmalloc

The kmalloc is first function to allocate memory in kernel. Use of this function is somewhat similar to malloc function used in user space. However, kmalloc requires one more argument in addition to memory size, which controls memory allocation procedure. Table 10.1 illustrates prototype of kmalloc function.

Table 10.1

```
void * kmalloc (size_t size, int flags);
```

The first argument to kmalloc specifies size of the memory to be allocated. The second argument specifies one or more (logical OR) of following flags which control memory allocation.

- GFP_KERNEL—Allocate physically contiguous memory. If memory not available, wait (thus sleep) until memory is available.
- GFP_ATOMIC—Allocate physically contiguous memory. Return immediately with NULL pointer if memory not available. Since kmalloc call with this flag never sleeps, this flag must be used for allocating memory in interrupt handlers or wherever sleeping is not allowed (for example after disabling interrupts or after taking a spinlock).
- GFP_DMA—Allocate physically contiguous DMA memory. A DMA memory is the one which can also be accessed by external devices without intervention of CPU. Thus if a device wants to write directly to memory, the driver must allocated DMA memory.

Memory allocated by kmalloc must be freed used kfree function. Table 10-2 illustrates prototype of kfree function.

Table 10.2

```
void kfree (const void * p);
```

This must be noted that kmalloc can not allocate memory more than 128 KB. Although on some architectures, it is possible to allocate more memory than 128 KB, you must not assume this to work on all architectures. Also you must not assume the allocated memory to be initialized. If you need to, you must explicitly initialize the allocated memory.

10.1.2 Vmalloc

As discussed, kmalloc allocates physically contiguous memory. Therefore, the allocated memory is contiguous in both kernel virtual address space and physical address space. However, kmalloc may fail if memory is fragmented.

To allocate larger memory than kmalloc can allocate, Linux kernel provides a function vmalloc which allocates memory that can be fragmented in physical address space but contiguous in kernel virtual address space. It means that, although kernel source code looks at it as contiguous memory, the memory is not really contiguous in RAM.

Having said that, memory allocated by vmalloc has certain limitations. Since it is not contiguous in RAM, it can neither be used for DMA purpose nor in interrupt context. If these limitations are not the case for your module, you can use vmalloc safely.

The memory allocated by vmalloc must be freed by vfree. Table 10.3 illustrates prototype of these functions.

Table 10.3

```
void *vmalloc(unsigned long size);
void vfree(void * addr);
```

10.1.3 Kmem Cache

Kmem cache is the best bet for kernel developers where it is needed to allocate similar objects very frequently. The kernel uses memory management algorithms to manage cache objects efficiently. Table 10.4 illustrates a small kernel module which creates, uses and destroys a kmem cache.

Table 10.4

```
#include <linux/module.h>
#include <linux/kthread.h>
static struct kmem_cache *cachep;
static struct task_struct *k1;
static int kthread1(void *arg);
int init_module(void)
{
        /* create cache */
        cachep = kmem_cache_create(
                    "my_cache",           /* Name */
                    64,                   /* Object Size */
                    0,                    /* Alignment */
                    SLAB_HWCACHE_ALIGN,   /* Flags */
                    NULL);                /* Constructor */
        if(cachep)
```

```
                printk("cache created\n");
        k1 = kthread_run(kthread1, NULL, "kthread1");
        return 0;
}
static int kthread1(void *arg)
{
        void *cache_obj;
        /* allocate object from cache */
        cache_obj = kmem_cache_alloc(cachep, GFP_KERNEL);
        if(cache_obj)
                printk("object allocated from cache\n");
        /* release object to cache */
        if (cache_obj) {
                kmem_cache_free(cachep, cache_obj);
                printk("object released to cache\n");
        }
        do_exit(0);
        return 0;
}
void cleanup_module(void)
{
        /* destroy cache */
        if (cachep)
        {
                kmem_cache_destroy(cachep);
                printk("cache destoryed\n");
        }
        return;
}
MODULE_LICENSE("GPL");
```

As shown above kmem_cache_create function creates a pool of objects which can be allocated and freed. Note that, kmem_cache_create does not take any argument for number of objects. This means that cache can grow or shrink at runtime. The constructor function of kmem_cache_create is called whenever new pages are allocated by cache.

There are certain limitations while using kmem cache in interrupt context:

- kmem_cache_create and kmem_cache_destroy can not be called from interrupt context
- kmem cache can not grow or shrink in interrupt context.

10.2 KERNEL THREADS

Kernel threads are light-weight processes which have independent execution flow just like other processes. Kernel threads must not be confused with user level POSIX threads and processes. For every user process there is one process context in kernel. Similar to this process context, one context exists for every kernel thread too. The only difference between these two context is that mm pointer in task_struct is NULL for kernel threads because kernel threads does not have corresponding user process.

A kernel thread can be created with kthread_create function. As shown in Table 10.5, the first argument to kthread_create function is the entry function of new kernel thread. The second argument is data which is passed as it is to kernel thread entry function. The third argument is name of the kernel thread which will be available in list of processes (ps -aux) after the thread is spawned.

It must be noted that a kernel thread created with kthread_create remains inactive (*i.e.*, does not start execution of the entry function) until it is waken up. Therefore function wake_up_process must be called after kthread_create to start the thread.

However, Linux provides a wrapper kthread_run which calls kthread_create and wake_up_process together. Therefore, kthread_run will create and start the kernel thread.

Stopping a thread is a little tricky. A kernel thread entry function cannot simply return without notifying to kernel. There are two ways to a kernel thread notifying kernel about exit as described below.

If a kernel thread is standalone *i.e.*, a thread which performs a certain work and finishes; then the thread must call do_exit function before finishing. The argument to do_exit is the return value from kernel thread which must either be zero or a negative value.

However, most of the kernel threads remain active throughout. Such kernel threads sleep when there is no work for them; and are woken up when some work is to be done. The threads do that work and go to sleep again; and repeat the loop. Such kernel threads must time to time check kthread_should_stop. If kthread_should_stop returns TRUE, the thread must exit.

The kthread_should_stop returns TRUE only if someone called kthread_stop on the thread. Therefore, for example a module unloading function can call kthread_stop for all the threads it spawned. This will cause, the kernel threads to find kthread_should_stop returning TRUE, and therefore all threads will exit.

It must be noted that kthread_stop can wake up the kernel thread only if the thread is sleeping in TASK_INTERRUPTIBLE state. If a kernel thread is waiting for a lock in TASK_UNINTERRUPTIBLE state, the thread will not be awaked. The thread comes to know about the exit command only when the thread calls kthread_should_stop function. Therefore, you must be very careful in acquiring semaphore or mutex in TASK_UNINTERRUPTILBE state.

Therefore, it is essential for module unloading function to wait until all threads call kthread_should_stop and then only module unloading function should proceed further.

It implies that kernel threads created by a module must not wait forever for a lock. Otherwise the kernel thread will not be able to call kthread_should_stop, and therefore module unloading function will keep waiting.

As a word of caution, you must not call kthread_stop on a thread which has called do_exit by itself.

Table 10.5 illustrates a simple module which creates and stops kernel threads.

Table 10.5

```
#include <linux/module.h>
#include <linux/sched.h>
#include <linux/kthread.h>
static struct task_struct *k1;
static int kthread1(void *arg);
int init_module(void)
{
        printk("kthread module inserted\n");
        /* create the thread */
        k1 = kthread_create(kthread1, NULL, "kthread1");
        /* start the thread */
```

```
        wake_up_process(k1);
        try_module_get(THIS_MODULE);
        return 0;
}
/* Thread entry function */
int kthread1(void *arg)
{
        unsigned long now;
        printk("kthread1 started.. \n");
        now = jiffies;
        while(jiffies < now + 60*HZ) /* 1 minute */
        {
                /* do some work */
                set_current_state(TASK_INTERRUPTIBLE);
                schedule_timeout(5*HZ);
                printk("kthread1 is running...\n");
        }
        printk("kthread1 exited\n");
        module_put(THIS_MODULE);
        do_exit(0);
        return 0;
}
void cleanup_module(void)
{
        printk("kthread module removed\n");
        return;
}
MODULE_LICENSE("GPL");
```

As shown above, this module creates a kernel thread using kthread_create function, and then starts it using wake_up_process function. The thread entry function is executed in separate and independent context from insmod. The function kthread1 waits for 60 seconds, and wakes up every 5 seconds; and then exits by calling do_exit function. Since this thread is self terminating, we don't call kthread_stop in cleanup_module function.

You must ensure that the module is not removed until the thread has completed execution; else a kernel crash will occur. To prevent this, we increment module count by try_module_get in init_module function; and decrement it by module_put function only after thread has finished execution. Therefore, it will prevent the user from inadvertently removing the module while thread execution is in progress.

Table 10.6 illustrates second and better way of controlling kernel threads.

Table 10.6

```
#include <linux/module.h>
#include <linux/sched.h>
#include <linux/kthread.h>
static struct task_struct *k;
static int kthread2(void *arg);
int init_module(void)
```

```
{
        printk("kthread module inserted\n");
        /* create and start the thread */
        k = kthread_run(kthread2, NULL, "kthread2");
        return 0;
}
/* Thread entry function */
int kthread2(void *arg)
{
        unsigned long now;
        printk("kthread2 started.. \n");
        now = jiffies;
        while((jiffies < now + 60*HZ) && !kthread_should_stop())
        {
        /* do some work */
               printk("kthread2 is running...\n");
               set_current_state(TASK_INTERRUPTIBLE);
               schedule_timeout(5*HZ);
        }
        while(!kthread_should_stop()) {
               set_current_state(TASK_INTERRUPTIBLE);
               schedule();
        }
        printk("kthread2 exited\n");
        return 0;
}
void cleanup_module(void)
{
        kthread_stop(k);
        printk("kthread module removed\n");
        return;
}
MODULE_LICENSE("GPL");
```

As shown above this module uses kthread_run function which creates as well as starts the thread. The kthread2 function remains in a loop until it has finished its work or function kthread_should_stop returns TRUE. Later when the module is removed then cleanup_module function calls kthread_stop. The kthread_stop function ensures that next call to kthread_should_stop returns TRUE. After this, the kthread_stop function waits until the thread has finished its execution.

Coming back to kthread2 function, observe the second while loop. This loop is required because if module is removed after 60 seconds; by then first while loop would have finished execution. But the thread must still not exit. It must exit only and only after someone has called kthread_stop.

Before concluding kernel threads it's worth noting that although a kernel thread is executed in separate context from insmod, yet both are related. To completely decouple them, you must daemonize the kernel thread by calling daemonize function.

Table 10.7 list prototype of kernel thread related functions.

Table 10.7

```
struct task_struct *kthread_create(int (*threadfn)(void *data),
                                       void *data,
                                       const char namefmt[],
                                       ...);
kthread_run(threadfn, data, namefmt, ...)
int wake_up_process(struct task_struct *p);
void daemonize(const char *name, ...);
int kthread_stop(struct task_struct *k);
int kthread_should_stop(void);
NORET_TYPE void do_exit(long code);
```

In addition to above described functions, there is one architecture specific function kernel_thread to create kernel threads. You need not use this function for new code but you may encounter this in old code. The function has following prototype (although it may vary for some architectures).

Table 10.8

```
int kernel_thread(int (*fn)(void *), void *arg, unsigned long flags);
```

10.3 INTER PROCESSOR INTERRUPTS

Linux kernel provides an interesting mechanism known as inter processor interrupts or IPI to send interrupts among processors in SMP system. This gives kernel programmers the ability to execute some function on other processors.

Table 10.9 illustrates functions involved in IPI mechanism.

Table 10.9

```
int smp_call_function_single(int cpu,
                    void (*func) (void *info), void *info, int wait);
void smp_call_function_many(const struct cpumask *mask,
    void (*func)(void *), void *info, bool wait);
int smp_call_function(void (*func)(void *), void *info, int wait);
```

Function smp_call_function_single can be used to run a function (second argument) on another one CPU (first argument). The third argument is passed to the second argument function as it is. If the last argument is TRUE, then caller is put to wait until function has completed execution on other CPU.

Other functions smp_call_function_many and smp_call_function are similar to smp_call_function_signle except that they allow function execution on more than one CPU and all CPU respectively.

Figure 10.1 illustrates call flow which can be implemented using IPI mechanism.

In Figure 10.1, a function kthread0 executing on CPU0 sends an inter processor interrupt to CPU1. The IPI interrupt handler at CPU1 invokes "IPI function" on CPU1. Then "IPI function" invokes or signals function kthread1 which also is executing on CPU1.

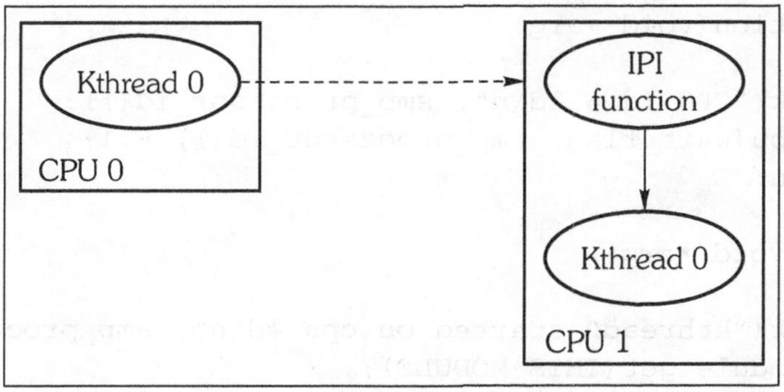

Figure 10.1

Table 10.10 illustrates an example of above mentioned IPI scheme.

Table 10.10

```
#include <linux/module.h>
#include <linux/sched.h>
#include <linux/kthread.h>
#include <linux/smp.h>
#ifndef CONFIG_SMP
#error "This program runs only on SMP"
#endif
static void ipi_function(void* arg);
static int kthread0(void *arg);
static int ktherad1(void* arg);
int init_module(void)
{
        struct task_struct *k0, *k1;
        if(!cpu_online(0) || !cpu_online(1)) {
              printk("CPU 0 or 1 is not online. Will not proceed
further\n");
              return 0;
        }
        /* create two kernel threads */
        k0 = kthread_create(kthread0, NULL, "kthread0");
        k1 = kthread_create(ktherad1, NULL, "ktherad1");
        /* force each thread to run on different cpu */
        kthread_bind(k0, 0);
        kthread_bind(k1, 1);
        /* start threads */
        wake_up_process(k0);
        wake_up_process(k1);
        printk("IPI module inserted\n");
        return 0;
}
static DEFINE_PER_CPU(int, wait_flag) = {0};
```

```
void ipi_function(void* arg)
{
        printk("CPU Id = %d\n", smp_processor_id());
        per_cpu(wait_flag, smp_processor_id()) = 1;
        return;
}
int kthread0(void *arg)
{
        printk("kthread0 started on cpu %d\n", smp_processor_id());
        try_module_get(THIS_MODULE);
        per_cpu(wait_flag, 0) = 1;
        /* wait for 10 seconds */
        set_current_state(TASK_INTERRUPTIBLE);
        schedule_timeout(10*HZ);
        /* send IPI */
        printk("Sending IPI from CPU 0 to 1\n");
        smp_call_function_single(1, ipi_function, NULL, 0, 0);
        module_put(THIS_MODULE);
        do_exit(0);
        return 0;
}
int ktherad1(void* arg)
{
        printk("ktherad1 started on cpu %d\n", smp_processor_id());
        try_module_get(THIS_MODULE);
        while(per_cpu(wait_flag, 1) != 1)
        {
              printk("ktherad1: wait_flag = %d\n", per_cpu(wait_flag,
 1));
              set_current_state(TASK_INTERRUPTIBLE);
              schedule_timeout(1*HZ);
        }
        printk("ktherad1: wait_flag = %d\n", per_cpu(wait_flag, 1));
        printk("ktherad1 exited..\n");
        module_put(THIS_MODULE);
        do_exit(0);
        return 0;
}
void cleanup_module(void)
{
        printk("IPI module removed\n");
        return;
}
MODULE_LICENSE("GPL");
```

The init_module function creates two threads kthread0 and kthread1. The module forces each thread to run on CPU0 and CPU1 respectively using kthread_bind function.

This module also illustrates per-CPU variables. A Per-CPU variable can be defined by DEFINE_PER_CPU macro. A per-CPU variable is actually an array of variables; one dedicated for each CPU. Therefore, every CPU accesses its own variable without being affected by same variable access on other CPU. To understand this, observe that kthread1 (on CPU1) is waiting for wait_flag to be 1. Even if kthread0 (on CPU0) sets wait_flag to 1, kthread1 continues to wait (because both threads are running on different CPU).

Later kthread0 sends an IPI to CPU1. Therefore, ipi_function is executed on CPU1. The ipi_function sets wait_flag to 1. Since both ipi_function and kthread1 are executing on CPU1, kthread1 comes out of loop and terminates.

10.4 SUMMARY

Linux kernel is a vast and interesting domain for learners especially for students. It opens a wide door of learning be it operating system, networking, file system or device drivers. Linux kernel is an open source project released under GPL license. This helps developers to carry out experiments and learn it easily.

10.5 ASSIGNMENTS

- Study and discuss about signal handling in Linux kernel
- Study and discuss about NPTL (Native POSIX Thread Library)

10.6 REFERENCES

- NPTL-http://en.wikipedia.org/wiki/Native_POSIX_Thread_Library

Index

A

B

C

D

E

F

G

I

J

K

L

M

N

O

P

W

X